Praise for

FREEZING COLD TAKES: ...

"Fred Segal's book is so good and so entertaining that it is bound to wind up as a national bestseller, one of the most popular books this decade. And if it's not, I certainly don't want to see these words rehashed on Freezing Cold Takes."

—Adam Schefter, ESPN's Senior NFL Insider

"I stand by every hot take I've ever had, including that Jimmy Clausen one that I'm sure you won't use. *(Editor's note: it's on page 101.)* Anyway . . . read this book, it's awesome!! (And it doesn't include too many of my takes, right Fred?)"

—Ian Rapoport, NFL Network Insider

"The number one rule to improve your knowledge is to admit and then learn from your mistakes, making *Freezing Cold Takes: NFL* a valuable reference book. Many will laugh at the awful analyses and misguided judgements inside, yet they serve as a tool to help improve and develop. In laughter comes learning."

—Michael Lombardi, author of *Gridiron Genius* and host of *The Lombardi Line* and *The GM Shuffle* on VSiN

FRED SEGAL

FREEZING COLD TAKES NFL

Football Media's Most Inaccurate Predictions—and the Fascinating Stories behind Them

FRED SEGAL

RUNNING PRESS

PHILADELPHIA

Copyright © 2022 by Frederick Segal
Cover copyright © 2022 by Hachette Book Group, Inc.

Hachette Book Group supports the right to free expression and the value of copyright. The purpose of copyright is to encourage writers and artists to produce the creative works that enrich our culture.

The scanning, uploading, and distribution of this book without permission is a theft of the author's intellectual property. If you would like permission to use material from the book (other than for review purposes), please contact permissions@hbgusa.com. Thank you for your support of the author's rights.

Running Press
Hachette Book Group
1290 Avenue of the Americas, New York, NY 10104
www.runningpress.com
@Running_Press

Printed in the United States of America

First Edition: August 2022

Published by Running Press, an imprint of Perseus Books, LLC, a subsidiary of Hachette Book Group, Inc. The Running Press name and logo are trademarks of the Hachette Book Group.

The Hachette Speakers Bureau provides a wide range of authors for speaking events. To find out more, go to www.hachettespeakersbureau.com or call (866) 376-6591.

The publisher is not responsible for websites (or their content) that are not owned by the publisher.

Print book cover and interior design by Amanda Richmond.
Cover Photo copyright © Getty Images/Barcin

Library of Congress Control Number: 2022015860

ISBNs: 978-0-7624-7545-2 (paperback), 978-0-7624-7546-9 (ebook)

LSC-C

Printing 1, 2022

For Brady and Violet

CONTENTS

INTRODUCTION

A BOOK ABOUT FREEZING COLD TAKES.
WHAT'S THAT?

Since 2015, I have chronicled unprophetic sports predictions on the internet. My Freezing Cold Takes Twitter, Instagram, and Facebook pages are, together, currently the preeminent digital platform specializing in highlighting incorrect sports prognostications. I have gained little fame and no fortune from the endeavor.

The concept of the Freezing Cold Takes Twitter feed is simple: It features sports quotes, analysis, and predictions from the past—whether from the media or the athletes themselves—that aged poorly or were, in hindsight, simply wrong. The feed's popularity rests on sports fans' deep-rooted desire for the media to be challenged on these prior comments. The way fans see it, writers, TV commentators, and radio personalities frequently point out athletes' and teams' mistakes, make sweeping declarations about a franchise's future, demand trades, suggest that coaches be fired, and anoint rookies as Hall of Famers. To sports enthusiasts, since the media consistently dishes out these criticisms, it's only fair for someone to call them out when their "hot takes" end up being "Freezing Cold Takes." Enter my humble Twitter feed.

In the hierarchy of journalistic importance, sports media's "accountability" for their incorrect predictions and commentary is on the lower end of the spectrum. Furthermore, the extent to which a person is held accountable when his or her Freezing Cold

Take is spread across social media is hardly very harsh. Yes, sometimes a subject will be ridiculed. As far as I've seen, the criticism and fun-poking have never had the slightest effect on a media figure's career.

A Freezing Cold Take can be a tweet from five years ago or a newspaper article from 1850. It can be about any topic and can be disseminated in any medium. One of the most common forms of Freezing Cold Takes arises from media predictions about a specific game. For example, in 2008, a majority of journalists and TV personalities produced Freezing Cold Takes when they predicted the New England Patriots, as 12-point favorites, would defeat the New York Giants in Super Bowl XLII in February 2008. The Giants pulled off one of the biggest upsets in NFL history and won 17–14.

A prediction is not the only type of commentary that can turn into a Freezing Cold Take. Another is subjective analysis about a player or team, whether in relation to the NFL Draft or any other time during or after the season. Consider any of the NFL Draft analysts in 1998 who opined that the Indianapolis Colts should have selected star college quarterback Ryan Leaf with the No. 1 overall pick in the NFL Draft over the other top quarterback prospect, Peyton Manning. In hindsight, many analysts probably regret that they suggested Leaf, whose NFL career was infamously terrible, while Manning, as the signal-caller, led the Colts to a Super Bowl win in 2007 and was recently inducted into the Pro Football Hall of Fame.

As one could guess, most media folks aren't thrilled when their old, inaccurate commentary is spread around the internet and mocked. But, surprisingly, that is not the primary grievance. It is that ridiculed past quotes don't usually contain enough context and do not fairly capture the circumstances surrounding the analysis at the time it was presented. The author of the ill-fated commentary often feels that any sound rationale used to come to his or her original conclusion is lost in the shuffle, and he or she is made to look like a complete absentminded fool. The appropriate context could provide the sportswriter with some sort of shame mitigation.

Generally speaking, the context that surrounds statements and ideas is a casualty of the digital age and the rise of social media. Thoughts expressed through social media platforms are more often shorter in length and contain less depth than those of traditional media, like newspapers. As ideas and thoughts are framed into shorter constructs, part of the context that supports them are carved out. Unless a reader has an independent awareness of the circumstances surrounding a remark, it may be impossible to fully understand the thought process behind why it was made.

With this book, I wanted to deviate from simply posting collections of Freezing Cold Takes in short, abridged quotes and passages. My aim here is to spotlight (okay, and mock in good humor) some of the most infamous NFL-related Freezing Cold Takes throughout history, and provide the appropriate context as to why they were made. While the Freezing Cold Takes in each chapter (and, in most cases, there are many) are interesting standing alone, exploring the circumstances that may have led to the ill-fated commentary is, in my opinion, just as or even more fascinating.

Keep in mind that not all quotes and statements in each story are Freezing Cold Takes. I have also included some accurate and prophetic commentary in various chapters, which also add context.

The stories offer a unique dive into NFL history from a different perspective than you might be used to. I hope you have as much fun reading it as I did writing it.

—Fred Segal, 2022

"THE PATRIOTS WILL REGRET HIRING BILL BELICHICK"

(2000 NEW ENGLAND PATRIOTS)

On January 4, 2000, Bill Belichick stood in front of the media at the New York Jets' facility in Hempstead, New York, and announced that he was quitting as head coach of the team. It was a position for which he hadn't even been formally introduced. Belichick, the team's defensive coordinator and associate head coach under Bill Parcells for the previous three seasons, had become the Jets head coach two days earlier after Parcells, following a disappointing 8–8 season, told team president Steve Gutman he was retiring. The six-year contract that Belichick had signed with the team in 1997 provided that he would become the Jets' head coach as soon as Parcells left. Thus, Belichick's naming was automatic.

"I'VE DECIDED TO RESIGN AS THE HC OF THE NY JETS"

Just prior to stepping to the podium, Belichick handed Gutman a piece of lined white paper stating, among other things, "I've decided to resign as the HC of the NY Jets." He cited the uncertainty of team ownership as the main reason for his departure. Owner Leon Hess had passed away eight months earlier, and his family was selling the franchise. While Hess and Belichick had been on good terms (Hess had even given him a $1 million bonus the year before in order to fend off potential suitors), he had no relationship with any of the potential buyers.

Many did not buy Belichick's "uncertainty of ownership" excuse. The Patriots were looking for a new coach, and Parcells and the Jets brass had become aware that New England had a strong interest in hiring Belichick. Just before Parcells stepped down as Jets coach, the Patriots had requested permission from the Jets to speak with Belichick about becoming their head coach and general manager. However, Parcells's abrupt departure had rendered the Patriots' request unworkable, because as soon as Parcells resigned, Belichick became the Jets' head coach contractually.

Belichick's brisk change of heart wasn't just a simple case of cold feet. The decision was a product of a complex situation that emanated from bitterness between Belichick, Parcells, and Patriots owner Robert Kraft, who had productive but complicated histories with each other.

At the center of the rancor was the acrimonious fallout from Parcells's leaving the Patriots three years earlier to coach the Jets. Parcells was the Patriots' head coach from 1993 to 1996. From nearly the moment Kraft bought the team in 1994, the two continuously butted heads. In 1996, Belichick was New England's defensive coordinator under Parcells. However, in contrast to Parcells, he developed a good relationship with Kraft.

In January 1997, after the Patriots lost Super Bowl XXXI to the Packers, Parcells made his intent clear to the organization that he wished to leave and take the head coaching job with the Jets. Since Parcells still had a year left on his contract, Kraft refused to release Parcells unless he received adequate compensation. NFL Commissioner Paul Tagliabue stepped in and ruled that because the Jets didn't own Parcells's rights, they could not hire him without the Patriots' permission. After weeks of unsuccessful negotiations, Tagliabue stepped in to arbitrate and eventually ruled that the Jets had to give the Patriots four future draft picks, including a first-rounder in 1999, in return for the termination of Parcells's contract by the Patriots. The Jets then hired Parcells. Belichick followed him and was installed as the Jets' defensive coordinator.

Three years later, when Belichick announced his resignation, he still had three years remaining on his $1.4 million-a-year contract with the Jets. Thus, there was no certainty that he would be legally able to negotiate with any other team. But two things were starting to become clear: First, Belichick did not want to remain with the Jets, and second, he coveted the Patriots' job.

One of Belichick's prime concerns about the Jets job was that he would not have the same level of control in New York as he would in New England. After his resignation, Parcells remained with the Jets as their director of football operations. Despite Parcells's assurance that Belichick would have unfettered control over football decisions, Belichick was unsure of Big Bill's role. It is easy to assume that he did not want Parcells breathing down his neck. Bob Glauber, a longtime columnist for *Newsday*, had known Belichick since he was the defensive coordinator of the Giants in the 1980s. "He bristles under that kind of power above him," Glauber said in 2020. "Especially ... [with] an opportunity to kind of run the show in New England."

"[BELICHICK] SHOULD BE DONE AS A HEAD COACH IN THE NFL, NOW AND FOREVER"

Many in the sports media skewered Belichick after his abrupt resignation. The day after his infamous press conference, Belichick was featured on the front page of the *New York Post* sports section with a picture of him on the podium under the headline "BELICHICKEN." *Post* columnist George Willis professed that Jets fans should "be breathing a sigh of relief," and were "very fortunate" because Belichick proved he wasn't man enough to fill Parcells's enormous shoes. Willis wrote, "If the Patriots want Belichick as their head coach, and he wants to go there, good riddance." *Sports Illustrated*'s Peter King thought Belichick "[broke] a contract he had no business breaking," and that his actions were "despicable and totally without honor." *Hartford Courant* columnist

Jeff Jacobs also questioned Belichick's inner fortitude. "That yellow line isn't the lane-divider on I-95 Northbound," he wrote. "It's the color of Belichick's backbone." A few weeks later, after Johnson & Johnson heir Woody Johnson had completed his purchase of the Jets, Jacobs wrote, "Do you think he can spare a little powder for Bill Belichick's diaper? Me thinks he soiled it when called to replace a legend."

Adrian Wojnarowski, now one of the most powerful and respected NBA reporters in the world, then a columnist at the *Record*, based in North Jersey, thought that Belichick did the Jets a favor by quitting. "Better they find out now, than [Jets president Steve] Gutman traipsing back to the podium with the same bewildered expression to announce his dismissal in two years," Wojnarowski wrote. "Belichick belongs in the darkened caves of film rooms, where he never, ever has to be responsible for a franchise." Ian O'Connor, in the (Westchester, New York) *Journal News*, echoed a similar sentiment. He called Belichick "a weasel of the worst kind," and declared that he "should be done as a head coach in the NFL, now and forever."

Belichick's first head coaching job was with the Cleveland Browns from 1991 to 1995. It was considered a failure, as he went 37–45 and was fired. He had ruffled fans' feathers with some of his roster moves (including releasing beloved quarterback Bernie Kosar) and constantly clashed with the media. Many of the Browns players didn't enjoy playing for him. "He was more negative than anything," Anthony Pleasant, a Browns defensive end under Belichick in Cleveland told the *Hartford Courant* many years later. "Guys would hate coming to work because of the atmosphere."

People familiar with Belichick's tenure in Cleveland were befuddled that he was such a hot commodity. In the *Dayton (Ohio) Daily News*, Greg Simms wrote: "I suspect he's the same little guy who is not ready for the big time." In a column skewering Belichick for his disloyalty, immaturity, and blatant disrespect shown to his mentor Parcells, *Akron Beacon Journal* scribe Terry Pluto, wrote that "The amazing thing is not that Belichick turned his back on the Jets. Rather, it's that any team wants to hire him at all."

New York Daily News columnist Filip Bondy was surprised as well. "Consider Belichick little more than a contested terrain in the ground war between Parcells and Kraft," Bondy wrote. "He is, after all, a mere defensive coordinator who suffered four losing seasons out of five as head coach of Cleveland. He's not Lombardi." Glauber, in *Newsday*, lamented how Belichick had "blown it." "He had the perfect opportunity with the perfect team, in the perfect city . . . to emerge from Parcells' formidable shadow." In the *Record*, columnist John Rowe wrote that the Jets should be relieved that Belichick didn't want to be their coach. "Even if Parcells doesn't return to the sidelines," Rowe explained, "they will be able to find someone better than Belichick."

Kraft told *Sports Illustrated* in 2017 that Modell warned him that if he hired Belichick, he'd be "making the biggest mistake of [his] life." Kraft also admitted that there were "people at the highest level of the league" telling him not to hire Belichick. "Nobody thought it was a good idea," Kraft said. He even had media people sending him videotapes of a couple of Belichick's press conferences in Cleveland as purported evidence of the coach's lack of communication skills.

"WHY ANY TEAM WOULD WANT TO HIRE THIS MAN AS A HEAD COACH IS BAFFLING"

As soon as he walked off that podium in Hempstead during that first week of 2000, Belichick immediately began his quest to join the Patriots. With the NFL prohibiting any team in the league from speaking with him, Belichick filed a grievance to attempt to have his Jets contract voided. Meanwhile, columnist Dan Pompei scorched Belichick in the *Sporting News*. "Why any team would want to hire this man as a head coach is baffling," he wrote. Pompei also hypothesized that Belichick was a coaching testament to the "Peter Principle," a theory which states that, in any hierarchy, a person tends to rise to the level of his incompetence. "Just because Belichick is a great defensive coordinator doesn't mean he can be an effective head coach." Another national journalist, Peter King, thought, like Pompei, that the Patriots should move their search in a different direction. "If I'm...Bob Kraft," King wrote on *Sports Illustrated*'s website, "I have to say no to Bill Belichick now." King didn't understand why the Patriots would consider bargaining with the Jets and potentially give up a high Draft pick for a coach with a career record of 37–45. "[Former Carolina Panthers head coach] Dom Capers [sounds] good to me," he wrote. Garry Brown, a columnist for the Springfield, Massachusetts daily, the *Union-News*, had similar thoughts. He decried Kraft for letting Parcells get away in 1997 and surmised that he would potentially be making another mistake in hiring Belichick. "Kraft could be headed for yet another blunder," Brown wrote. "That would be the hiring of Bill Belichick as his new head coach...Belichick appears to be a [previous Patriots head coach Pete] Carroll type—well suited to be an assistant coach, ill-suited to be the head man."

Eventually, after several legal attempts by Belichick to extricate himself from his Jets contract had failed, Parcells and Kraft put their differences aside and struck a deal. The Patriots gave up a package of draft picks, including the Patriots' first-round pick (No. 16 overall) in the 2000 Draft, to the Jets, solely for the right to sign Belichick. On January 27, 2000, New England introduced Bill Belichick as their new head coach.

"PARCELLS SNOOKERED BOB KRAFT AGAIN . . . [I] WOULDN'T HIRE BELICHICK TO RUN A BURGER KING"

Immediately, questions arose about whether Belichick was worth the first-round pick the Patriots had surrendered. "I'm kind of a little surprised," said ESPN analyst Ron Jaworski. "Giving up a No. 1, I think is a lot...I would think there were other qualified coaches out there so you don't have to give up a No. 1, who should be a Pro Bowl player." In the (Rochester, New York) *Democrat and Chronicle*, columnist Bob Matthews wrote, "I'd give up the no. 16 pick overall in the draft for Bill Parcells, but I wouldn't give up the 61st pick for Bill Belichick." Boston-based radio host Ted Sarandis was convinced that "Parcells snookered Bob Kraft again," and that he "wouldn't hire Belichick to run a Burger King." The *Boston Herald*'s Karen Guregian, in a column to which she now refers as "one of the most idiotic things I've ever written," enumerated NFL coaches she thought were worth first-round picks. Among them: Vince Lombardi, George Halas, Paul Brown, Bill Parcells, Joe Gibbs, Don Shula, Chuck Noll, Tom Landry, and Bill Walsh. Belichick, she concluded, was not on their level. "Sorry folks. Bill Belichick does not fit the mold. He is not in that coaching stratosphere," she proclaimed. Ian O'Connor, in a *Journal News* column, wrote that Belichick was "a man you wouldn't want running your $2 hot dog stand," and that he thought the Patriots would regret hiring him. "Soon enough," O'Connor added, "the Patriots will discover that they did bad business. They hired a head coach with a losing record and personality to match."

"BILL PARCELLS JUST COST THE JETS A COUPLE OF CHAMPIONSHIPS, BY SCARING OFF THE BEST COACH IN FOOTBALL"

Of course, hindsight shows us that in hiring Belichick, the Patriots made the best business decision in the history of the franchise—possibly the history of the league. "It's turned out to be probably the greatest trade in NFL history," Guregian said in 2020. While technically it wasn't a trade, it is hard to argue with her sentiment. The 2021 season was Belichick's 22nd in New England. During that time, the Patriots have amassed a 254–99 regular-season record, as well as a 30–12 playoff record. They have also won nine conference titles and six Super Bowls during his tenure with the team.

In a 2017 interview with the *Boston Globe*, O'Connor said he believes that Belichick is the greatest NFL coach of all time and admits his mistakes from 2000. "I didn't think he had the human relations skills to lead an organization," O'Connor said. With respect to his initial assessment of the hire, he feels his column after the Patriots hired Belichick is "probably the worst article I have ever written." In a twist of fate, in 2018, he published a book titled *Belichick: The Making of the Greatest Football Coach of All Time* about Belichick's rise to legendary coaching status. The irony is not lost on him. "I'm fascinated by how he became what he became. My penance." Guregian has also come to terms with her ill-fated column. She now believes that "Belichick has probably jumped ahead" of all the great coaches she listed as worthy of a first-round pick.

Bondy formally admitted his mistake when, in Belichick's fifth season, the Patriots were preparing for their third Super Bowl appearance. He wrote a column in the *New York Daily News* calling himself a "moron" and a "knucklehead" and wrote that if he were granted a do-over, he would pursue an angle that read something like "Bill Parcells just cost the Jets a couple of championships, by scaring off the best coach in football." Bondy posited that Parcells still being on staff with Belichick was actually a valid and legitimate concern, writing that Parcells "did no favors with his post-coaching administrative career," which was brief and unproductive. He continued: "Who wanted this guy Parcells hanging around, forever threatening by his mere existence to overshadow and undermine the next head coach? Certainly not Belichick."

The *Cleveland Plain Dealer*'s Bill Livingston, who covered Belichick when he was coach of the Browns, seemed to understand this from the beginning. "Parcells, who remains with the Jets as a 'consultant,' would get all the credit for victories and none of the blame for defeats," he wrote in January 2000, right after Belichick resigned from the Jets. "Big Tuna would have been looking over [Belichick's] shoulder, and it is unduly stressful laboring for a boss with a clue."

Glauber said that his piece the day after Belichick's 2000 Jets resignation press conference was one of the most conflicted he has ever written and, because he was so surprised, he didn't know what to think. "It was one of the most abrupt, stunning, weird moments that I've ever had in covering sports for more than 40 years."

Reflecting over 20 years later, Bondy believes his lack of knowledge of the NFL may have handicapped him a bit in covering this situation. "I would be the first one to admit I have never been an expert on American football," he recalled in 2020. "During my long career, I was never [a full-time beat writer] in the NFL, so my bad take on this issue should come as no surprise."

Perhaps Bondy's most prescient point in his 2005 mea culpa piece, which many would probably argue still holds merit, is that the media, with all their opinions and access, are still heavily insulated from many of the major issues that affect the decision making of a franchise and its staff and that, as readers, we should take their opinions with a grain of salt. He wrote, "If there was any proof that the media know next to nothing about the layered vagaries and trade secrets of professional football, it was their nasty farewell to a future Hall of Fame coach."

"TRADE DAN MARINO. KEEP SCOTT MITCHELL"

(1993 MIAMI DOLPHINS)

Although the words were the same size as the others on the page, they stood out like a defensive lineman standing next to a kicker. "Trade Dan Marino. Keep Scott Mitchell." That was the lede of Greg Cote's column in the November 1, 1993 edition of the *Miami Herald*. It is the only portion that anyone remembers. It now lives in infamy. Cote brainstormed an idea that was then considered unimaginable: The Miami Dolphins should consider trading their most iconic player. And as if that were not enough, he suggested that the team ship off the legendary quarterback in favor of a relatively unknown backup who had only played in two-and-a-half games.

MARINO THE BELOVED

Dan Marino is a South Florida sports hero. One of the greatest passers of his generation, he is the Miami Dolphins' most famous and beloved player. Before the NBA's Miami Heat drafted Dwyane Wade in 2003, Marino was *the* face of South Florida professional sports and, in 1993, he was at the peak of his reign.

After he threw for over 5,000 yards and led the Dolphins to a Super Bowl appearance in just his second season in 1984, Marino burst into NFL superstardom. With him, expectations skyrocketed. Fast-forward to 1993. Despite racking up impressive passing numbers, Marino had yet to take the Dolphins back to the promised land. At 32 years old, his proverbial clock was ticking down, and his chances for capturing the elusive title were dwindling.

Prior to the start of the 1993 season, the Dolphins were predicted by many to win their division and represent the AFC in the Super Bowl in Atlanta. That path seemed steady as the Dolphins won three out of their first four games. But on a cold October day in Cleveland, the road to Atlanta became severely obstructed.

INTRODUCING SCOTT MITCHELL

Dan Marino had rarely been hurt and hadn't suffered any major injuries as a Dolphin player. Since becoming the Dolphins' starting quarterback six games into his rookie season in 1983, Marino had only missed two games due to injury, and that was during that rookie season. But on Sunday, October 10, 1993 in Cleveland, in his 145th consecutive game for the Dolphins, Marino's luck ran out. With Miami up 10–7 over the Browns in the second quarter, Marino ruptured his right Achilles tendon throwing a screen pass, ending his season in a flash.

Marino's backup, Scott Mitchell, a 6-foot-6, 230-pound 25-year-old southpaw, had been drafted by the Dolphins in the fourth round of the 1990 NFL Draft out of the University of Utah and had served as Marino's backup the previous three seasons. By 1993, Mitchell's only substantive professional experience was one NFL regular-season pass in a game against Seattle in 1992 when Marino sat out a play after a hit to the head. Mitchell had also played the previous summer for the Orlando Thunder of the now-defunct World League of American Football. He came into the game in Cleveland having thrown only eight passes in his entire NFL career.

After throwing a disastrous 99-yard interception, returned for a touchdown on his first pass, Mitchell settled down and led the Dolphins on two touchdown drives in the second half. The Dolphins won 24–14. No one had thrown for two touchdowns in a single game for Miami since Don Strock accomplished the feat in 1983.

The Dolphins proceeded to win their next two games with Mitchell at the helm. His best performance was in his second start, a home game against Kansas City on Halloween where he led Miami to a 30–10 blowout win over Joe Montana and the Chiefs.

Against the AFC's fifth-ranked pass defense, Mitchell completed 22-of-33 passes for 344 yards, threw three touchdowns and zero interceptions, and was named AFC Offensive Player of the Week. After two-and-a-half games, he was 44-of-62 for 652 yards and had six touchdowns and one interception, all for an outstanding quarterback rating of 119.2. If he had had enough throws to qualify, such a rating would have been the highest in the league at the time.

"YOU SEE [MITCHELL] DROP BACK AND THINK 'THAT'S MARINO.' EXCEPT HE'S LEFTHANDED"

Mitchell's performances were enough to raise eyebrows. Ahead of Miami's upcoming game against the New York Jets, an article in the *Asbury Park Press* contained the headline MITCHELL LOOKING A LOT LIKE MARINO. Jets defensive end Marvin Washington was intrigued by Mitchell as well. "Sometimes you look at it on film," Washington said, "you see him drop back and think 'that's Marino.' Except he's lefthanded." Cote was perhaps the most impressed. The day after the Chiefs game, he wrote his now-infamous article, the one that would follow him throughout his career, which started: "Trade Dan Marino. Keep Scott Mitchell. There. That's what the unspeakable looks like in print. It may be time to start thinking about it. Much too early to let the idea set in cement, obviously— but not to weigh the increasing possibility."

In the piece, Cote lamented that Marino would be 33 years old in 1994 and would be coming off a serious injury. Additionally, he noted that Scott Mitchell would be an unrestricted free agent at the end of the season. Moreover, a new salary cap was about to be implemented. To be able to pay more money to younger players, teams were unloading veterans with high salaries. With Mitchell playing so well, Cote figured that there was no way that the Dolphins would be able to keep both Mitchell, who would cost an estimated $3 million per year, and Marino, who was due around $5 million a year. So, in Cote's eyes, why not think about going with a young potential star and unloading Marino while he still had value?

The article immediately gained traction in South Florida, and Cote was quickly maligned. "I instantly knew what I had written was a pretty explosive thing to write in the Miami market," Cote recalled in 2020. That same day, in the afternoon, Cote was invited to be a guest on *Sports Jam*, a local sports TV program on Miami-based WPLG Channel 10, in front of a live audience at Don Shula's All-Star Café in Miami and hosted by former Dolphins wide receiver and longtime Miami sports broadcaster Jimmy Cefalo. The interview with Cote was a remote with Cefalo at the restaurant and Cote standing in front of the *Miami Herald* building in downtown Miami. As a joke, Cote's face was pixelated on TV so it could not be seen and his voice was disguised as if he were in the witness protection program. When he was introduced, he was mercilessly booed by the restaurant audience.

Prior to the internet and social media, a local sports column would rarely be seen outside its market. But Cote's piece spread quickly and triggered a great debate throughout the country. Although most of the reactions to the article were hostile and negative, the idea was not completely shunned. "I think they should trade Marino. He's been overrated for years," said one fan on a phone-in hotline to the *Fort Lauderdale Sun-Sentinel*. "We have a future with Mitchell as a quarterback, and he is giving other members of the team a chance," another added.

A few days later, Armando Salguero, another *Miami Herald* writer, played counterpoint to his colleague Cote's piece and wrote that Cote's suggestion to trade Marino was "blasphemy!" and such a consideration was "obscene." Furthermore, Salguero pointed out, there was an issue about Marino's trade value. How much could the Dolphins really get for a 32-year-old quarterback coming off a torn Achilles? One NFL GM told Salguero at the time, "I would not give up a first-rounder for him. And the Dolphins probably wouldn't let him go for anything less than two first-rounders. It would be a tough sell in both directions."

The buzz from the column seeped into the locker room. "It does make some sense," Marino said about Cote's suggestion. But Marino did express a hint of annoyance about the situation. "I've only been out two games, and here people have me traded." The article never made it awkward for Cote to be around Marino, but he doubts Dan was too thrilled with him. "Privately, he probably thought I was an asshole... But he was always kind to me." Mitchell's agent, Tony Agnone, made sure to clear up any question that the article was not an actual controversy. "From a logical standpoint, you might make a case for it," Agnone said at the time. "But from a realistic standpoint, it's not going to happen. Scott has played two-and-a-half games, and Marino has played 11 years and is going to the Hall of Fame." But Mitchell wasn't surprised that there were people broaching the topic. "There was all kinds of discussion, not just in South Florida, but across the NFL and across the nation," he said in 2020. "The Dolphins had been Dan Marino for so many years, and I don't think people expected the backup that no one had heard of, to come in and play so well."

According to former Dolphins wide receiver O. J. McDuffie, who was a rookie in 1993, trading Dan Marino was not on anyone's radar in the Dolphins locker room. "No, no, no... not in a million years... We were just buying time until Danny got back. [He] was on fire at that point."

Cote, and his column, continued to be the subject of much discussion throughout the course of the week. Later in the week, he told

George Diaz of the *Orlando Sentinel*, "I'm wearing my bulletproof vest and surviving the firestorm down here." In a follow-up column Cote wrote four days later, he explained that readers were flooding his message line, he had been receiving hate mail, and that local radio call-in shows were "engorged." In addition to the *Sports Jam* hit, he appeared on TV and radio interviews across the country. The backlash, he believed, was predicated on one big misunderstanding. "I am not an animal!," he wrote. Readers had misconstrued his message. He was not championing a "Dump Marino" campaign, he claimed. Instead, he was just putting it out there as something that people should consider. "All I'm saying, bottom line, is that this may become an issue the club must deal with and weigh strongly, so let's talk about it."

The following Sunday, the Jets handily beat the Dolphins 27–10 at Giants Stadium, which put the brakes on the Marino trade talk. "Thank God for one thing," wrote *Sun-Sentinel* staff writer Charles Bricker a few days after. "Scott Mitchell's soiree in New Jersey over the weekend will put an end to the trade Dan Marino drivel for at least a week." After the game, Jets quarterback Boomer Esiason excoriated Cote's suggestion to trade Marino. "Whoever wrote that better have his head examined," Esiason said. "One of the main reasons we won is that the Dolphins didn't have Dan Marino and they are a much different team without him."

The week after the Dolphins' loss to the Jets, Mitchell hurt his collarbone on the side of his throwing arm in a win over Philadelphia and was ruled out for at least a month. After a miracle win over the Cowboys on Thanksgiving, the Dolphins lost their final five games and missed the playoffs. Mitchell started the final two games of the season, but he wasn't 100 percent. "I could barely pick my arm up," he remembered.

"[SCOTT MITCHELL] IS HOPEFULLY THE MISSING PIECE OF THE PUZZLE THAT WILL ONE DAY TAKE THE DETROIT LIONS TO THE SUPER BOWL" (1994–1998)

The Dolphins did not trade Dan Marino. Mitchell did become a free agent and turned his seven starts into a three-year, $11 million contract with the Detroit Lions. It included a $5 million signing bonus. In 2022, that kind of money is small potatoes for an in-demand free agent quarterback, but back in 1993, it was a small fortune. With that contract, however, came pressure. At the press conference introducing Mitchell to the Lions, head coach Wayne Fontes glowingly stated, "This guy is hopefully the missing piece of the puzzle that will one day take the Detroit Lions to the Super Bowl."

Mitchell's tenure in Detroit is a subject of debate. In four seasons as a starter, he led the Lions to the playoffs three times. In 1995, Mitchell's best season as a pro, he threw for almost 4,300 yards, 32 touchdowns, and only 12 interceptions. However, in his time with Detroit, the team never went further than the first round of the playoffs. In 1998, Mitchell was benched for backup Charlie Batch after the second game of the season and never earned his job back. He played three more seasons, all unmemorable—one with the Ravens and two with the Bengals. In 10 total games with the two teams, he threw four touchdowns and 15 interceptions.

Mitchell hung up his cleats after the 2001 season. He sometimes looks back to what could have been with the Lions. After the 1996 season, Fontes was fired and offensive coordinator Tom Moore, who had developed a high-powered Lions offense that fit Scott Mitchell's strengths, moved on. The Lions hired Bobby Ross to replace Fontes. According to Mitchell, Ross just didn't give a formerly great offense a chance to succeed. "I had really good years in Detroit," Mitchell said in 2020. "We made the playoffs, and we would have continued." His frustration does not stem from the way that they played but that the Lions kept changing things around so often. "If you really understand how hard it is to win in the NFL, and to win Super Bowls, you would want to exercise more patience with teams."

In 2011, the NFL Network aired a program listing the "Top 10 NFL Worst Free Agent Signings." The Lions' signing of Scott Mitchell in 1994 was rated No. 9. Some interviewed for the program thought that was a bit unfair. "Scott Mitchell just gets totally destroyed in history," said Giants play-by-play announcer Bob Papa. "He wasn't as bad as everybody says he was ... [he] wasn't the greatest free agent signing, but there's been a lot worse than that." Aaron Schatz of the stats and analytics–based website Football Outsiders also defended Mitchell on the broadcast. "People forget just how good Scott Mitchell's season was in 1995," he said. "In our play-by-play breakdowns, he comes out as the best quarterback, most valuable quarterback in the league."

"LOOK, THEY WEREN'T WINNING WITH [MARINO]"

Ironically, Marino, who was on a supposed career downslide, lasted almost as long as Mitchell. He produced incredible statistics and had a marvelous career, but he never made it back to the Super Bowl. Marino retired after the 1999 season and was inducted into the Pro Football Hall of Fame in 2005.

Does Marino's lack of postseason success, in some way, vindicate Cote? Cote thinks so.

"The way it turned out, what Dolfan can honestly say the Fins might not have benefited from the change I wrote about? It was worth considering, which essentially is all I said," he wrote in 2016. "Look, they weren't winning with him."

Decades later, the fact that someone put Mitchell in the same sentence with Marino, one of the legends of the game, is going to be ridiculed, especially given how Mitchell's tenure with the Lions is generally perceived. It is a perception that Mitchell believes is unfair. "It's frustrating because there is nothing I can do about it… I was a very good player in the NFL, and I don't have any problem with that," he said. "It's just that being in a better situation would change things."

In hindsight, would things have been different in 1993 if he hadn't injured his collarbone? Mitchell thinks it is possible. "Had I not got injured, that season would have been different for our team," he said. "Especially if we go to the playoffs and do well in the playoffs." If such was the case, the trade-Marino conversation, which fizzled after the injury, may not have subsided. "I'm gonna play another 12 to maybe 14 years in the NFL at that point… I'm not so sure that the discussion wouldn't have become reality."

While it is impossible to know if Mitchell could have taken the Dolphins to greater heights after 1993, it is an objective fact that Marino did not. In the remainder of Marino's career, the Dolphins didn't even make it back to the AFC Championship. Mitchell thinks that may have been different if he remained in Miami. "Being in the same system, I would have done very well in Miami—I have no question about doing very well." With an offense Mitchell was comfortable with, and many years left in the tank, could it have been much worse for the Dolphins? While most will still scoff at the thought of trading Marino being anything but sacrilege, in retrospect, Cote believes his suggestion wasn't so far-fetched. But the reality is, as time passes, that kind of context fades away, and all that remains are the words *Trade Marino. Keep Mitchell*, which will live on forever.

"CHIP KELLY IS THE ANSWER TO OUR CITY'S PRAYER"

(2013–2015 PHILADELPHIA EAGLES)

On the opening Monday of the 2013 NFL season, the league and its fans were witnesses to the launch of what was supposed to be a new era of professional football: the Chip Kelly era. On *Monday Night Football*, the regular season's biggest stage, Kelly, the Philadelphia Eagles' new head coach and famed offensive innovator, made his NFL coaching debut. Two minutes into the third quarter, many were convinced that Kelly would materially change professional football and instill fear into defensive coordinators across the league. This sentiment would be short-lived.

THE CHIP KELLY EXPERIMENT

Before Kelly arrived in Philadelphia, he was the hottest coach in college football. As the University of Oregon's offensive coordinator from 2007 to 2008 and head coach from 2009 to 2012, he presided over one of the most dynamic offenses in the nation. Under Kelly's tutelage, Oregon implemented a high-octane, no-huddle offense that was virtually unstoppable in the Pac-10 Conference. In four years as Oregon's head coach, he led the Ducks to a 46–7 record. From 2009 to 2012, Oregon averaged an NCAA-leading 43.6 points per game. In 2010, Kelly led the program to its first National Championship game, losing narrowly to Auburn.

Kelly's offense at Oregon was so swift, it was referred to by some as the "Blur" because the team moved so fast and frenetically that the defensive players on the field often couldn't catch their breath. Most no-huddle offenses take 20–25 seconds from when the ball is spotted until the next snap. Oregon, at its fastest, averaged around 15 seconds. Defensive players would sometimes fake injuries just to slow things down. It was like nothing college football had ever seen, and had never been implemented in the NFL, at least as a team's normal offense.

Hired by the Eagles in 2013, Kelly replaced longtime head coach Andy Reid, who was terminated after a 4–12 campaign in 2012. Kelly was hailed as an offensive mastermind. However, there were questions about whether his Oregon offense could translate to success in the pros. Centered on tempo, Kelly's offense strived to snap the ball quickly at the line of scrimmage and used a variety of formations to keep defenses off-balance and create mismatches. One concept he frequently utilized was the "run-pass option," or "RPO." With an RPO, the quarterback, after the snap, reads the reaction of a defender, then decides whether to hand the off the ball or throw a quick pass.

There have been teams in NFL history that used predominantly no-huddle offenses to much success. But by 2013, only Peyton Manning, Tom Brady, and a few others were frequently running no-huddle plays. Most teams in the NFL did not do it consistently throughout the course of a game. Even when they did, it was at a much slower pace than what Kelly's college team was running. His Blur offense at Oregon was noticeably different. So much so that it was frequently categorized as a "gimmick" and viewed by some as a college offense that could not function as efficiently in the NFL.

"THEY TOLD US THEY WERE GONNA GO FAST. I'VE NEVER SEEN IT THIS FAST" (2013)

The fascination with Kelly's offense was palpable on the *Monday Night Football* broadcast. The game was at FedEx Field in Landover, Maryland, against defending NFC East Champion Washington. As soon as the Eagles began their opening drive, ESPN play-by-play commentator Mike Tirico focused on their offensive tempo and counted the number of seconds it took for the Eagles to run each play.

On their first drive, Eagles' quarterback Michael Vick immediately got to work. First, a 6-yard pass to wide receiver Riley Cooper. Then a 28-yard pass to tight end Brent Celek. A 16-yard pass to wide receiver DeSean Jackson and a 6-yard run by running back LeSean McCoy followed. By the time the fifth play was snapped, an incomplete pass from Vick, only 1:27 had come off the clock. After a few more plays, Jon Gruden, Tirico's partner on the broadcast, was blown away. "They told us they were gonna go fast. I've never seen it this fast," he said.

The Eagles kept their foot on the gas until a backward pass got away and was returned by Washington for a fluke touchdown. Despite this setback, that first drive set the tone. After the Eagles kicked a field goal, they immediately received the ball back following a Washington fumble. Soon thereafter, Vick threw a pass down the middle to wide receiver DeSean Jackson for a 25-yard touchdown. A few minutes into the second quarter, up 12–7, Vick hit tight end Brent Celek in the middle of the field for a 28-yard touchdown. The Eagles got the ball back again with over four minutes left in the quarter and, after a heavy dose of LeSean McCoy runs, Vick scored a three-yard touchdown on a zone read quarterback keeper. Philly was up 26–7 at the half.

The halftime stats were off the charts. The Eagles had 21 first downs, while Washington ran 21 plays. Philadelphia ran 53 plays in the first half, the most in the NFL in 15 years. After cornerback Cary Williams intercepted a Robert Griffin III pass on Washington's first drive of the third quarter, the Eagles immediately took advantage and scored on the second play of the ensuing drive, as LeSean McCoy ran through a gaping hole and cut outside, hardly touched, for a 34-yard touchdown run. Philadelphia led 33–7. It could not have gone better for Kelly in his debut.

"THE REVOLUTION HAS BEGUN INDEED" (2013)

In that first game, Chip Kelly had the football world convinced his offense was going to be a problem for the rest of the league. Numerous media members and other analysts chimed in on Twitter throughout the game.

> Keep in mind these vaunted NFL Defensive Coordinators have had 8 months to slow down this "gimmick college offense"
>
> —ESPN college football analyst Kirk Herbstreit

> NFL GMs are sitting at home drooling over this Chip Kelly offense, and they are gonna want [then sophomore University of Oregon quarterback] Marcus Mariota to run it for the team
>
> —*Bleacher Report* NFL Draft analyst Matt Miller

> Wow, you think Chip Kelly's offense will work in the NFL? You have your answer now
>
> —Former Philadelphia Eagles quarterback Donovan McNabb

> I kept hearing (and strongly disagreeing) all off-season that NFL D coaches would figure out this Saturday offense. Uhmm...I don't think so.
>
> —Super Bowl–winning quarterback and ESPN analyst Trent Dilfer

Man, every def coordinator who has Philly on their schedule is gonna have nightmares tonight. #boogieman

—Former NFL quarterback, and ESPN college football analyst Danny Kanell

This is not an "after one game" thought. Many of us who followed Oregon knew [what] Chip Kelly's tempo was going to mean to the NFL.

—NFL.com draft analyst Lance Zierlein

When I talk to guys who have coached with or against Chip Kelly, the most common reason they think he'll succeed is "he's too smart to fail."

—*Sports Illustrated* NFL writer Albert Breer

Happy National Chip Kelly NFL Offensive Revolution Day.

—CBS Sports's Bill Reiter

Just wait until Chip Kelly gets his quarterback.

—CBSSports.com college football writer Dennis Dodd

That sound u hear is the phone ringing of any spread up tempo offensive coach in college football.

—Former NFL defensive tackle and Tampa area radio host Booger MacFarland

McCoy's touchdown run was the last time the Eagles scored that night. The offensive juggernaut slowed down a little and Washington closed the gap to make it look close, but the Eagles won 33–27. McCoy finished with 31 carries for 184 yards and a touchdown. Jackson finished with seven catches for 104 yards and a touchdown. Vick threw for 203 yards and two touchdowns and ran for 54 yards and a touchdown.

Chip Kelly's opening NFL act continued the next day. A THING OF DEBUTY, read the headline on the cover of the next day's *Philadelphia Daily News*, followed by a subhead: "The Revolution Has Begun Indeed." In *Business Insider*, sports reporter Tony Manfred wrote that the game gave viewers a "glimpse of what football will look like in the future." Later that week, the *Philadelphia Business Journal* reported that demand for Eagles tickets on the secondary market was up 175 percent.

More praise for Kelly rolled in throughout the week. "The Eagles offense isn't a fad," said Colin Cowherd on his national radio show *The Herd* on ESPN Radio. "They're technology advancing… and we're NEVER going back to dial-up." Former Cowboys and twice Super Bowl–winning head coach Jimmy Johnson was also impressed. "I love it," he told *USA Today* after the game. "That was thoroughly impressive. He is going to give defensive coaches fits." *Toronto Star* columnist Cathal Kelly wrote that Chip Kelly is going to change the NFL forever by starting the no-huddle trend that will eventually eliminate the huddle altogether.

Include ESPN analyst and former Eagles quarterback Ron Jaworski among the impressed. "[The Eagles' win] changed the landscape of the NFL from a philosophical, schematic approach to how the game is played," he said the week following the Eagles' opener. "It was spectacular, and it will be sustainable."

Longtime commentator Dan Dierdorf raved about how perfectly some of the Eagles' personnel fit in its new offensive scheme. "In this offense, you've got to have players who are good in space, and Chip Kelly has three of the best space players in the NFL in

Vick, McCoy, and Jackson," he said. "These three guys were just made for this offense."

Local Philadelphia sportswriter and radio personality Angelo Cataldi acted like Kelly was a gift from the heavens. Included in Cataldi's *Metro Philadelphia* column:

> Chip Kelly is the answer to our city's prayer, a man who follows no rules and suffers no fools. He is a visionary in a city blinded by 53 years of football futility. He is the best reason—if not the only reason—to fall back in love with sports right now in Philadelphia...
>
> Kelly is more than just a tactical wizard. He makes everybody around him better. Mike Vick looks like he's 25 again. LeSean McCoy had the game of his life. DeSean Jackson is not just a deep threat anymore...And every one of them believes in the new coach. They love the guy...
>
> Everybody loves Chip Kelly because he is exactly what we have lacked for more years than we can calculate. He is smarter than the rest, and equal to the task. Even after just one game, there is no denying the new direction he is charting for a city desperate to celebrate a championship in the sport we love the most.
>
> Welcome to Philadelphia, Chip Kelly. You got here just in time.

The euphoria from that great night wore off quickly. The Eagles lost their next three games. But they eventually turned it back around. After Michael Vick went down with a hamstring injury in

Week 5, second-year backup Nick Foles took over at quarterback and ended up having a breakout season. Foles made the Pro Bowl and posted an astounding ratio of 27 touchdowns against only two interceptions. In the Eagles' eighth game, playing the Raiders in Oakland, Foles threw seven touchdowns, tying an NFL record. The Eagles won seven out of their last eight games and the NFC East before losing a heartbreaker in the Divisional Round of the playoffs at home to New Orleans on a last-second field goal.

Ultimately, Kelly's first season in Philadelphia was a success. The Eagles improved their win total from the year before by six games, and the new offense showed great potential, especially by the end of the year. Foles turned out to be the biggest surprise of the season, especially because he lacked a common trait possessed by all of the Chip Kelly's Oregon quarterbacks and by Michael Vick: speed. At Oregon, Kelly invariably used dual-threat quarterbacks. Foles was a tall pocket passer who was slow on foot. But in 2013, the Foles-led offense was very proficient. He seemed like a revelation. Others also shined. McCoy won the NFL's rushing title, running for 1,607 yards, a franchise record. Jackson also had a career season with 82 catches for 1,332 yards and nine touchdowns. Philly.com's sports editor Matt Mullin was excited about the future. "The rest of the NFC East should be concerned," he wrote. "Chip Kelly isn't going anywhere, and he's only going to get better."

"THANKS TO CHIP KELLY, THE FUTURE'S SO BRIGHT, WE GOTTA WEAR SHADES" (2014)

The end-of-the-season optimism was high in Philadelphia. A few days after the playoff loss, *94WIP* Philadelphia Sports Radio host Glen Macnow made a declaration: "It's going to happen [eventually]. [The Eagles] will win a Super Bowl with Chip Kelly." Cataldi maintained the rosy, unwavering belief in Kelly he had expressed in September: "Thanks to Chip Kelly, the future's so bright, we gotta wear shades." In *Metro Philadelphia*, writer Mike Greger wrote: "[The 2013 season] was the tip of the iceberg. With a franchise quarterback firmly in place, along with an ever-improving defense and some of the best skill players in the league, the sky isn't falling in Philadelphia. If anything, the Eagles are the sky."

While Kelly continued to look to supercharge his offense, he was still trying to adapt to personnel management in the NFL. With his first season in the books, he began to assert more control over the Eagles' roster.

Kelly's personnel moves generated much less enthusiasm than his offense. In April 2014, he made the first of many controversial roster decisions. At Kelly's behest, the Eagles released wide receiver DeSean Jackson without giving a specific reason. This was the same DeSean Jackson who had caught over 80 passes in 2013. In addition (as described in a later report by NJ.com), during the months leading up to the 2014 Draft, Kelly began to undermine general manager Howie Roseman and the Eagles' scouting department. According to a former Eagles front-office official, "[R]ight before the draft, the scouts set the board. Then Chip got a hold of it and totally turned it around…Anybody that Chip didn't want, that player's card got removed from the board and thrown in the trash." The draft turned out to be less than fruitful. In terms of drafted players, just one Eagles draftee, third-round pick wide receiver Jordan Mathews, turned out to be a productive player for the franchise.

There were high expectations going into the 2014 season, but it didn't turn out quite like 2013. The Eagles led the division most of the season but collapsed at the end, losing three out of their last four to finish 10–6 and miss the playoffs. There were numerous injuries on the offensive line, plus a four-game suspension to star right tackle Lane Johnson for using performance-enhancing drugs. McCoy still had a productive season, but Foles regressed. After an unimpressive span, where he turned the ball over far too much, he broke his collarbone during the Eagles' ninth game of the season. Philadelphia had to turn to Jets cast-off Mark Sanchez to run the offense the rest of the way.

"HE WAS THE WORST COMMUNICATOR OF ANY COACH I'VE EVER BEEN AROUND" (2015)

By early 2015, Kelly had gained even more power. When the 2014 season ended, Roseman fired Tom Gamble, Kelly's hand-picked VP of player personnel. Infuriated, Kelly convinced Eagles owner Jeff Lurie to demote Roseman and give Kelly full control over the roster. Kelly then proceeded to blow the roster up, disposing of most of the remaining players from the Andy Reid era, including key contributors to the team that had won 20 games the previous two seasons. He even traded Foles, who in December 2013 Kelly had called the Eagles' "starting QB for the next 1,000 years" for the oft-injured and former No. 1 overall draft pick (2010) Sam Bradford.

Next on the chopping block was McCoy. Kelly shipped the running back to the Buffalo Bills for linebacker Kiko Alonso, who had missed the 2014 season because of an ACL injury. After that, Kelly released veteran defensive lineman Trent Cole and offensive lineman Todd Herreman, and elected not to re-sign free agent wide receiver Jeremy Maclin. Maclin was coming off a 1,300-yard, 10-touchdown season. To replace McCoy, he gave a hefty five-year, $42 million contract to Cowboys free agent running back and 2014 NFL rushing champion, DeMarco Murray. He also signed Seahawks cornerback Byron Maxwell to a six-year, $63 million deal.

The 2015 season was a disaster. The Eagles' offense slipped down to the bottom third in the league. In *Football Outsiders* final DVOA (Defense-adjusted Value Over Average) rankings of total offense for the 2015 season, the Eagles finished 22nd out of 32 teams, down from seventh in 2014. It was a far cry from Kelly's Oregon days.

The only time the Eagles' offense really resembled the Blur from Kelly's Oregon days was during that first half against Washington in 2013. From then on, the Eagles began taking it much slower between plays, while every so often "sprinkling" the faster up-tempo stuff.

As the 2015 season went along, Kelly's offense became more predictable and one-dimensional. Opponents began to figure out how to change coverages to counter Kelly's RPO attacks. Murray only got half the carries he had when he won the rushing title at Dallas. By Week 13, Murray had been demoted to second string for the faster and smaller Darren Sproles. Murray played in only two games where he had over 20 carries. On December 30, with one game left in the season and the Eagles sitting on a 6–9 record, owner Jeffrey Lurie fired Kelly.

Despite Kelly's 26–21 record over three seasons as head coach, Lurie had seen enough of him. His drastic roster decisions were costly, and the relationships between Kelly, Lurie, and the Eagles' front office, had fractured. Numerous people spoke out about Kelly's lack of communication skills. Merrill Reese, the play-by-play announcer for the Eagles for 40 years, said he had absolutely no relationship with Kelly. "He was the worst communicator of any coach I've ever been around," Reese later recalled.

Some went even further. Cornerback Brandon Boykin, who is Black, said that although he didn't believe Kelly was racist, he didn't relate to players, and was "uncomfortable around grown men of our culture." A few months before the 2015 season began, former Eagles offensive lineman Tra Thomas, who worked as a staff intern in 2013–2014, said, "[Certain Eagles players] feel like there is a hint of racism" in the Eagles' locker room. Some current Eagles' players, former Oregon players, and former coaches have since spoken out against the racism claims and defended Kelly.

Not long after Kelly was given the pink slip in Philadelphia, he was hired as the new head coach of the San Francisco 49ers. The Niners were in complete rebuilding mode, but Kelly didn't last long enough to see the team revive. In his only season as head coach, San Francisco went 2–14 and he was unceremoniously fired. As of 2022, Kelly is back in college, as the head coach of UCLA, where he was hired after the 2017 season.

While Chip's offensive "revolution" didn't materialize as planned, he did play a role in the modernization of pro offenses. Although not the first coach to use the RPO in the NFL, Kelly was the first to make it a staple in the league. Since 2013, the RPO has been adopted by many teams who have expanded it and developed more complex and effective variants.

Kelly's successor in Philadelphia, Doug Pederson, with assistance from offensive coordinator Frank Reich, integrated some of Kelly's RPO concepts into his offense with the Eagles. In 2017, when Eagles starting quarterback Carson Wentz went down with an ACL injury, Foles, who was brought back to Philadelphia before the 2017 season as a backup, took over and was masterful executing RPOs throughout the playoffs. His denouement came at Super Bowl LII in Minneapolis, where he was named MVP after leading Philadelphia to a 41–33 victory over Tom Brady and New England. It was the first Super Bowl title in the history of the Eagles franchise.

CULTURE VERSUS SCHEME

When Kelly was hired by the Eagles, the underlying question above all else was whether his offensive scheme would work in the NFL. Most in the NFL world seemed to have an overwhelming belief that if it worked, everything else would fall into place. Although his offenses weren't as dominant as in college, Kelly fit the bill as an offensive mind at the next level. But when it came to most of the other responsibilities of an NFL head coach—like building a culture, making sound decisions, and managing personnel—he was in over his head.

In 2014, an NFL Films camera and microphone once caught Chip Kelly on the sidelines before a Sunday night game saying, "Culture wins football," and that "Culture will beat scheme every day." In his case, it was rather prophetic.

"HOW COULD THE RAVENS PASS UP LAWRENCE PHILLIPS, TAKE OT JONATHAN OGDEN, AND DRAFT 'SMALLISH' RAY LEWIS?"

(1996 BALTIMORE RAVENS)

"**A**"—that's the grade the *Dallas Morning News* gave the Arizona Cardinals' 1998 NFL Draft class. In 2001, the *Arizona Republic* accorded the Dolphins the same grade. In 2005, *Florida Today* gave the Packers a "D." But the Cardinals never called home to brag. The Dolphins never posted the grade on the team refrigerator. The Packers didn't bring back a signed copy and beg for extra credit. These grades don't count. They have never counted. In truth, they don't mean anything. What counts is winning. After the 1998 Draft, the Cardinals had one winning season out of its next ten. From 2001 to 2022, the Dolphins have been one of the league's least successful franchises. The year they got a "D," the Packers selected Aaron Rodgers in the 2005 Draft. As of 2022, he is still Green Bay's starting quarterback, and because of him, the Packers have been perennial contenders for the majority of the time.

The annual ritual of grading NFL Draft results as soon as the draft is completed is popular but nonsensical. It would be much more reasonable to wait a few years to see how the selections perform. However, since sports fans have an insatiable appetite for analyzing everything about their team in real time, it has become tradition for hordes of draft analysts and "experts" to immediately grade each team's draft class as if they were scoring an elementary school paper.

For a prime display of imprecision in the draft grade process, consider the grades given to the Baltimore Ravens and the St. Louis Rams after the 1996 Draft.

THE INAUGURAL BALTIMORE RAVENS SEASON (1996)

The Baltimore Ravens' first season in the NFL was 1996. The year before, the team was located 400 miles north, in Cleveland, Ohio, and were known as the Cleveland Browns. But at the end of the 1995 season, Browns owner Art Modell was frustrated in his failed attempts to convince the City of Cleveland to build a new football stadium that he relocated the organization, including its staff, and its players to Baltimore and started anew as the Ravens.

The 1996 NFL Draft was also the first in which Ozzie Newsome, then the Ravens' director of football operations, was the final decision maker. Newsome played tight end for the Browns from 1978 to 1990 and set franchise records in both receptions and touchdowns. In 1999, he was inducted into the Pro Football Hall of Fame. When his playing career ended, he became an executive in the Browns front office and moved to Baltimore with Modell in 1996, where he eventually became the first Black general manager in NFL history.

THE LAWRENCE PHILLIPS CONUNDRUM

The Ravens held the fourth overall pick in the 1996 Draft. Newsome had his eye on a handful of players, including University of Nebraska running back Lawrence Phillips. For three years, Phillips had been one of the most prolific and electrifying running backs in college football. Many thought he had "can't miss" superstar talent. Some experts believed he was the best overall player in the draft. However, Phillips came with baggage. Based on a few serious incidents during his tenure in Nebraska, many teams had significant concerns about his character. He was enough of a risk that a few teams said they would not select him in any round.

Going into his junior year in 1995, Phillips was considered a Heisman Trophy candidate. However, after an early September game, Phillips was arrested for breaking into backup quarterback Scott Frost's apartment and assaulting Phillips's ex-girlfriend, who was there hanging out with Frost. Phillips proceeded to drag her by the hair down a flight of stairs. It wasn't his first run-in with the law during his time at Nebraska, but it was certainly the most troubling.

After the arrest, Phillips was suspended by the team indefinitely. Eventually, he pled no contest to a misdemeanor, received probation, went to counseling, and apologized to the victim. After six games without Phillips, Nebraska head coach Tom Osborne made a controversial decision and lifted his suspension. Later, in the Fiesta Bowl in January 1996, Phillips ran for 165 yards and scored three total touchdowns as Nebraska blew out Florida 62–24 to win its second straight National Championship.

While everyone marveled in the Cornhuskers' dominant performance that night, many expressed disappointment that Phillips was allowed to play. "Shining moment is tainted," was the headline on Jason Whitlock's column in the *Kansas City Star* the next day. *Baltimore Sun* staff writer Don Markus called the Huskers' title the "the worst story of the year" and wrote that Nebraska was "the feel-bad" team of the season. But despite all the dissent surrounding Phillips's participation, the Fiesta Bowl turned out to be a great showcase for Phillips for the upcoming NFL Draft evaluation season. Going into the 1996 Draft, one of the Ravens' biggest needs was at running back. In 1995, as the Cleveland Browns, the team had only five rushing touchdowns.

JONATHAN OGDEN AND RAY LEWIS: THE BEST PLAYERS AVAILABLE

While Phillips was high risk, UCLA's Jonathan Ogden was the polar opposite. The 6-foot-8, 318-pound behemoth offensive tackle, who won the 1995 Outland Trophy (awarded to college football's best lineman), was the best offensive line prospect in the draft.

His senior season had been sensational. He did not give up a single sack, and had no character concerns.

Before the draft, the Ravens did not expect to have a chance to pick Ogden. Most mock drafts had him going third to Arizona, with Phillips falling to Baltimore at fourth. The Ravens were preparing to choose between Phillips and Illinois defensive lineman Simeon Rice, but, surprisingly, Arizona drafted Rice. The Ravens then made a stunning decision. They passed on Phillips and selected Ogden: They felt he was the best player available.

Perhaps the pick should not have been so stunning. On paper, Ogden was the safest pick in the Draft and he was almost certain to be great. However, there was one problem: Ogden had played left tackle at UCLA, and Baltimore already had a left tackle, Tony Jones. Jones was one of the premier left tackles in the league, having started 99 consecutive games for the Browns. But, after they made the pick, the Ravens announced that Ogden had agreed to move to guard, a position on the offensive line that he had never played, and that Jones would stay a left tackle.

Apparently, part of the reason the Cardinals passed on Ogden was that he insisted he wanted to play left tackle (if true, it was a stance he must have dropped instantly after he was drafted by Baltimore), and the Cardinals already had a left tackle, veteran Lomas Brown.

The Ravens also had acquired the 49ers' first-round pick from a trade between the two teams before the 1995 Draft. That became the 26th overall pick in 1996. There, Baltimore snagged University of Miami linebacker Ray Lewis. Lewis was the runner-up for the 1995 Butkus Award for college football's best linebacker. While he was a well-respected prospect, Lewis's "flaw," and the principal reason he was available when the 26th pick came around, was his size. "He didn't have the ideal measurables," Phil Savage, then the

Ravens' director of college scouting, recalled years later. At just 6-foot, 235 pounds, he was a bit on the small side for a linebacker, and scouts were skeptical. "There's a feeling that if a middle line-backer isn't 6-foot-2 and 250 pounds, they can't do it," said Marvin Lewis in 2018. Lewis was the Ravens' defensive coordinator in 1996.

"[PHILLIPS] WOULD HAVE BEEN A CLASS-A CITIZEN . . . BALTIMORE WOULD HAVE BEEN PROUD"

Although he was happy with Ogden, Modell had been set on selecting Phillips. He admitted that the Ravens would have picked the running back if the Cardinals didn't throw the curveball and pass on Ogden for Rice. Even after Arizona took Rice, Modell was still pushing for Phillips, but Newsome overrode him and picked Ogden, avoiding the onslaught of negative publicity the team would have faced for drafting Phillips.

The St. Louis Rams ended up taking Phillips with the sixth overall pick. Their front office was ecstatic. According to Hank Goldberg, who was reporting from the Rams' headquarters on ESPN's draft broadcast, when the Ravens selected Ogden, a loud roar of excitement arose from their draft room.

If the Rams had any concerns about Phillips's legal issues, owner Georgia Frontiere wasn't showing it. "If it helps our team," she said soon after the pick was announced, "that's all I care about."

Despite passing on him, Modell was quick to defend Phillips from critical comments by the press. He made sure to point out that if the Ravens would have drafted Phillips, he would have been confident in the selection:

> I had no qualms about taking [Phillips], because I
> felt, based on our investigation, that he was subject

to quick and complete rehabilitation and that he
would have been a class-A citizen and a man the City
of Baltimore would have been proud of.

The Ravens owner even went as far as to make it clear that
he believed that Phillips's ex-girlfriend, the victim of his assault,
shouldered at least some of the fault for the running back's actions. According to Modell, she "provoked" Phillips's attack on
her. "That doesn't excuse his behavior but you've got to understand
[Phillips's] background," Modell said. "This was the love of his life.
Someone he could cling to. He had no mother, no father . . . and she
turned out to betray him."

Modell's victim-blaming comments were met with a fair share
of criticism, but there was no significant fallout and the words
were essentially forgotten within days. This is a prime illustration
of how the NFL community's perception and understanding of do-
mestic violence has evolved. If an NFL owner made similar comments today, he or she would likely face substantial backlash and
significant damage to his or her reputation.

"WE THOUGHT ART MODELL WAS SMARTER THAN THIS. PHILLIPS SHOULD HAVE BEEN THE PICK"

The post-draft rankings for the Ravens were not complimentary.
Tampa Bay Times NFL reporter Rick Stroud included the Ravens
in his list of draft "losers," decrying the fact that they "plan to try
and move Ogden to [guard]—a position he's never played." *Miami
Herald* columnist Greg Cote gave the Ravens' draft a "C-minus"
and called the Ogden pick "odd" because the offensive line was already a Ravens strength going into the draft.

The Ravens were also skewered for passing on Phillips. The *Chicago Sun-Times* asked, "How could the Ravens pass up Lawrence Phillips and take OT Jonathan Ogden with the intent of playing him at guard?" Len Pasquarelli, an *Atlanta Journal-Constitution* NFL writer, gave the Ravens a "C," reasoning that the team "passed on the draft's best player [Phillips]," while also wondering, "Where does Ogden play?" *Los Angeles Times* columnist Bill Plaschke listed the Ravens as one of the teams in the draft that "stumbled." "We thought Art Modell was smarter than this," Plaschke wrote. "Phillips should have been the pick there."

It wasn't just the Ogden pick that was criticized. Randy Lange, a reporter for the (North Jersey) *Record*, wrote that Ray Lewis was the Ravens' "worst buy" of the draft. "Lewis," Lange wrote, "like [linebacker] Craig Powell [the Browns' first-round pick in 1995, who only lasted one season with the franchise] a year ago, was forced into Round 1." Stroud wrote in his next-day draft column that "after the [Ravens] failed to address their running back needs, they drafted smallish LB Ray Lewis." Plaschke was also lukewarm about the Lewis pick, questioning why Baltimore would take the linebacker when Texas A&M running back Leland McElroy was available.

"I REALLY BELIEVE THAT [ST. LOUIS] IS THE PERFECT SPOT FOR LAWRENCE PHILLIPS"

Anchored by Phillips, the Rams' 1996 Draft class was critically acclaimed. Former NFL quarterback Joe Theismann, one of the main analysts on ESPN's draft broadcast, loved Phillips's fit in St. Louis. "I really believe that this is the perfect spot for Lawrence Phillips," Theismann said. "I still believe that this is the kid that we're gonna be talking about a year from now as being a sensation in the National Football League."

ESPN's draft expert Mel Kiper Jr., broadcasting with Theismann, slammed the pick. The Rams needed a revamp of offensive talent, but Kiper didn't think that a risk like Phillips was worthy of being the sixth pick when there were other quality running backs in the draft pool. "It's too deep a year for running backs. You can get an [Ohio State running back] Eddie George…" he said. Theismann did not share Kiper's opinion. He told Kiper:

> I don't agree with either of your points to be honest
> with you Mel…I think, as we've said and most
> people have conceded, take the problems off the
> field away, everybody's called him the best player in
> the draft, you have to sooner or later let the talent
> go. This is not a league of angels. There are people
> that have had problems but they've gotten over
> them. I think this is a young man who will put this
> behind him and will be a better football player.

Rams head coach Rich Brooks felt the same way as Theismann. "We obviously don't think this is a major risk," he said. In addition to Phillips, the Rams traded down to 18, and selected wide receiver Eddie Kennison. A speedster from LSU, Kennison was expected to be drafted later in the first round. One pick later, the Indianapolis Colts selected Syracuse wideout Marvin Harrison 19th. Harrison spent his entire career with the Colts, set numerous NFL and team receiving records, and, in 2016, was inducted into the Hall of Fame.

In the second round, St. Louis chose Tony Banks, a quarterback from Michigan State. Banks was thought to have the size

(6-foot-4½, 220 pounds), mobility, and arm talent, but he was a questionable decision maker. He threw 15 interceptions to only nine touchdowns his senior year. Nevertheless, Brooks saw him as the quarterback of the future.

The Rams front office received very high marks for their picks. If this was grade school, they certainly would have made the honor roll. Pasquarelli gave the Rams an "A-plus." Stroud listed St. Louis as one of his "top bananas," mostly for drafting "arguably the best player in the draft [Phillips]," and wrote that "if personal demons can be exorcised, Phillips could be one of the best running backs in league history." Stroud also added that "at least the Rams got rid of one headache by unloading slumping running back Jerome Bettis to Pittsburgh." Bettis ended up having a Hall of Fame career for the Steelers.

Plaschke added to the compliments. Like many others, he lauded St. Louis for choosing Phillips and dumping Bettis. Plaschke also gushed that the Rams acquired the draft's "most promising quarterback" in Tony Banks. Mike O'Hara, in *USA Today*, also had fine things to say. "Instant offense with RB Lawrence Phillips and WR Eddie Kennison, and a QB of the future in Tony Banks in the 2nd round," he wrote. "Grade: A-minus." Vinny DiTrani, in the *Record*, gave the Rams an "A," because their "offense was upgraded 100 percent." The *Buffalo News*'s Milt Northrop listed the Rams as one of his "big winners" of the draft. "St. Louis had the nerve to take Lawrence Phillips," Northrop wrote, "and didn't have to trade up to get him." The *Dallas Morning News* called the Rams the "kings of their draft class." "Could a team have done any better?" asked the *Chicago Sun-Times* about the Rams. "They got the best player in the draft, RB Lawrence Phillips, with the sixth pick, [and] a potentially great receiver in Eddie Kennison... The Rams should get impact that is immediate and long term."

THE RAVENS STRIKE LIGHTNING IN A BOTTLE. TWICE

So, what actually happened? For the Ravens, they struck lightning in a bottle—twice. Both Ogden and Lewis had Hall of Fame careers. Each started immediately for the Ravens and made instant impacts. Ogden played at guard his rookie season, after which the Ravens traded Jones to Denver and Ogden was able to move back to tackle, his more natural position. In 12 seasons, he was a four-time All-Pro, and was selected to the Pro Bowl 11 times. He is now considered by many to be one of the greatest tackles ever to play in the NFL.

Ray Lewis became one of the premier defensive players in the league and is regarded by most to be the best linebacker of his era. In his rookie season, he led the team in tackles; in his second season he led the NFL in tackles. In 2000, he won his first of two NFL Defensive Player of the Year awards. That same year, the Ravens won their first Super Bowl, and Lewis was named MVP of the game. Lewis retired after the 2012 season. His final game was in February 2013, at Super Bowl XLVII, where the Ravens won their second championship.

THE RAMS' PICKS UNDERWHELM, AND PHILLIPS FLAMES OUT

The Rams' selections didn't fare nearly as well, despite the team's supposedly magnificent draft. They posted losing records the three seasons following the draft. Banks was their starting quarterback for most of that period, and while he occasionally put up nice numbers, he turned the ball over far too much, took a ton of sacks, and generally became a huge liability. After the 1998 season, the team traded Banks to none other than…Baltimore. He never became a star and retired in 2005.

Kennison had a tremendous rookie year but fell off the next two, after which the franchise traded him to New Orleans. He eventually went on to play for a total of five teams throughout a solid 14-year career. Ironically, the Rams won the Super Bowl the year after Kennison and Banks were traded.

Phillips did not reach his potential. He played only one-and-a-half seasons in St. Louis, scoring 12 touchdowns in 25 games. After repeated instances of misconduct, he was released in November 1997. Soon after, he was signed by the Dolphins but only lasted two games in Miami—he was cut after he was involved in an incident in a South Florida nightclub, to which he eventually pled no contest. After he put up a productive season in Barcelona in the now-defunct NFL Europe, the 49ers took a flier on him in 1999. But after struggling on the field and openly denouncing his coaches and authority figures off it, he was released by the Niners after only a few months. He went on to play a few seasons in the Canadian Football League, and by 2003 he retired.

After Phillips's football career ended, he started to get into more significant legal trouble. He went to prison in 2006, eventually being sentenced to a total of 31 years for crimes including assault with a deadly weapon, assault with great bodily injury, and false imprisonment. In 2015, he was charged with killing his prison cellmate. Before his trial, he committed suicide.

"WE FACTOR WHO'S THE BEST PLAYER"

The 1996 Draft was the beginning of a stellar executive career for Newsome. By the time he stepped down as general manager after the 2018 season, Newsome oversaw 192 picks in all. As of 2020, 15 of those picks became first-team All-Pros, 31 became Pro Bowlers, and three were inducted into the NFL Hall of Fame. One of those

Hall of Famers is Ogden, a 2013 inductee, whose selection was announced in February of that year, one day before the Ravens won Super Bowl XLVII. Newsome introduced Ogden at the induction ceremony that August. He was the first Ravens player to be inducted. Lewis followed in 2018. Free safety Ed Reed, the Ravens' first-round pick in 2002, was inducted in 2019.

The fact that Baltimore drafted Ogden when it already had a solid left tackle and that it chose "smallish" Ray Lewis, in lieu of its major "need" for a running back, foreshadowed Newsome's draft strategy during his tenure. "We do not—especially on the first day of the draft or the top four picks—factor in 'need,'" Newsome said in 2007. "We factor who's the best player." This policy helped turn the Ravens into solid contenders throughout Newsome's tenure as general manager.

Ozzie Newsome stepped down as the Ravens' general manager after the 2018 season. As of 2022, he is still an active part of the franchise but with a lesser role in the front office. "Ozzie is the foundation of the Ravens," Ravens coach John Harbaugh said in 2013. Although there is a sentiment from some fans and experts that his draft results had declined toward the end of his tenure, Newsome is still one of the most important and impactful general managers of the past thirty years. He has earned that respect even though he began his front-office career with a mediocre draft grade average. He gives hope to C-students everywhere.

"I'M TELLING YOU,
[THE CHARGERS]
HAVE SOMETHING
SPECIAL HERE
[WITH RYAN LEAF]"

(PRESEASON PERFORMANCE TRAPS)

"I know it's only preseason, but…" Famous first words. Some write them, others speak them, almost all think them. But, at some point, almost everybody ignores them. The NFL preseason is where dreams come alive and delusions are enabled. It is a special time where a single performance can confirm the most tenuous biases and create jaded declarations of hope.

In the preseason, most teams' playbooks consist of basic schemes, and each team plays its second-, third-, and even fourth-string players for significant portions of the games. Many of the players who play in the preseason games won't even be on any teams' active roster when the regular season starts. All things considered, it's not the time to properly assess any player's performance. Also, exhibition games don't count toward each team's records, so by the time the regular season kicks off, anything notable that happened during the preseason is practically forgotten.

If they're being honest with themselves, most fans and members of the media know not to take players' achievements during the preseason too seriously. However, every year, regardless of the warning signs, many are victimized by "preseason performance traps," when the football world interprets a player's (the majority of the time, a quarterback's) positive preseason performance as more significant than it is. The phenomenon has been around for decades but has become more prevalent in recent years as social media apps like Twitter allow people to express their thoughts about a game as it's going on in real time.

Preseason performance traps apply to players and teams of all shapes, sizes, and characteristics, and they occur in many different scenarios. A few examples are listed and described below.

AN "UNDERDRAFTED" ROOKIE WHO PLAYS WELL IN HIS PRESEASON DEBUT

Ryan Mallett, a tall, strong-armed quarterback with a lightning-quick release, was touted as a likely first-round pick throughout his two seasons as the starter at the University of Arkansas, where he threw for close to 7,500 yards and 62 touchdowns. However, during the 2011 Draft, several character issues scared teams from spending a high draft pick on him. He ended up slipping to the third round, where the Patriots grabbed him with the 74th overall pick. A large faction of analysts thought he was drafted significantly lower than his talent suggested.

Mallett took all of New England's second-half snaps during the Patriots' first preseason game, a home win over Jacksonville. Facing mostly the Jaguars' third- and fourth-string defenses, he led New England on four touchdown drives. He finished the game 15-of-21 for 171 yards and a touchdown pass.

Soon after the game, the plaudits started rolling in for the rookie quarterback. NFL Network analyst Bucky Brooks declared that the game proved Mallett was the steal of the draft. ESPN NFL reporter Chris Mortensen relayed that he had already heard from one general manager who was second-guessing himself for not picking Mallett. Fox Sports' NFL writer Peter Schrager, after having touted Mallett during the 2011 Draft, reiterated that he was "shocked and disturbed" over the fact that the Bengals' first-round pick, quarterback Andy Dalton, was selected before Mallett. To Schrager, the Arkansas gunslinger slipping to the third round was "MIND BOGGLING."

Ultimately, Mallett proved to be worth even less than a third-round pick. In two seasons with the Patriots, he completed only one regular-season pass. New England traded him to Houston in 2014. He played four more seasons in the NFL with Houston and

Baltimore, but never became a full-time starting quarterback and was out of the league by 2018.

AN "OVERDRAFTED" ROOKIE WHO PLAYS WELL IN HIS PRESEASON DEBUT

With the 16th overall pick in the 2013 Draft, the Buffalo Bills selected Florida State quarterback EJ Manuel. The media reaction was overwhelmingly negative. But unlike the previous example, where people questioned why Ryan Mallett wasn't drafted *high enough*, the Bills were criticized for drafting Manuel *too high*, because he was graded as a second-round prospect on most analysts' draft boards and was deemed by many to be a "project." The preseason was Manuel's first chance to prove the critics wrong.

During Buffalo's first preseason game, a 44–20 Bills win in Indianapolis, Manuel completed 16-of-21 passes for 107 yards and a touchdown. For some people, it was already enough to justify Manuel's draft position. "Finally, the Bills have their QB in [EJ Manuel]," tweeted CBS Sports' Adam Schein. NFL Network analyst and Hall of Fame defensive lineman Warren Sapp also had high praise: "EJ Manuel has command and control of this offense like no rookie I've ever seen." An article on the website *Bleacher Report* surmised that Manuel "has proven his worth," and that he looked poised "to show why he was the top quarterback taken in [the draft]."

In the end, Manuel did not turn out to be first-round quality and was not the answer for the Bills. He started 10 games in 2013 but missed six after suffering two separate knee injuries. Once healthy again, he lost his job to Kyle Orton after the first month of the 2014 season and was relegated to the bench the following two years. Buffalo let him go after the 2016 season. He went on to play a few unremarkable seasons in Oakland before retiring in 2019.

A MASSIVELY HYPED ROOKIE WHO LEADS THE TEAM ON A FEW PRESEASON TOUCHDOWN DRIVES

EJ Manuel was a disappointment, but he is never mentioned in the conversation of top draft busts. Usually, the most memorable draft busts are players who fall short of meeting the high expectations thrust upon them after an extraordinary amount of hype surrounded them throughout the NFL Draft process and beyond.

"There was a magic to Rick Mirer's game. A refreshing, positive energy"

When a quarterback is the subject of persistent fanfare before and after the draft, one single positive performance during a preseason game may be enough, for some, to justify the hype surrounding him. This happened with Seattle Seahawks rookie quarterback Rick Mirer in 1993. His first preseason start elicited a textbook preseason performance trap.

A highly touted prospect out of Notre Dame, Mirer was the second overall pick in the 1993 Draft and was viewed as the key piece to a rebuild of a Seahawks franchise that had finished a dismal 2–14 in 1992. Mirer played in the second half of his first preseason game and started the Seahawks' second, a home matchup against San Francisco in the Kingdome. Taking advantage of favorable field position resulting from numerous 49er turnovers, Mirer led Seattle on four straight scoring drives. All in all, he went 6-of-12 for 87 yards in limited action and threw two touchdowns.

To most, Mirer's rookie debut was a nice start, but nothing memorable. But to *Seattle Times* writer Steve Kelley, it meant much more. Mirer's performance convinced Kelley of the team's inevitable future prosperity with the young quarterback. In his game column, Kelley wrote, among other things:

[Mirer] looked as comfortable as a 10-year veteran. He was as tough as oak, quick as a twitching muscle.

There was a magic to Rick Mirer's game. A refreshing, positive energy.

[The starting quarterback] job should be Mirer's. Not merely because of what he did last night, but because of what he will do in November of this year and in many autumnal Sundays to come.

Mirer is the best news the Seahawks have had since they drafted [eventual Hall of Fame defensive tackle] Cortez Kennedy.

The curtain on the Seahawks' future rose last night in the Kingdome.

The Seahawks need a hope for the rest of the 1990s... They need Rick Mirer.

Mirer's career arc did not reach the heights Kelley intimated. As a rookie, Mirer started every game for Seattle and finished fifth in the AFC in completions and yards. However, he threw 17 interceptions and only 12 touchdowns, and the Seahawks finished 6–10. He never improved. In the four seasons Mirer spent with the franchise, the Seahawks never finished with a winning record. He spent the remainder of his career as a journeyman backup and retired in 2004.

"[Ryan Leaf is] going to be a topic of conversation around here for 15 years"

In the hierarchy of NFL Draft busts, Ryan Leaf may be the crown prince. Drafted right behind Peyton Manning at number two overall by the San Diego Chargers in 1998, Leaf was pegged as a can't-miss prospect. Stunningly, he became possibly the biggest draft flop in NFL history.

With the excessive amount of hoopla surrounding Leaf throughout the draft process, it was practically impossible not to believe the accolades bestowed upon him. The moment he was drafted, virtually everyone assumed he would be an NFL superstar.

Leaf's NFL career began promisingly. In his second preseason start, a 41–27 win over the Rams in San Diego, he played the entire first half and was 13-of-22 for 200 yards passing, including a passing touchdown and a rushing touchdown. The showing was enough for *San Diego Union-Tribune* columnist Nick Canepa to essentially anoint Leaf a future Chargers legend. In his next-day column, Canepa explained that this was a rare occasion he wouldn't curb his enthusiasm about one game. "If you think we're making a big deal out of Ryan Leaf, you're wrong," he wrote. "He's going to be a topic of conversation around here for 15 years." Canepa continued:

> With a great quarterback, you always have a chance,
> which was how it was when [famed Chargers
> quarterback and Hall of Famer Dan Fouts] walked
> our turf…Judging by what I saw last night, there's
> no reason to believe [the Chargers can't be serious
> contenders for a long time]…I'm telling you, we
> have something special here.

Leaf's rookie season was a disaster from which he never recovered. He threw two touchdowns and 15 interceptions, and he lost his starting job after nine games. He was released by the Chargers after only two years and was out of the league after just three seasons, never to return. His quick descent to rock bottom, including drug addiction and a prison stint, and his eventual recovery, are well documented. The Chargers eventually gained stability at quarterback in 2006 when Philip Rivers became the starter and held on to that role for 14 straight seasons (where he played the majority of his likely Hall of Fame career).

A NEW QUARTERBACK OF A HISTORICALLY BAD TEAM WHO PERFORMS WELL IN THE PRESEASON

Unlike the Chargers, many teams lack consistency at quarterback for extended periods. The longer a team goes without a capable signal-caller, the more likely the football media and the team's fans will overextend their acclaim whenever the team has a quarterback who shows even the slightest bit of promise.

The Cleveland Browns have been the 21st century's poster child for NFL quarterback instability. Since they rebooted the franchise as an expansion team in 1999 (after the original Browns left Cleveland in 1996 and became the Baltimore Ravens) up through 2021, the Browns have been perpetually bad. During this period, they have made the playoffs just twice and have had only three seasons with a winning record. A huge factor in the Browns' long stretch of futility is their inability to find any consistency at quarterback. Like their win-loss record throughout the past 23 years, the Browns' record on choosing quarterbacks isn't very good. Since 1999, the Browns have had 30 starting quarterbacks. At least a handful of them performed well enough in the preseason to lure people into the mistaken belief that change was on the horizon.

"Jake Delhomme [is] just what [the] doctor ordered for [the] Browns."

After the Browns' first decade of subpar quarterback play, there was a little bit of optimism in the air about the 2010 season when they brought in Jake Delhomme. He was a 12-year veteran with a solid track record. In the seven years before he arrived in Cleveland, Delhomme led the Carolina Panthers to three playoff berths, including a trip to the Super Bowl in 2004 and an NFC Championship Game appearance in 2006.

In the Browns' 2010 preseason opener, a 27–24 win in Green Bay, Delhomme, in his only drive, went 6-of-7 for 66 yards, and led the team to a touchdown. About the drive, the AP's Tom Withers wrote: "One drive: 11 plays, 80 yards in under six minutes. That's all it took for Jake Delhomme to convince many Cleveland fans that the Browns' seemingly endless problems at quarterback are history... It was an opening act to behold." Two games later, in Detroit, Delhomme completed 20-of-25 passes for 152 yards and a touchdown, during which *Sports Illustrated*'s Peter King tweeted, "Jake's reborn." In his *Cleveland Examiner* column the following day, under the headline "Jake Delhomme just what doctor ordered for ailing Cleveland Browns," Browns writer Greg Swartz wrote that "a comeback player of the year award isn't out of the question" for Delhomme, who had the worst season of his career the year before.

It didn't work out that way. Delhomme suffered a high ankle sprain in Week 1, and didn't play again until Week 5. He started three more games for the Browns in 2010, but by the end of the year, he lost his starting job. He finished the season with two touchdowns and seven interceptions. The Browns ended up with a 5–11 overall record. Delhomme was released just before the start of the 2011 preseason.

"[With Colt McCoy], Cleveland may have solidified the [quarterback] position for the next [10 years]"

Next man up: Colt McCoy. In 2011, McCoy was the clear-cut starter going into Browns camp. In his rookie season the year before, he started eight games and showed promise.

A prolific four-year starter at quarterback at the University of Texas, McCoy went into the 2010 Draft facing questions about his size (6-foot-1, 215 pounds) and arm strength. As a result, he slipped to the third round, where the Browns grabbed him with the 85th overall pick.

Despite having the starting job in the bag, McCoy still had to prove that he could lead the team to success. It didn't take long to convince people he was capable. In the Browns first preseason game, McCoy, playing in just three series, went 9-of-10 for 135 yards and threw a touchdown pass. A few days later, ESPN's Merril Hoge posited that "Cleveland may have solidified the [quarterback] position for the next [10 years]."

Almost a week later, McCoy played even better when he threw three touchdowns at home against the Lions. During the game, ESPN's John Clayton tweeted that McCoy might be the "most improved QB in football." A few days after, Cleveland-based writer Branson Wright wrote a blog for the *Cleveland Plain Dealer* in which he proclaimed that, with McCoy, "the Browns have a potential franchise quarterback for the first time since the '80s when they had [Browns legendary quarterback] Bernie Kosar" from 1986 to 1993. Later in the preseason, Peter King predicted that McCoy would be one of the league's five breakout stars of 2011. King also requested his Twitter followers to "mark [his] words" that Browns team president Mike Holmgren would be sold on McCoy by season's end.

Ultimately, McCoy started 13 regular-season games for Cleveland in 2011. While he wasn't awful, he failed to convince the Browns brass that he was the team's long-term answer. After suffering a concussion in Week 14, he missed the rest of the 2011 season. He never started another game for the Browns, who released him after the 2012 season. McCoy has been a journeyman backup in the league ever since.

"Believe it, Browns fans. It's time to buy into Brandon Weeden"

In 2012, the Browns installed 28-year-old rookie first-round draft pick Brandon Weeden at quarterback, but he struggled. He started 15 games and threw 14 touchdowns and 17 interceptions for a Browns team that went 5–11.

Before the 2013 season, Cleveland hired a new head coach, Rob Chudzinski, who, in turn, brought in Norv Turner as offensive coordinator. Turner, who called the offensive plays for two of the three Cowboys' Super Bowl winning teams in the '90s, was considered by many to be an offensive genius. He was pegged as the guy to mold Weeden into a reliable quarterback and transform the Browns offense into a productive one.

Weeden started off the 2013 preseason hot. In six drives, he led the team to three touchdowns and two field goals. Many believed Turner was behind Weeden's fast start. ESPN's Ed Werder tweeted about "the Norv Turner impact." Syracuse.com writer Ryan Talbot chalked up Weeden's seeming improvement to "the power of Norv." Writer Andrea Hangst was so impressed with Weeden's play, she was convinced Weeden was a changed player. "Believe it, Browns fans: Weeden is living up to his first-round billing," she wrote in a *Bleacher Report* article titled "It's Time to Buy into Brandon Weeden After Another Dominant Preseason Outing."

None of this proved to be true. Weeden battled injuries but still struggled when he was healthy. By the eighth week of the season, he permanently lost his job. The Browns finished the season at 4–12, and, soon thereafter, Turner was fired, along with the rest of the coaching staff. Weeden was released three months later.

"[DeShone Kizer] is the future for the Cleveland Browns...[He] is the next generation of QB"

In 2017, DeShone Kizer was the odd man out of a first round of a draft that included quarterbacks Mitch Trubisky, Patrick Mahomes, and Deshaun Watson. A 21-year-old signal-caller out of Notre Dame, Kizer, along with Trubisky and Watson, were projected to be first-round picks during the months leading up to the draft, but at some point Mahomes surpassed him, and Kizer slipped to the second round, where the Browns grabbed him.

Kizer was 6-foot-4 and 235 pounds, quick on his feet, and had great arm strength. Critics were intrigued by his tools. After a few positive performances during the preseason, many were bullish on his future. Former NFL wide receiver Nate Burleson, one of the hosts of the NFL Network TV show *Good Morning Football*, fawned over Kizer throughout the preseason. "[Kizer] is the future for the Cleveland Browns," he said. "[He] is the next generation of QB." Burleson also predicted that Kizer would lead the Browns to seven wins. CBS Sports analyst London Fletcher was also all-in on Kizer. "When I watch him, he's a special quarterback," Fletcher tweeted just before the start of the 2017 regular season.

Kizer started in Cleveland's final preseason game and played well enough to win the starting job. Statistically he wasn't great, but he made enough eye-popping plays to put himself on the radar. The day after that game, Steven Ruiz, a columnist for the *USA Today* website For the Win, published an article titled "The Browns' 18-year search for a quarterback is finally over." In it, he wrote, "At long last, the Cleveland Browns have real hope at the quarterback position." While he admitted that Kizer had a long way to go, he surmised that he was not the same "pretender" as every other touted prospect that had come to Cleveland during the past two decades with franchise quarterback aspirations. "This time it feels different," he wrote. "This time it *is* different."

It was only different in that it was worse. Kizer won the starting job and started 15 games, throwing 11 touchdowns and 22 interceptions. The Browns did not win a single game in 2017, becoming only the third team in NFL history to finish a season winless and only the second to finish 0–16. Kizer was traded to Green Bay a few months after the season ended and was cut after the following season. Through 2021, he has yet to make another active NFL roster.

THE PHYSICALLY GIFTED, BUT INCONSISTENT, QB WHO HAS PLAYED WELL IN THE PRESEASON

Leading up to the 2014 Draft, some draftniks were impressed with Virginia Tech quarterback Logan Thomas, and particularly with his physical tools. But even though the 6-foot-6, 250-pound quarterback was blessed with tremendous speed, arm strength, and athleticism, he was only considered to be a mid- to low-round draft prospect. While he sometimes showed flashes of brilliance during his college career, he was inconsistent, and struggled with his accuracy. With his freakish physical attributes, many suggested he would be a better prospect as a tight end. However, the Arizona Cardinals and its head coach and renowned quarterback mentor, Bruce Arians, disagreed. Arizona drafted Thomas in the fourth round with the intention of having him play quarterback.

Thomas's potential was on full display during his first preseason game. Playing the entire second half of Arizona's 32–0 win over

Houston, Thomas completed a combined 11-of-12 passes for 113 yards and threw a touchdown and no interceptions. ESPN's Ron Jaworski called him the best of the 2014 rookie quarterbacks he had seen. Rivals.com college football analyst Mike Farrell proudly declared that he was "one of the few who still thinks [Thomas] can be very very good." On NFL.com, media personality Adam Schein wrote:

> Some draft gurus and members of the media elite think Logan Thomas has no future in the NFL at quarterback. Those folks are wrong. On the other hand, my guy Phil Simms—who said on our CBS draft preview show that Thomas was the true QB sleeper in this class—is oh so right.

The week after the first preseason game, Arians was asked about the critics who had said Thomas should play tight end. "They're eating a lot of crow this week," he replied. "So that's fun."

Thomas made the Cardinals roster as a quarterback in 2014. He played in two regular-season games and completed one pass. While Thomas may have shined in a few of his preseason appearances as a rookie, he never could impress on the practice field, as the same inconsistency issues, particularly with his accuracy, continued to plague him. He was released in 2015 and didn't make another active roster until Buffalo signed him in November 2016, after he had switched to tight end. The new position has served him well. Thomas has played tight end for Buffalo, Detroit, and most recently Washington. In 2020, he had his best season, catching six touchdowns. In 2021, Thomas signed a three-year contract extension with Washington worth $24 million.

A SECOND-YEAR QB WHO HAD A TERRIBLE ROOKIE YEAR, BUT PLAYED GREAT THE FOLLOWING PRESEASON

While Logan Thomas found new life as a tight end, a few years earlier Blaine Gabbert was in his second season trying to prove himself worthy as a quarterback.

In 2013, Gabbert, the Jaguars' 10th overall pick in the 2011 Draft, was coming off a dreadful rookie season and was fighting for his starting job. But he had spent the off-season trying to improve. This included time with new Jaguars head coach Mike Mularkey, who tweaked his mechanics. Gabbert's outlook seemed positive after his first two preseason games in which he completed 18-of-26 passes for 174 yards, three touchdowns, no interceptions, and a passer rating of 126.1. During the second game, after Gabbert's second touchdown pass, CBS Sports' Pete Prisco tweeted, "Where are all the Gabbert rippers?" To which former Jaguars All-Pro offensive lineman and 2022 Hall of Fame inductee Tony Boselli replied, "It doesn't fit their script!" Peter King was also impressed. "Your magic spell is working, Mike Mularkey," he wrote in his weekly "Monday Morning Quarterback" column in SI.com later in the week.

Turns out, Gabbert was still Gabbert. The Jaguars won two games in 2012. Gabbert contributed 10 unmemorable starts before succumbing to injury. He was released by the Jaguars in 2014. That was essentially the end of his career as a first-string quarterback in the NFL.

A TEAM THAT UNDERWENT A MAJOR OFF-SEASON ROSTER REVAMP, THEN DOMINATED THE PRESEASON

Teams that make a significant number of important roster moves in the off-season are prime candidates to fall victim to a preseason performance trap. When such a team looks sharp and improved during its preseason games, the roster overhaul is usually cited as the primary reason why. One example of a team that followed this script is the 2015 Philadelphia Eagles.

After posting identical 10–6 records in his first two seasons (2013–2014), Eagles head coach Chip Kelly added head of football operations (i.e., general manager) to his title. In his new role, Kelly made a bevy of unpopular off-season moves. A few of them involved trading some of the team's most prominent players, including running back LeSean McCoy and quarterback Nick Foles. To replace them, Kelly brought in veterans Sam Bradford and 2014 rushing champion DeMarco Murray.

With the new personnel, Kelly's high-tempo offense was unstoppable in their first three preseason games, all wins, as the Eagles scored 115 points. In the third game, a 39–26 victory over the Packers, Bradford was 10-of-10 with 121 yards passing and three touchdowns. ESPN Fantasy Football expert Matthew Berry was watching the game, and was very high on Chip Kelly's offense. "The Eagles are gonna be awesome this year," he tweeted. "I want as many [Philadelphia] players as I can get [on my Fantasy Football teams]."

The bullishness was palpable in the City of Brotherly Love. "Get excited about this Eagles team," wrote Andrew Porter on CBS Philadelphia's website. "You're allowed." Longtime Philadelphia sportswriter and TV analyst Ray Didinger was also amped up. "I'm telling you—if you want to put this team in the conversation of a team that can go all the way, I mean right now, I'm not gonna tell you no," he said on the *94WIP Morning Show* in Philadelphia.

Some couldn't wait for the regular season to start. Former Eagles linebacker and Philadelphia radio personality Ike Reese was literally salivating: "My mouth is watering, waiting for this offense to take the field Monday night [for the Eagles regular-season opener] in Atlanta." (Lehigh Valley, Pennsylvania) *Morning Call* writer Nick Fierro was amazed by the team's cohesiveness after Kelly had brought in a considerable number of new players. "The chemistry on this squad is almost as scary as the talent," he wrote. "The Eagles should be good for 12 [wins], an NFC East Division title and at least one home game in the playoffs, if not two."

Unfortunately for the Eagles and their fans, preseason success did not translate to the regular season. The team started off 1–3, and the offense that was "high-powered" in the warm-up games sputtered all season long. They finished 7–9 and missed the playoffs, and Kelly was fired in the second to last week of the regular season.

LET'S GET CYNICAL

Chronic cynics can be a drag. But if there were ever a time to be a skeptic, it would be during the NFL preseason. Legacies rarely begin or end during an exhibition game. The highlights, the performances, and the narratives all vanish as soon as the regular season starts. The games are hardly ever replayed, the moments are scarcely relived, and the traps are practically impossible to avoid. The only real certainty of an NFL season is that a fair amount of people will be thinking the same thing by the end of September: "It was just preseason, I should have known better."

"NO POINT IN KEEPING
TOM COUGHLIN
AROUND"

(2004–2007 NEW YORK GIANTS)

The script was already three-quarters written. A lame duck NFL coach had barely limped into keeping his job for another season. It was an all-too-familiar story. It just needed its inevitable and predictable ending, which appeared to be approaching.

By the second week of January 2007, Tom Coughlin's fate seemed all but sealed. He was closing in on the end of his third season as head coach of the New York Giants and had lost the confidence of the fans, the media, and, most importantly, many of his players.

A few weeks earlier, Coughlin had hit the rock-bottom moment of his tenure in New York. It was Christmas Eve, Week 16 of the 2006 regular season, and the Giants were sloughing through a humiliating thrashing by the New Orleans Saints. During the third quarter of what would eventually be a 30–7 Saints win, fans at Giants Stadium commenced a "Fire Coughlin" chant, which persisted throughout the rest of the game. When the game finally ended, Coughlin and his team were booed off the field by a majority of the 20,000 fans who remained. The Giants fell to 7–8 after the loss with only one more game left in the regular season. But despite the losing record, they somehow had a chance for a playoff spot. The Giants were hanging on by a thread.

"GUYS ABSOLUTELY HATE TOM COUGHLIN" (2004–2005)

The Giants hired Coughlin in 2004 to elevate a franchise coming off a 4–12 season. After winning the NFC Championship in 2000 under Coughlin's predecessor Jim Fassel, the team's progress stagnated. In the final few seasons under Fassel's leadership, the Giants became undisciplined, made critical special teams' errors, had trouble closing out games, frequently committed brainless penalties, and suffered defensive meltdowns.

One of the team's principal motivations in hiring Coughlin was to reduce the mistakes that had been plaguing the team during the previous few years. As a strict, detail-oriented disciplinarian, Coughlin was touted as the perfect man to get the team on the right track.

As soon as he arrived in New York, Coughlin preached discipline. He came armed with a strict list of rules and requirements for his players, which included prohibitions against jewelry anywhere in the stadium and sunglasses on the sidelines, a traveling dress code, and, most notoriously, an ironclad timeliness policy that required players to arrive at meetings at least five minutes early. If a player ran afoul of any of these guidelines, he would end up with a monetary fine.

Over a year earlier, Coughlin had ended an eight-year stint as the head coach of the Jacksonville Jaguars, where he built the team from an expansion franchise to a contender that twice made it to the AFC Championship game. However, by the end of his tenure, his players and coaching staff started to grow tired of his demanding personality. After going 6–10 in 2002, the Jaguars' third straight losing season, Coughlin was fired.

During the 2004 off-season, Giants defensive lineman Michael Strahan, the heart and soul of the team's defense and an eventual Hall of Famer, had begun to hear some troubling stories about his new coach. "At least 10 players who had played for him in the past talked to me about Coughlin," he remembered. "Nine out of the 10 complained about his unusual rules and rigidity. One player called him an abusive warden."

It didn't take long for Coughlin's authoritarian act to rub his players the wrong way. In September, three defensive players filed complaints with the NFL Players Association after Coughlin fined each of them $500 for not arriving at a meeting early enough.

Strahan was fined $1,000 for the same reason. "I absolutely hated the man," Strahan recalled.

Strahan wasn't alone. "Guys absolutely hate Tom Coughlin," one Giants player told the *New York Post* during the 2004 season. "He's not the type of coach we're going to go and put everything on the line for. Guys don't play for him; we play because we have to play and you're not going to win that way." In early September, on the pregame show *Fox NFL Sunday*, analyst and Hall of Fame quarterback Terry Bradshaw called Coughlin "mean," "hateful," and "a jerk." That same Sunday, on CBS's pregame show *NFL Today*, studio analyst Shannon Sharpe, a former NFL tight end, said that he "would rather die in an abandoned building alone, and my family not know what happened, than play for [Coughlin]." Around the same time, Coughlin was voted "NFL's worst coach" by a *Sports Illustrated* poll of current and former players.

By 2006, Coughlin still hadn't let up on his disciplinary approach. Once, during training camp, wide receiver Plaxico Burress told Coughlin two weeks in advance that he would be late to the facility on a specific Tuesday to attend his pregnant wife's ultrasound. Coughlin still fined him $2,000 for missing a meeting.

"But I told you in advance," Burress said to Coughlin.

"Yeah, but you were just telling us you weren't going to be there. You missed a meeting and that's a fine."

After the 2006 season ended, another player spoke with the *New York Post*: "[Coughlin's] a lot to handle," the player said. "He just yells to yell. Everyone's sick of it. When you win, you can deal with it. When you don't win, you don't want to deal with anything."

And they weren't winning. At least, they weren't winning *enough*. In his first three seasons, Coughlin had yet to elevate the franchise to the heights expected when he was hired. The Giants lost 10 games in 2004. In 2005, they won the NFC East division but were dispatched by the Carolina Panthers 23–0 in the Divisional Round of the NFC Playoffs, and with a losing record going into the final game, 2006 looked like a dud as well.

Perhaps the most disappointing trend during Coughlin's first three seasons in New York was that the undisciplined gameplay that had plagued the team during the previous regime persisted. The team continued to make mental mistakes and commit a boatload of penalties. From 2004 through 2006, the team finished as one of the top 10 most penalized teams in the NFL.

Coughlin's militaristic style wasn't the only thing that drew his players' ire. His game planning and in-game coaching were also areas of concern. On a few occasions, running back Tiki Barber, the team's most dynamic player, took shots at Coughlin's preparation and strategy. One highly publicized comment Barber made was after the Giants' shutout loss to the Panthers in the 2005 playoffs. Barber said that he thought "in some ways, [the Giants] were outcoached." Star tight end Jeremy Shockey was also critical at times. In July 2006, Shockey professed how much he loved playing as part of his previous coach Jim Fassel's offense before Coughlin came on in 2004. Later that year in September, after the Giants' 42–30 Week 3 loss at Seattle, Shockey told the media that the Giants got outplayed and outcoached.

"[COUGHLIN] IS FIRED . . . HE LOST THE FOOTBALL TEAM AND IT'S JUST TOO LATE" (2006)

By the end of the 2006 calendar year, the Giants' immediate future did not look bright. A few months earlier, Barber, only 31, and playing the best football of his career, shocked everyone and professed his intent to retire at the end of the 2006 season. In addition, concerns were growing about Eli Manning, the team's franchise quarterback. Manning, who was in his third season in the league, possessed all the tools necessary to be a star NFL quarterback, but was plagued by streaky and unsteady play.

After a great start to the 2006 season, Manning struggled through much of the second half of the season, and the Giants ended up losing six out of their last eight games. During that eight-game stretch, Manning had a few awful performances. In addition to the Christmas Eve massacre against the Saints, where he completed only nine passes for 74 yards, he completed less than 50 percent of his passes and threw two interceptions during a 26–10 Week 11 loss at Jacksonville. From the (Westchester, New York) *Journal News*:

> It has come down to a matter of confidence with
> Manning, something that has appeared in short
> supply over the 2–6 ending to the regular season.
> Mechanically, he is a mess, having reverted
> to throwing off of his back foot even when not
> pressured. Mentally, he has pressed to make throws,
> only to see them wind up at his receivers' feet.

As for Coughlin, the debacle on Christmas Eve was the final straw for many in the local media. After that game, even though the Giants still had a chance to make the playoffs, the local media had seen enough. They led their own "Fire Coughlin" chant by way of the pen.

"Of course, Tom Coughlin should be fired," New Jersey–based Giants writer Stephen Edelson wrote in the *Asbury Park Press*. "Regardless of…whether the Giants make the playoffs…it has become clear that it's time to change the culture that exists within this storied franchise. Blow the whole thing up and start over if necessary." *New York Post* Giants beat writer Paul Schwartz wrote that "the entire operation must be imploded." In the *New York Times*, columnist Selena Roberts was also blunt: "You have to consider the judgment of [the Giants ownership] in placing this coach with this team."

Tara Sullivan, a columnist for the (North Jersey) *Record*, was even more ruthless. "Barber is on his way out...Giants' fans can only hope he takes coach Tom Coughlin with him," she wrote. "Because it's become painfully obvious that these players are done playing for [him]...They're a joke. A disgrace to their uniforms."

Some thought Notre Dame head coach Charlie Weis would be a better fit for the Giants. As the New England Patriots' offensive coordinator, Weis was the architect of the offense that won three Super Bowls from 2001 to 2004. In 2004, before Coughlin was hired, Weis was considered for the Giants job, but he ultimately signed on with Notre Dame, where he went on to have success in his first two seasons. By 2006, he was a hot commodity and, to many, a great fit for the Giants in 2007. "[John] Mara and Steve Tisch, the [Giants] co-owners, need to find out what it will take to get Charlie Weis out of his Notre Dame contract," wrote longtime *New York Daily News* columnist Gary Myers. *New York Post* columnist Steve Serby had the same opinion. "[The Giants should] go after Weis the way Lawrence Taylor went after quarterbacks," he suggested. "Weis would be the closest thing to a young Bill Parcells." This was not the first time Serby advocated for Weis. In December 2003, before the Giants hired Coughlin, Serby wrote, "[Weis] owns a genius offensive mind that is imaginative, creative, adaptable and versatile enough...to ensure that [the Giants] never underachieve again."

Ultimately, the Giants were fortunate to have avoided Weis. He struggled at Notre Dame after 2006 and was fired at the end of 2009. After unimpressive stints as an assistant coach on the NFL and college levels, he went on to a disastrous two-and-a-half years (2012–2014) as the head coach at the University of Kansas. He hasn't coached since 2014.

After the Saints drubbing, the Giants closed out the 2006 regular season with a convincing 34–28 win over Washington and squeaked into the playoffs with an 8–8 record. In what would be his final win as an NFL player, Tiki Barber ran 23 times for 234 yards and three touchdowns.

The Giants' season ended the following Sunday in Philadelphia when they lost to the Eagles 23–20 in the NFC Wild Card Round on a last-second field goal. The loss further highlighted the lack of discipline that was supposed to have been corrected under Coughlin—the team wasted time-outs in crucial periods of the game, committed three straight fourth-quarter penalties on the same drive, and racked up five false starts.

After the playoff loss, many believed it was a foregone conclusion that the Giants would soon be looking for a new head coach. On Fox's postgame show, Bradshaw agreed. "[Coughlin] is fired," Bradshaw said. "He lost the football team and it's just too late." ESPN commentator Sean Salisbury also called for Coughlin to be fired. In a column later in the week, veteran *Boston Globe* scribe Dan Shaughnessy wrote about "The Final Days of Tom Coughlin in New York," and lamented that longtime Giants general manager Ernie Accorsi, who had announced earlier in the year that he was retiring at the end of the 2006 season, would be "[finishing] a great career on such a low note."

Once the Giants' season ended, columnists throughout the area continued the fire Coughlin campaign. "No point in keeping Coughlin around," was the headline on Keith Idec's column in North Jersey's *Herald-News*. Myers also suggested that the Giants should sack their head coach. "Coughlin must go," he wrote. "Too many players have tuned him out. He has taken this team as far as he can." Also, in the *Record,* columnist Ian O'Connor wrote that "Coughlin should be fired today," and in the *New York Post,* Serby pleaded for the Giants to "fire him now!!!"

"SELLING MEDIOCRITY" (2007)

The discussion was all for naught. The Giants didn't hire a new coach in 2007. Less than a week after the season ended, co-owners Mara and Tisch announced that they were extending Coughlin's contract for another season. "Tom Coughlin is our coach for 2007 and hopefully for many years after that," Mara said. In reaction to the news, Serby wrote in the *New York Post* that keeping Coughlin was a sign that the Giants were "selling mediocrity, and stiff-arming the notion that if you never dare to be great you will never be great." *New York Post* columnist Mike Vaccaro wrote that it was the worst possible thing they could have done. The way he saw it, the team "was keeping their coach a virtual lame duck for another 12 months."

Mara's statement about retaining Coughlin was an example of a "dreaded vote of confidence." It had the opposite effect intended and crystallized the fact that Coughlin's job status was tenuous at best.

Precedent has long established that a coach who produces a lackluster season following a dreaded vote of confidence almost always receives a pink slip shortly thereafter. Often the coach doesn't even make it through the next season. Coughlin's story seemed destined to end in that fashion.

"[HE] ROBBED ME OF THE JOY I FELT PLAYING FOOTBALL" (2007)

After the playoff loss to the Eagles, Barber followed through on his plan and officially retired. One of the most prolific offensive players in Giants history, Barber still holds numerous individual Giants franchise records. He concedes that much of that success came during Coughlin's tenure, part of which he attributes to Coughlin and his staff and their work with him, including helping him hold onto the football better, as Barber fumbled the ball at least eight times each season from 2000 to 2003.

In February 2017, just over a month after the Giants playoff loss to the Eagles, Barber signed a multiyear, multimillion-dollar contract with NBC as a year-round correspondent on the *Today Show* and as an analyst for the Sunday night NFL pregame show *Football Night in America*. When he was introduced by the network at a press conference, Barber immediately took shots at his former coach and his coaching style. He intimated that it was Coughlin's unyielding personality, along with the constant, physical grind from the coach's demanding practices, that had driven him out of football. Predictably, the media rolled with it, and it became a frequent topic of discussion the following week.

Barber later admitted that he made a pointed effort to talk about Coughlin at the press conference in order to generate buzz for the launch of his NBC career. "I knew enough about New York sports media to know that anything I said would get played up in columns and news stories the next day," he recalled. "I needed to make a little splash."

A couple of months later, before the start of the 2007 season, Barber released his autobiography *Tiki: My Life in the Game*. In it, he elaborated further about Coughlin. Among many other thoughts about his former head coach, he wrote that Coughlin "robbed me of what had been one of the most important things I had in my life, which was the joy I felt playing football," and that "if Tom Coughlin had not remained as head coach of the Giants, I might still be in a Giants uniform."

Barber wasn't done dishing on his former team. A few months later, he turned his attention toward quarterback Eli Manning.

Just over three years earlier, the Giants had acquired Manning during the 2004 NFL Draft, at which point he was essentially anointed the franchise's future savior. The San Diego Chargers had selected Manning with the first overall pick. But not long thereafter, they traded him to the Giants. In return, San Diego received the player the Giants selected at No. 4 overall, North Carolina State quarterback Philip Rivers, along with four future draft picks. It was a hefty price for the Giants to pay for one player, and through the 2006 season Manning had not lived up to the billing.

Manning was a man of little emotion. "[He] never uttered a single curse word in the huddle the three years I played with him," Barber remembered. He was practically unflappable, even during the worst situations on the field. It was an asset much of the time, but when the team was struggling, the perception that Manning had a laid-back attitude led to questions about his competitiveness. Fair or not, to some in the media, his demeanor did not exude leadership.

During his first *Football Night in America* broadcast, before a Giants preseason game, Barber drilled down on Eli. "He hasn't shown leadership," Barber said. "[Manning's] personality hasn't been so that he can step up, make a strong statement and have people believe that it's coming from his heart...Sometimes it was almost comical the way that he would say things." The comments really pissed Eli off. So much so that he responded to them publicly, something he rarely did. "I guess I could have questioned [Tiki's] leadership skills last year with calling out the coach and [discussing] retiring in the middle of the season, saying he lost all the heart," Manning said.

A SOFTER TOUCH FROM COUGHLIN (2007)

During the off-season and training camp, Coughlin made a series of adjustments to his coaching style. He replaced his defensive coordinator and defensive backs coach. He also made Kevin Gilbride, who took over temporarily at the end of 2006, the permanent offensive coordinator. But the most surprising and noticeable change was the fact that Coughlin came into camp with a softer personality and exuded a genuine intent to be nicer and warmer to his players. He was committed to becoming more approachable and making players feel more comfortable in reaching out to him.

Coughlin's personality change was likely a directive straight from the top. "[Mara and Tisch] were going to fire Coughlin, even after he got into the playoffs, unless they heard the right things from him in the postseason interviews," remembered Myers. One of those things was that Coughlin would try to loosen up a bit. "They told him," Myers added, "we see how you are with your grandchildren, we know that there is that side of you." Coughlin seemed to get the message.

"THE HOUSECLEANING'S COMING. BRINGING COUGHLIN BACK . . . HAS MERELY EXTENDED THE PROBLEM" (2007)

Despite Coughlin's gentler approach, the 2007 season started disastrously. The Giants gave up a whopping 80 points and 846 total yards in their first two games, both losses. The defense was porous, and the team continued to rack up bad penalties.

After the Giants' second loss, a 35–13 blowout by the Packers at the home opener at Giants Stadium, Coughlin's job status looked bleak. "How fired is Tom Coughlin?" longtime *Denver Post* sportswriter Jim Arsmtrong asked rhetorically in his Monday column. The *Asbury Park Press*'s Stephen Edelson, who had written nine months earlier that Coughlin should be fired, still felt the same way. "The housecleaning's coming," he wrote. "Bringing Coughlin back for another season has merely extended the problem another year, rather than giving the fresh start everyone deserved."

The following Sunday, on *NFL Today*, former NFL quarterback and CBS analyst Boomer Esaison wrote off the team's playoff chances:

> How are the Giants going to get back to the playoffs?
> I don't see it... If you can't get off the field on third
> down, you can't stop the opposing team's passer, you
> can't stop their big running backs or their tight ends,
> you know what? That's gonna continue the rest of
> the year and I think this team is heading south.

But the Giants were a better football team than they had shown those first two games. Beginning a few weeks later, the team fired off a six-game winning streak. New defensive coordinator Steve Spagnuolo transformed the Giants' defense into the team's best unit. Additionally, Coughlin's changes to his approach were noticeable. He was having fun, and the team was more relaxed on the field. "Tom lightened up," Plaxico Burress recalled. "He was like the total opposite of what he had been before."

When Mara and Tisch had met with Coughlin at the end of the 2006 season, an important topic of discussion, other than Coughlin needing to lighten up, was the team's franchise quarterback. In his first three seasons, Eli Manning had shown potential that he could become the star quarterback they all thought he would be when they drafted him. But he wasn't there yet. He was inconsistent and had as many bad moments as good. The owners wanted Coughlin to assure them that he had a plan in place for Eli to progress to his full ability.

To work with Manning, in addition to the permanent appointment of Gilbride to run the offense, Coughlin also brought in quarterbacks coach Chris Palmer, considered a "quarterback guru."

Eli had played adequately during the team's six-game win streak despite playing in pain with a separated shoulder. But on November 25, Eli had a nightmare game that gave even the most confident supporters second thoughts. In a 41–17 shellacking by the Vikings at Giants Stadium, Manning threw four interceptions, *three* of which were returned for touchdowns. It was the Giants' worst home loss in eight years.

A day later, Manning was grilled by the press, who asked him why, during such an embarrassing performance, he was so calm and didn't scream at any teammates or show emotion. The following Sunday, on ESPN's *NFL Countdown* pregame show, panelist and former NFL wide receiver Keyshawn Johnson rhetorically asked, "What quarterback in the National Football League has won anything quiet, just walking into the line of scrimmage quiet?"

Doubts about the Giants' franchise quarterback were at an all-time high after the Vikings game debacle. A few days later, Giants general manager Jerry Reese said that "Eli Manning has gotten skittish, for whatever reason." Esaison, who in addition to being a CBS commentator, was (and as of 2022, still is) also a local radio host in the New York market, started to wonder whether Eli could handle playing in New York. "Maybe he should be in Jacksonville. Maybe he should be in Atlanta or New Orleans," Esaison said. "New York is going to chew him up right now—and it has chewed him up for the last four years."

Approaching the regular-season finale at New England, the Giants were 10–5 and had clinched the fifth seed in the NFC Playoffs. Thus, from a playoff seeding standpoint, the game was meaningless because the Giants were locked in the fifth spot and would remain there regardless of the outcome. However, contrary to conventional wisdom, Coughlin did not bench his starters. It was a plan with which many disagreed. "[Coughlin] needs to take advantage of being locked into the No. 5 seed by sitting guys who could benefit from a week off," wrote Myers in the *Daily News*. Bob Glauber, in a *Newsday* column, wrote that playing the whole game at full strength would be "foolhardy." (Rochester, New York) *Democrat and Chronicle* columnist Bob Matthews felt the same way. "Anything beyond appearances by [Giants] star players would not be reasonable."

The Giants lost to New England, 38–35, but the Patriots didn't cruise to victory as they had during most games that season. Coughlin's squad actually outplayed New England for the first three quarters and led 28–14 in the fourth before the Pats pulled away at the end. Manning, who had been struggling since the end of November, threw four touchdowns and went toe-to-toe with the league's MVP, Tom Brady. The performance gave him a jolt of confidence, and plenty of reason for optimism going into the playoffs. It set the tone for the most improbable postseason run in NFL history.

"THE GIANTS HAVE NO CHANCE WHATSOEVER": A PLAYOFF RUN FOR THE AGES (2008)

On the Tuesday before the Giants' first playoff game, a wild card contest at Tampa Bay, Bucs cornerback Ronde Barber told his twin brother Tiki on *The Barber Shop*, their weekly show on Sirius Satellite Radio, that he was happy about the matchup. "Of course we want to play the Giants," he boasted. The message was clear: The Giants were not a team to fear. Tampa, unlike the Giants, rested many of their top players before their last game, a fact that former NFL head coach Jimmy Johnson could not overlook. "Tampa rested their players, and they are healthier," he said when he predicted that the Bucs would win on *Fox NFL Sunday* the morning of the game. His fellow co-hosts, Howie Long, Terry Bradshaw, and Frank Caliendo, all agreed.

The Giants turned out to be a tougher opponent than Ronde Barber thought. His brother's former team eliminated the Bucs 24–14. Next, despite Johnson, Long, Bradshaw, and Caliendo all quickly and decisively picking against them, the Giants traveled to Dallas and avenged two regular-season losses by beating the Cowboys 21–17.

The following week, in Green Bay, playing for the NFC Championship, the Giants beat the Packers in one of the coldest games in NFL history. The wind chill at kickoff was—23 degrees Fahrenheit. The game turned out to be Hall of Famer Brett Favre's final game with the franchise.

The Giants arrived in Glendale, Arizona for Super Bowl XLII as 12-point underdogs against what was generally thought to be an invincible New England squad. The consensus opinion was that, while the Giants had made a valiant effort in the postseason, the game would be the end of the Giants' fairy tale playoff run.

Some of the most prominent people in the media thought the Giants didn't have a prayer. Bradshaw, who hadn't been shy in taking potshots at the Giants and their coach, unsurprisingly proclaimed that he thought "The Giants have no chance whatsoever of winning this football game." One confident New England fan started a website called 19-0.org because he was so sure the Patriots would win and complete the season with a perfect 19–0 record. The site started selling Patriots T-shirts that said 19–0, with the words PERFECTION and DYNASTY below. They sold 700 shirts in the week leading up to the Super Bowl, before the NFL shut it down.

During media day, five days before the game, Plaxico Burress predicted that the Giants would win 23–17. When word about that reached Patriots quarterback Tom Brady, he laughed, and said, "We're only going to score 17 points? OK. Is Plax playing defense? I wish he had said 45–42 and gave us a little credit for more points."

Remarkably, Burress ended up overestimating the point total. In one of the greatest upsets in NFL history, the Giants made Bradshaw and others eat their words by defeating the Patriots 17–14. Manning threw two touchdowns, including a 13-yard pass to Burress with less than a minute left in the game. The most notable play of the game occurred on the Giants' final drive with the Giants down 4 with just over a minute remaining in the fourth quarter. On third and five from New York's 44-yard line, Manning escaped a sack and threw a prayer to wide receiver David Tyree in the middle of the field, who caught the ball for a 32-yard gain, using his helmet as support. Four plays later, Manning threw the game-winning touchdown to Burress, and the rest was history. Coughlin and the Giants were Super Bowl champions. Manning was named Super Bowl MVP.

Despite being awarded MVP honors, Eli Manning's performance may not have been the best of the night. Some bestowed that distinction on defensive coordinator Steve Spagnuolo and the Giants' defense. Spagnuolo changed the Giants' defensive front throughout the game. He had defensive end Justin Tuck line up in different spots on the line of scrimmage and ran creative blitzes on almost 30 percent of the Patriots' snaps. The different looks and constant pressure confused and frustrated Tom Brady all night.

Spagnuolo also devised clever coverage schemes to keep Patriots wide receiver Randy Moss, the best pass catcher in the NFL at the time, in check. Although Moss was able to catch a touchdown in the fourth quarter, he finished the game with only five total catches, far below his season average.

Many media folks had been critical of Coughlin's plan to play the Giants' final regular-season game at full strength. But it paid off. Besides injecting confidence into Eli Manning, it allowed the Giants' first-team defense to gain experience playing and understanding the Patriots' offense, which likely played a big part in the coaches' development of the defensive strategies that were so successful in the Super Bowl. Myers, one of the scribes who was critical of Coughlin's strategy for the regular-season finale, later admitted the head coach's shrewdness. "With [that] three point loss, the Giants convinced themselves they could play with anybody," he wrote a few days after the Super Bowl triumph. "As it turned out, Coughlin made the smartest move of his career."

"TIKI BARBER WATCHED HIS FORMER TEAMMATES WIN THE HOLY GRAIL" (2008)

For both Coughlin and Manning, the Super Bowl win was a spectacular triumph over their critics. Ironically, their most prominent critic was there, front and center, to watch the entire thing. Tiki Barber was in attendance covering the game. When Barber retired, he may have anticipated that NBC would send him out to Arizona to cover the Super Bowl, but there was likely very little chance he expected to witness his former coach and quarterback hoisting the Lombardi Trophy.

After the game, with ticker tape and confetti spread across the field, Tiki interviewed numerous celebrating Giants players.

When he caught up with Eli Manning, he was in the stadium's tunnel, still in uniform and wearing a Super Bowl Champions hat and oversized novelty T-shirt over his shoulder pads. Despite the awkwardness of the situation, Barber and Manning were respectful toward each other throughout an uneventful interview.

At 5:00 a.m. the following day, on a rainy and windy morning in Glendale, Barber stood across the street from University of Phoenix Stadium for a live hit for NBC's *Today*. From the studio in New York, host Meredith Viera introduced him: "Our own Super Bowl vet, Tiki Barber, watched his former teammates win the holy grail." She then offered him congratulations, as if he were still a member of the team.

For a situation akin to covering the joyous wedding of a recent ex-girlfriend, Tiki handled himself with class. He praised Manning's performance during the game and throughout the playoffs and described how he was rooting for his former team in the press room.

COUGHLIN'S GIANTS AFTER 2008

After the glorious night in Glendale, there was much optimism for the Giants' future. However, winning the Super Bowl did not catapult the franchise as most believed it would. In 2008, the Giants were the No. 1 overall seed in the playoffs, but were upset at home by the Eagles in the Divisional Round. They proceeded to miss the playoffs the following two seasons. By the end of the 2010 season, Coughlin found himself in an eerily similar predicament to the one he had faced just four years earlier. He had come practically a full circle and was back in the hot seat.

In 2011, entering Week 16, the Giants had lost five of their previous six games. Then, like déjà vu, they squeaked into the playoffs and went on another magical playoff run that culminated in a 21–17 victory over the favored Patriots in Super Bowl XLVI. Eli Manning, who threw for almost 5,000 yards and 29 touchdowns that season, won his second Super Bowl MVP award.

The Giants never made the playoffs again under Coughlin. After the 2015 campaign, the team's third straight losing season, the front office finally pushed Coughlin out. He had caught lightning in a bottle twice, but he couldn't do it again. Eli Manning retired four years later.

While his Giants' tenure didn't end well, Coughlin's legacy was cemented by the 2007 and 2011 seasons. The first Super Bowl was his ultimate vindication. His willingness to make changes in his personal approach was a major factor in the 2007 playoff run. "Right after the [2006 season] I began evaluating and trying to find ways in which I could be better," he said in 2007, a couple of days after his first Super Bowl triumph. "You have to learn and be prepared to make the adjustments and change."

Tiki Barber's relationship with the Giants' organization and its fans hasn't been the same since his retirement. His productivity on the field will always be overshadowed by his exit and his polarizing comments shortly thereafter. In 2010, Barber was named one of the annual inductees into the Giants Ring of Honor. By that time, morale around the franchise was at a low ebb. They had missed the playoffs in 2009 after finishing 8–8 and were off to a 1–2 start in 2010, including two straight bad losses in the previous two weeks. In the days leading up to his Ring of Honor induction ceremony, which would take place during halftime of the Giants' Week 4 home game against the Bears, Barber told the media that Coughlin's control of the team was "slipping away," and that the coach's job was in "crisis." It was no surprise that he was loudly booed by the Giants faithful at the induction ceremony. By 2011, Barber's TV career had fizzled out. Soon thereafter, he tried to make a comeback in the NFL, but no team was interested. Currently, in 2022, Barber co-hosts a national sports radio show in New York for CBS Sports Radio that airs every weekday afternoon. Also, since 2019, Barber has been a broadcaster for weekly NFL games on CBS as a color commentator.

Barber has said numerous times that he has no regrets about walking away from the game when he did. Regarding his comments about Coughlin and Manning in the months after his retirement, Tiki said in 2013, "Maybe people weren't ready to accept strong opinions from recently retired athletes." He also contends that if he had come back, the team probably would not have gone to the Super Bowl. "The dynamics of the team shifted when I left, and Eli became that guy who had to take all the pressure on his back," Barber said. "And at the time, incorrectly, I didn't think he could handle it." In December 2008, he sat down with Eli for a one-on-one interview for NBC and admitted that Eli proved him wrong.

Tara Sullivan, one of the columnists who on Christmas Day in 2006 called for Coughlin's firing, also admits she was wrong, but stands by what she wrote in her column. "It was entirely based on what I was seeing on the field," she said in 2020. "The whole narrative [when Coughlin was hired in 2004] was that 'We are going to make these guys tougher . . . they are going to be disciplined,' and then to watch that product, in that New Orleans game . . . it looked like it was going in the wrong direction." The fact that Coughlin flipped the script in 2007 turned out to be a good thing for local columnists like her. "I love the fact that Coughlin proved me wrong . . . because it meant that I got to cover one of the greatest stories."

Myers, who covered the Giants for the *New York Daily News* for 29 years before retiring in 2018, also has no regrets about his column. "I still contend that what I wrote in 2006 was right on the money [at that time]," he said in 2021.

Often, people are bewildered by poorly aged sports commentary, and think, "How could he or she have actually thought this?" That being said, folks may be lenient in judging the criticism levied at Coughlin during his first three seasons with the Giants—after all, by the end of 2006, his tenure with the team looked hopeless and his fate seemed inevitable. The local media was calling for his ousting, and as the 20,000 people at Giants Stadium on Christmas Eve 2006 made clear, Giants fans wanted him to be shown the door, too. By then, few, if anyone, predicted that Coughlin would be around after 2007, much less win a Super Bowl. It is a feat even the Giants players would never have guessed. "We even shocked ourselves," Michael Strahan said after the Super Bowl XLII triumph.

Hindsight is rarely forgiving, but at least those who whiffed on this story are in good company.

"BRIAN BROHM HAS
MORE UPSIDE THAN
AARON RODGERS"

(2008 GREEN BAY PACKERS)

T oday, footage from NFL Drafts is widespread. TV coverage and expert analysis of practically every draft pick is instantly spread across the internet. As a result, draft analysts know that every word they say about any draft pick during a broadcast will likely live on long after the draft. This was not the case in 2008. Back then, archived video clips were not as prevalent digitally, and most of the ones that were could only be found on YouTube. Prior to 2010, the majority of the draft coverage that you could find on the internet was from the first round and usually only included the first few picks. That means thousands of regrettable statements made by analysts during draft broadcasts throughout the years were never revisited or scrutinized. Unless ESPN or the NFL Network decide they want to roast their own, lots of great material to ridicule is going to remain stacked in their archives collecting dust. However, occasionally, among the scarce material available, classic Freezing Cold Takes are hiding below the surface, waiting to be discovered. Such was the infamous "Brian Brohm over Aaron Rodgers" clip from the 2008 NFL Draft.

BRETT FAVRE "RETIRES" (MARCH 2008)

When Green Bay selected Louisville senior quarterback Brian Brohm in the second round of the 2008 NFL Draft, it immediately triggered speculation about what that meant for Aaron Rodgers, the team's recently installed starter at the position. Rodgers, the Packers' first-round pick in 2005, had been the backup to Packers legend Brett Favre for the previous three seasons. He had rarely seen the field, playing in only seven regular-season games, throwing 59 total passes and one touchdown. Rodgers only saw significant action in one game, in 2007, on Thanksgiving against the

Cowboys in Dallas, when he played two-and-a-half quarters after replacing Favre, who had injured his elbow. But that was about to change. A month before the 2008 Draft, the 38-year-old Favre announced his retirement and the franchise expressed a complete commitment to Rodgers as the team's quarterback of the future. Despite the front office's vote of confidence, Rodgers was still an unproven backup. Whether he had the talent to be a high-level starting quarterback in the NFL was yet to be seen. To many, he was not a slam dunk.

Favre's breakup with Green Bay became messy. In July, he wanted to come back, but the Packers wouldn't guarantee him the starting job. Essentially, the franchise had moved on. The Packers ended up trading him to the Jets, causing resentment among many fans. The support for Rodgers within the franchise was strong, but it didn't seem that fans would be very patient if he didn't play well.

BROHM: A LOUISVILLE LEGEND

Brian Brohm had been a productive three-year starter at the University of Louisville. A hometown kid from a football family, he broke out during his junior year in 2006 when the Cardinals finished the season with a 12–1 record. He was named MVP in the 2007 Orange Bowl, a Louisville win over Wake Forest. Most analysts believed Brohm would have been a first-round pick in the 2007 Draft if he had declared after his junior year, but he chose to stay for his senior season. He said he wanted to try to lead Louisville to a National Championship and, in the process, further enhance his draft stock. In June 2007, ESPN's premier draft guru Mel Kiper Jr. ranked Brohm as the No. 1 player on his 2008 Draft "Big Board." Further enhancing the hype, a photo of Brohm, standing in front of two of his Louisville teammates, was featured on the cover of *ESPN The Magazine*'s 2007 college football preview.

The preseason buzz about Brohm's impending senior season fizzled fast. Louisville struggled under a new head coach, finished 6–6, and failed to make a bowl game. Individually, Brohm performed relatively well, throwing for 4,024 yards and 30 touchdowns. However, he also threw 12 interceptions, which was as many as he had thrown in the three previous seasons combined. Ultimately, his draft stock took a hit. By the time April rolled around, the majority of projections had him slotted for the late first or early second round.

"[BROHM IS] PROBABLY THE MOST READY TO PLAY [AN NFL GAME]"

Despite Louisville's disappointing season, many openly wondered why Brohm wasn't receiving more love from the draftniks. Even with Boston College's Matt Ryan and Delaware's Joe Flacco in play, there were still a few who thought that Brohm should be considered the top quarterback of the bunch. A Cardinals scout told the *Milwaukee Journal Sentinel* that he thought Brohm was "more polished, more ready" than Ryan, who was the top quarterback on almost everybody's board and a projected top five pick. Another scout told the *Green Bay Press-Gazette* that he thought Brohm "is probably the most ready to play" in an NFL game. Before the draft, Kiper said that Brohm was "his guy at No. 2" in terms of quarterbacks on the draft board.

Perhaps the biggest Brian Brohm advocate was longtime Louisville writer Rick Bozich. The week before the draft, Bozich wrote in the *Courier-Journal* that the love of Ryan over Brohm was "puzzling." He had covered Brohm since he was in 10th grade at Trinity

High School in Louisville, so he knew him well. "I watched Brohm make most of his important throws at U of L, the ones that won the Orange Bowl, beat West Virginia and made the Cardinals seem like a cinch to hang 40 points on any defense with even tiny flaws," he wrote. He also cited Ryan's interception rate in 2007, which was higher than Brohm's. "One thing I do not see when I look at Ryan's passing performance is a guy who was mistake-free in the short-to-medium passing game."

"ACTUALLY I DO LIKE BROHM BETTER THAN AARON RODGERS"

Despite the high praise, Brohm slipped to the late second round where Green Bay grabbed him with the 56th pick. Ryan was picked third overall by the Atlanta Falcons and Flacco went to the Ravens at 18th overall. When the Brohm pick was announced at Radio City Music Hall in New York, it drew a mini-ovation from a row of Packer fans in the first mezzanine.

From a television programming standpoint, the Packers' live selection of Brohm during the second round was unmemorable. For a few years, it was a moment that very few, if any, people ever thought about. It probably would have been long forgotten by now if it hadn't been for a YouTube account with the handle "packersinsider." About a month after the draft, the account posted a five-minute video of alternative coverage of the draft aired on ESPNNews, one of ESPN's secondary channels. It features a panel of ESPN experts, including ESPN analysts Merril Hoge, Robert Smith, and Todd McShay, in a studio along with host Rece Davis. When the clip begins, the Packers had just selected Brohm in the second round. After announcing the Packers selection, Davis told the panel, "Now you have Brohm and Rodgers, both with the opportunity long term to be the Packers quarterback." Right away,

Hoge, a veteran NFL analyst and former league player, confidently, and without hesitation, asserted, "Actually I do like Brohm better than Aaron Rodgers," noting that Brohm played in two pro-style systems at Louisville.

McShay went even further. "I like him," he told Davis. "I honestly think Brian Brohm, two years from now, could be the starting quarterback of the Green Bay Packers." He then added, that "Brohm's upside is greater than that of Aaron Rodgers." McShay explained that his pre-draft ratings for Rodgers and Brohm were very similar. Three years earlier—before the Packers selected Rodgers, who played at University of California–Berkeley, in the first round of the 2005 Draft—McShay had rated him as early second-round caliber. He thought Rodgers had no creativity coming out of college, and McShay had concerns about the system run by Cal head coach Jeff Tedford. Hoge expounded further, stating:

> When Rodgers was coming out, the one thing he lacked was anticipation. He had to see a route, come open, see a wide receiver come open, and that's just disturbing. When you are thinking about transitioning, Brohm does not do that. He will throw with anticipation, and that is a huge advantage going into the next level.

"[PACKERS GM TED] THOMPSON HAS BROUGHT IN A POLISHED ROOKIE WHO WILL BE PEEKING OVER RODGERS' SHOULDER RIGHT FROM THE START"

Rodgers was given the keys to the kingdom as soon as Favre retired. However, he must have had some concerns that the Packers selected a quarterback so early in the draft during the year he was finally taking over as the Packers' quarterback. "[Packers GM Ted] Thompson has brought in a polished rookie who will be peeking over Rodgers' shoulder right from the start," wrote Tom Oates in the *Wisconsin State Journal*. Some loosely compared the situation to three years earlier, when Favre was firmly entrenched as the Packers' quarterback and Green Bay selected Rodgers in the first round. Nevertheless, the same day the Packers picked Brohm, Thompson and head coach Mike McCarthy allayed any immediate concerns and made it clear that Rodgers was the clear-cut starter.

Once training camp commenced, it quickly became apparent that Rodgers had nothing to worry about. Brohm struggled mightily. On his first pass attempt in the Packers' first preseason game, he threw an interception on a badly overthrown ball, finishing the game 8-of-17 for 70 yards and a 33.9 passer rating. "I think that wasn't good for his confidence," said Bozich in 2020. "[Before the NFL], he never really struggled that much." By the time the preseason ended, he was surpassed as the number two quarterback by fellow rookie Matt Flynn, picked by the Packers in the seventh round. While the Packers didn't make the playoffs in 2008, Rodgers proved his worth. He threw for over 4,000 yards, with 28 touchdowns and 13 interceptions. By the end of October, Green Bay had given Rodgers a six-year, $65 million contract extension, signifying that they planned for Rodgers to be the team's starting quarterback for years to come. Any issue about Brohm replacing Rodgers was already ancient history.

As for Brohm, his press clippings and his perceived talent proved to be a mirage. After one year at Green Bay as third-string quarterback, where he never took a regular-season snap, he was waived. He then signed with Buffalo and played two more seasons, starting two games and losing both, throwing zero touchdowns and five interceptions. After that, he bounced around the (now-defunct) United Football League and the Canadian Football League for five years before calling it quits. As of 2022, he is the quarterbacks coach and co–offensive coordinator at Purdue University, where his brother Jeff is the head coach.

Bozich now concedes that the draft projections showing Matt Ryan ranked higher than Brohm were accurate. "In retrospect, the NFL people were right," he said. "[Ryan] definitely has a more dynamic arm and can make throws that Brohm couldn't make, but from what I saw in college, I thought Brohm was the better player." One thing Bozich can't reconcile is how Brohm's NFL career turned out. "I can't believe he didn't make it at least as a backup somewhere," he wondered. "I look at some of the guys that hang around the league for a long, long time, and I look at what happened in [Brohm's] career. I don't get it."

Rodgers has, of course, gone on to become a Packers legend. He led the Packers to a Super Bowl championship in 2010 and was named the MVP of the game. He was also the NFL's Most Valuable Player in 2011, 2014, 2020, and 2021. As of 2022, at 38 years old, he remains the starting quarterback for the Packers.

"THE JETS JUST GOT THE STEAL OF THE DRAFT, THEIR FUTURE STARTING QB, BRYCE PETTY"

(NFL DRAFT FREEZING COLD TAKES)

The NFL Draft is the NFL off-season event of the year. It also produces the highest number of Freezing Cold Takes of any sports-related event on earth. Every year, analysts, commentators, scouts, coaches, fans, players, random people on the street, and the girl next door are among the folks who publish quotes, analysis, and any other commentary regarding how the draftees will perform in the future.

Take an adventurous trip down memory lane with this long list of NFL Draft–related Freezing Cold Takes.

QUARTERBACKS

"The Giants' first-round choice of . . . Phil Simms of Morehead State drew a chorus of boos from the packed gallery at the Waldorf, and the cat-calls continued—'Put down the phone and try praying!' and 'Phil Who?'"

—From an article by Larry Fox in the *New York Daily News* (1979)

"I don't understand it . . . I don't know who is going to work with him down there. Where is the great quarterback coaching genius? I don't see where he is going to get this great coaching that's going to overcome the problems that he's had . . . I think they need help in other directions."

—Paul Zimmerman ("Dr. Z"), writer for *Sports Illustrated* and analyst on ESPN's Draft coverage, after the Miami Dolphins selected Dan Marino with the 27th overall pick (1983)

"After this draft is history, ten years from now, [Tony] Eason will be the one player remembered. Even more so than Elway."

> —Chicago Bears general manager
> Jim Finks to Paul Zimmerman, during a
> pre-draft conversation between the two;
> Dr. Z told viewers about the exchange during
> ESPN's coverage of the 1983 Draft

"I feel any team that needs a quarterback and bypasses John Friesz will be making the biggest mistake since the five teams that bypassed Danny Marino."

> —Dave-Te Thomas, NFL Draft analyst and
> founder of *NFL Draft Report* (1990)

"[With Andre Ware at quarterback], the [Detroit Lions will] drive better than anything that's ever come out of a Ford, Chrysler or GM plant."

> —Bob Sansevere, staff columnist, *St. Paul
> (Minnesota) Pioneer Press* (1990)

"If I was New England, I would take Rick Mirer. The reason I would take Rick Mirer is because I think that he could sell tickets in the New England area to the Notre Dame fans."

> —Joe Theismann, ESPN NFL broadcaster
> and draft analyst, just before the start of the
> 1993 Draft, explaining why he believed the
> Patriots, who owned the No. 1 overall pick,
> should pick Rick Mirer over Drew Bledsoe (1993)

"Everybody should have drafted Jake Plummer. He's another Joe Montana...Potentially, he's a Hall of Famer."

> —Bill Walsh, Hall of Fame and former
> San Francisco 49ers head coach (1997)

"[Danny Wuerffel's] a winner. What else could you want? If a team needs a quarterback, they better take him."

> —Mike Holovak, Houston Oilers
> director of scouting (1997)

"I say it's a no-brainer for the Colts to take [Ryan] Leaf...The name of any big-time professional game is still talent, and Leaf clearly has more of it than [Peyton] Manning will ever dream of."

> —Vic Carucci, columnist *Buffalo News* (1998)

"Without a doubt, Peyton Manning will be [the 1998 Draft's biggest flop for] whoever has the misfortune to draft this overrated collegian."

> —Kevin Flowers,
> *New Castle (Pennsylvania) News* (1998)

"He is the quarterback we clamored for, the potential savior cut in a city's battling image... He's daring. He's poised. He's a clever playmaker, a mobile thinker who will turn Soldier Field into Sunday at the improv...Already, [Cade] McNown sounds like a folk hero in the making."

> —Jay Mariotti, columnist
> *Chicago Sun-Times* (1999)

"Obviously, [Tom Brady] has a great future in New England—as a practice squad quarterback."

—Alan Greenberg, *Hartford Courant* columnist (2000)

"I see Brett Favre in this group [of QBs in the 2004 Draft class]...That's who [J. P.] Losman is going to be...100 percent."

—Charley Armey, former NFL general manager (2004)

"Will ['draft project' Ben Roethlisberger] help this year? No. Will [he] help next year? Probably not."

—Rick Green, writer, *Erie (Pennsylvania) Times-News* (2004)

"In five years we will talk about Kellen Clemens the way we talk about Tom Brady."

—Ron Jaworski, ESPN NFL analyst (2006)

"Dolphins could have had their next Dan Marino if they had selected Brady Quinn."

—Pete Prisco, CBS Sports NFL writer (2007)

"Mike Greenberg can't contain his excitement about the Jets & [Mark] Sanchez. He really believes Broadway Joe has met his match."

—Official Twitter account of the ESPN TV show *SportsCenter* (2009)

"If you are betting against this [Pat White] being a big-time quarterback, don't...I want the ball in his hands."

—Mike Mayock, NFL Network Draft Analyst (2009)

"I love, love, love this pick for Carolina. Jimmy Clausen. Man, teams are going to be sorry . . ."

—Ian Rapoport, *Boston Herald* reporter (2010)

"If [Tim] Tebow isn't a [Jacksonville] Jaguar by tonight, it's my opinion the franchise is gone within three years."

—Tim Brando, CBS Sports NFL broadcaster, on the day of the first round of the 2010 NFL Draft (2010)

"I love [Jake] Locker. I'm a 'Locker Stocker,' man!"

—Jon Gruden, ESPN television analyst and former NFL head coach, during ESPN's coverage of the 2011 Draft

"LOVE IT. Christian Ponder to the Vikings. He will have a long successful career in Minnesota. Sleeper of the draft."

—Barrett Sallee, *Bleacher Report* college football writer (2011)

"The Cardinals should give up the [fifth overall pick in the draft to trade] for [veteran NFL quarterback] Kevin Kolb."

—Charley Casserly, NFL Network analyst and former NFL general manager (2011)

"I don't see Russell Wilson being anything more than Seneca Wallace. I'm higher on Josh Portis as a prospect."

—Hugh Millen, 950 KJR-AM, Seattle (2012)

"Dak Prescott is a backup in [the] NFL. At tight end."
—Colin Cowherd, host of *The Herd* on
ESPN Radio (2014)

"Johnny Football will bring a buzz to Houston. And
that buzz is good. There will be a lot of excitement.
I'll buy two tickets if he goes to Houston...I don't
feel like I'm overdrafting...If I'm a quarterback
coach, this is what I want to mold for my future in
the modern-day NFL."
—Jon Gruden, during ESPN's coverage
of the 2014 Draft, arguing why the
Houston Texans should draft
Johnny Manziel first overall (2014)

"The Jets just got the steal of the draft, their future
starting QB, Bryce Petty."
—Skip Bayless, host of *First Take*
on ESPN (2015)

"[DeShone] Kizer...is going to make millions and
millions of dollars. Multiple time Pro Bowler."
—Dan Wolken, *USA Today*
sportswriter (2016)

"HACKENBERG TO THE JETS!!! YES!!!!...I'm
100% all-in on Christian Hackenberg...A steal,
so pumped...I've knocked down every single
'Hackenberg sucks' argument."
—Jason McIntyre, *Fox Sports 1* personality
(and big New York Jets fan) (2016)

"Chiefs are STOOPID."

—Tony Massarotti, sportswriter and host
of *Felger and Mazz* on 98.5 the Sports Hub
(Boston), after Kansas City traded up from
pick No. 17 to No. 10 in the first round
of the 2017 Draft, and then used the
No. 10 to select Patrick Mahomes (2017)

"It is unprecedented to see a player like [Patrick Mahomes], a first-round player, who has so many flaws and different things that you try to fix. I don't know how you fix this."

—Bucky Brooks, NFL Network analyst (2017)

"[The] Chiefs just made the dumbest move of the draft. Mahomes has a cannon, but he freelances way too much."

—Mike Farrell, Rivals.com,
national recruiting director (2017)

"It won't happen, but if Louisville were really thinking about Lamar Jackson's future, they would move him to WR. That's where he will play in the NFL."

—Booger McFarland, ESPN college
football analyst (2017)

"I would consider any team that used a first-round pick on Josh Allen to be the biggest loser of the first round. No good NFL quarterback has ever had statistics as bad as Allen's in college."

—Rodger Sherman, writer, *The Ringer* (2018)

"Cincinnati should keep veteran Andy Dalton and trade back to get more quality picks."

>—Michael Robinson, NFL Network analyst and former NFL wide receiver, when asked what the Bengals should do with the No. 1 pick in the 2020 Draft, which they eventually used to select Joe Burrow (2020)

RUNNING BACKS

"The . . . Bears chose Walter Payton [with the fourth overall pick], and a man in the front row [at the draft] booed . . . He identified himself as a Chicago businessman . . . He was disappointed that the Bears had not grabbed a lineman."

>—Excerpt from Red Smith's *New York Times* article from the 1975 Draft

"[Emmitt Smith will] be a good player in this league, but it'll be a short career. When he loses a step, that'll be it."

>—Ray Perkins, Tampa Bay Buccaneers head coach (1990)

"[Emmitt] Smith should be a solid, productive player, but he's no game-breaker. He's what Herschel Walker has slumped into—a plodding, straight-ahead type who won't outrun anyone."

>—Kevin Lyttle, columnist, *Austin American-Statesman* (1990)

"Blair Thomas will be a hero in New York. He has no holes as a player or person."

> —Joe Mendes, New England Patriots director of player development, after the New York Jets selected Thomas No. 2 overall (1990)

"Meet Curtis Enis. I admit to Enis Envy...he's exactly what the good doctor ordered [for the Bears]."

> —Jay Mariotti, columnist, *Chicago Sun-Times* (1996)

"Ten years from now, I can almost guarantee that this gaffe will rank alongside Sam Bowie over Michael Jordan as one of the worst draft picks ever."

> —Elliott Smith, columnist, *Odessa (Texas) American*, after the 1999 Draft, referring to when the Colts, with the fourth overall pick, passed on Ricky Williams to select Edgerrin James

"Brandon Weeden and Trent Richardson in the same backfield next year? That's pretty freaking cool."

> —Stewart Mandel, *Sports Illustrated* college football writer (2012)

"Anyone else thinking Trent Richardson is the next truly great NFL running back? Like, Adrian Peterson good?...If I'm wrong on [Richardson], I'm 'Dewey-beats-Truman' wrong."

> —Gregg Doyel, CBS Sports writer (2012)

"Wayne Gallman >>>> Derrick Henry when it comes to their careers at the next level."

> —Todd Fuhrman, CBS Sportsline
> gaming analyst (2012)

"I would rather have Kenneth Dixon than Derrick Henry."

> —Matt Miller, NFL Draft analyst,
> *Bleacher Report* (2016)

WIDE RECEIVERS

"[Dolphins third-round draft pick] Larry Shannon [is]... probably a step faster than Randy Moss... He's bigger, he's taller, he's faster [than Moss]."

> —Miami Dolphins head coach
> Jimmy Johnson (1998)

"[The] Colts reached."

> —Warner Hessler, writer (Newport News,
> Virginia) *Daily Press*, on the Colts using
> the 30th overall pick in the 2001 Draft to
> select Reggie Wayne (2001)

"This was the easy part. Charles Rogers was the right pick, such an obvious pick, even the Lions couldn't miss the can't-miss guy. Lions fans should enjoy this. It's their reward for the 5–27 penance of the past two seasons."

> —Bob Wojnowski, *Detroit News* columnist
> (2003), after the Lions selected Charles Rogers
> with the second overall pick in the 2003 Draft
> just before the Texans selected wide receiver
> Andre Johnson with the No. 3 pick (2003)

"I'll see you at his Hall of Fame induction."
                —Mel Kiper Jr., ESPN lead draft analyst, to
                colleague Merril Hoge about University of
        Southern California wide receiver prospect Mike
        Williams, who was selected by the Lions with the
                10th overall pick in the 2005 Draft

"Matt Jones, a WR-TE hybrid freak of nature, was
a great first round pick. He will become a great
weapon for [Jags starting quarterback] Byron
Leftwich."
                —Walter Cherepinsky, NFL draft analyst &
        creator of NFL website WalterFootball.com (2005)

"Jay Cutler says THANK YOU. Kevin White will
be a BEAST. Extremely confident and backs it up.
Big/strong/fast/tough."
                —Skip Bayless, host of *First Take*, on ESPN,
                        after the Bears selected Kevin White
                        with the No. 7 overall pick in the 2015 Draft

TIGHT ENDS

"[Rickey] Dudley will be a factor [for the Oakland
Raiders] for 12 years."
                                —John Marvel, writer
                        Contra Costa (California) Times (1996)

"People are high on Arizona TE [Rob] Gronkowski?
I don't see it. At all."
        —Greg Bedard, *Boston Globe* NFL reporter (2010)

"The thought of the New England offense plus
[C. J.] Spiller is scary—the thought of the New
England offense plus Rob Gronkowski is something
defensive coordinators can live with."

—Gregg Easterbrook, writer, ESPN.com's
Page 2, questioning why New England,
before using the 42nd pick to select
Gronkowski, didn't try to use the
pick to trade up for an "impact player"
like Spiller or Derrick Morgan (2010)

DEFENSE

"[Buffalo Bills]: Worst Pick: Bruce Smith DE,
Virginia Tech: Smith is a happy-go-lucky guy who
tends to be lazy. He also likes to eat."

—Joel Buchsbaum, NFL Draft
analyst, in a newspaper feature where
he chose the best and worst pick
each team made during the 1985 Draft

"[Chris Doleman] is a projection...He's a down
lineman that is projecting to linebacker, and there
used to be a rule of thumb, when you are drafting
this high [fourth overall] you take sure things not
projections."

—Paul Zimmerman ("Dr. Z"), writer
for *Sports Illustrated*, and analyst on
ESPN's draft coverage (1985)

"Should the Panthers use the second overall pick on North Carolina DE Julius Peppers? ... I say trade down in the first round with the intention of selecting [defensive tackle] Ryan Sims."

—Dan Arkush, executive editor,
Pro Football Weekly (2002)

"Charles Woodson ... won't have the impact short-term [of running back Curtis] Enis, nor the impact long-term [of quarterback Brian] Griese."

—Kevin Flowers,
New Castle (Pennsylvania) News (1998)

"Let's face it: [Ed] Reed is a pick without pizazz."

—Mike Preston, columnist,
Baltimore Sun (2002)

"With [defensive tackle Vernon] Gholston now in New York, [Jets head coach Eric] Mangini has hit another one out of the park. Excellent selection."

—Matt Sohn, *Pro Football Weekly* (2008)

"[The Houston Texans] will rue the night they took Pizza Boy J. J. Watt over Nick Fairley, Houston lover."

—Chris Baldwin, *CultureMap Houston* (2011)

"Luke Kuechly at No. 10 to Panthers is not going to work out well."

—Andrew Perloff, producer, the
Dan Patrick Show (2012)

"TONY MANDARICH IS IN A CLASS BY HIMSELF ... IT DOESN'T GET ANY BETTER THAN THIS"

(1989 GREEN BAY PACKERS)

I f there were a Mount Rushmore of draft busts, Tony Mandarich's heavy face and mullet would be carved in it. A behemoth offensive line prospect out of Michigan State University, who was lavishly praised by virtually every prognosticator, Mandarich was a spectacular flop after being drafted second overall by the Packers in the 1989 Draft.

"THE INCREDIBLE BULK" (1989)

Perhaps the defining image of the phenomenon that was Tony Mandarich was the *Sports Illustrated* cover, issued a few weeks before the draft, which featured an image of the lineman and included the headline THE INCREDIBLE BULK, along with the subhead "Best Offensive Line Prospect Ever." The now-infamous cover portrayed a towering 6-foot-6, 315-pound Mandarich with his shirt off standing on a mountaintop in front of beautiful sunset.

Throughout the rich history of the NFL, many prospects have been universally forecasted to be great NFL players. However, very few, if any, were viewed *more* favorably than Mandarich. Experts and commentators around the country confidently described him as a sure thing, a prospect guaranteed to be a perennial All-Pro and possibly an NFL immortal. Most of the tales about the Mandarich hype don't even do it justice. To this day, his story of great expectations versus dismal reality is basically unparalleled.

Virtually anyone who scouted, evaluated, or even mentioned Mandarich before the 1989 Draft utilized the maximum amount of hyperbole to describe him. He didn't give up a single sack and recorded 50 pancake blocks during his senior season in college. His film was off the charts. In 2009, former Rutgers defensive lineman Kory Kozak described watching Mandarich's game tape in 1988 while preparing to play Michigan State in the first game of the season:

> Watching the Rose Bowl [against USC on January
> 1, 1988], we saw Mandarich pancaking [future
> first-round defensive lineman] Tim Ryan from
> USC on one play, driving him out of film frame the
> next... It wasn't only Ryan. We saw an All-America
> defensive end pinned to the ground by Mandarich,
> a linebacker from Wisconsin on skates 10 yards
> downfield, a defensive tackle from Ohio State curled
> up in the fetal position. The worst was the Iowa
> team captain who went for the trifecta: on skates
> for 10 yards, pinned to the ground, and then curled
> up in the fetal position... [Mandarich] drove a
> Northwestern player into the end zone, pancaked
> him, and then told the player to "stay there."

"THIS IS A DIFFERENT PLAYER. WE'LL NEVER HAVE ANOTHER"

In the weeks and months leading up to the draft, the praise for Mandarich's size and ability poured in. "He's faster than any offensive lineman in pro football," Michigan State head coach George Perles said. "There's probably nobody faster in the world at his weight. This is a different player. We'll never have another." Joe Wooley, the director of player personnel for the Eagles, said, "If you want to put a 9.0 on him (the highest grade in the National Football Scouting system at the time), you can go ahead and do it... He's a man among children." The Browns did give him such a grade. It was their first 9.0 since O. J. Simpson.

There were enough glowing evaluations of Mandarich to fill a book all by themselves. Among them:

> "A once-in-a-lifetime impact starter."
>
> —*Ourlads' Guide to the NFL Draft*

> "A freak of nature."
>
> —Cleveland Browns scout Mike Lombardi

> "The best offensive lineman I have ever graded in my years of researching the draft."
>
> —Mel Kiper Jr.

> "Mandarich is out of this world."
>
> —Veteran draft analyst Joel Buchsbaum

> "A surer thing than most quarterbacks he will ever have to protect."
>
> —Don Pierson, writer, *Chicago Tribune*

> "An instant starter and probable Pro Bowl performer right out of the blocks. All the Packers have to hope is that he doesn't hurt too many of their defensive players before the preseason opener."
>
> —Larry Dorman, writer, *Miami Herald*

> "I've been in football 29 years and I've never seen a more outstanding offensive lineman."
>
> —Former Philadelphia Eagles head coach Dick Vermeil

"Could be the best tackle ever."

—Brian White, writer, (Southwest Florida)

News-Press

"He's the best I've seen in a long, long time."

—Mike Allman, Seattle Seahawks

director of player personnel

"He's the finest pure offensive tackle I've ever seen come out of the draft."

—Steve Ortmayer, director of player

development for the San Diego Chargers

"Mandarich is in a class by himself... It doesn't get any better than this behemoth."

—Vinny DiTrani, writer, (North Jersey) *Record*

A contributing factor to Mandarich's mythological pre-draft portrayals was his otherworldly February Pro-Day performance at Michigan State. The workout astonished the NFL scouts in attendance. "Someday, we'll be able to tell people we were here when this happened," said Dallas Cowboys offensive line coach Jim Erkanbeck. Mandarich weighed in at 304 pounds and ran a 4.65 forty-yard dash, an unfathomable time for a lineman of his size. He also bench-pressed 225 pounds a staggering 39 times. It was described by Dolphins director of player personnel Chuck Connor as "a running back's workout in a 6-foot-5, 303-pound body."

The pro-day workout, along with the video clips of Mandarich destroying defensive linemen in the Big Ten, added to the folkloric conception of Mandarich that had been forming for months. Two months later, when the *Sports Illustrated* cover hit the stands,

Tony Mandarich became more than just a prospect. He was a phenomenon.

The Green Bay Packers held the No. 2 pick in the draft behind the Dallas Cowboys, and were in line to take Mandarich. Dallas, desperate for a quarterback, was slotted to pick UCLA quarterback Troy Aikman. According to the Giants' director of player personnel, Tom Boisture, the Packers were lucky. "[Packers General Manager] Tom [Braatz] should spend all his time in church praying that Dallas takes Aikman…" Boisture said. "You can get quarterbacks. You can't get Mandariches. He's like what O. J. was for a running back. Pound-for-pound he's the best athlete I've seen. And there's a lot of pounds there, baby."

"OUR TRAINER TALKED TO THEIR TRAINER, OUR DOCTOR TALKED TO THEIR DOCTOR . . ."

The *Sports Illustrated* cover may have made Mandarich look like the second coming of the Hulk, but the lengthy piece inside the edition, written by Rick Telander, wasn't nearly as kind. Telander had flown to Los Angeles, where Mandarich was training before the draft, to follow him around for a few days for the story. It portrayed Mandarich as a Guns N' Roses blasting, bandanna-wearing, weightlifting Neanderthal who chugged caffeine. While he didn't directly come out and say it, the tone of Telander's article implied that perhaps Mandarich's physique wasn't sculpted entirely by legal means.

Telander was familiar with the college football steroid culture. Less than a year earlier, in October 1988, he collaborated with University of South Carolina defensive lineman Tommy Chaikin to publish a first-person account in *Sports Illustrated* of Chaikin's steroid abuse and the physical and mental toll it had taken on him. Chaikin also alleged that there was widespread steroid use among the players in the South Carolina program that was tacitly approved by the coaching staff. It turned into a major scandal. A subsequent internal investigation determined that several coaches had been involved in the distribution of steroids to athletes at the University. Three South Carolina coaches ended up pleading guilty in federal court on misdemeanor charges involving distributing steroids to the players.

Many others were suspicious of Mandarich. When he arrived at Michigan State his freshman year, Mandarich weighed 255 pounds. By the time he left a few years later, he was up to 315 pounds and looked like he could bench-press a large building. Mandarich did not take kindly to steroid speculation. He became increasingly annoyed with questions about his body. When prompted, he would cite the drug tests he passed when he played for Michigan State and the one he took before the NFL Scouting Combine in Indianapolis during the months leading up to the 1989 Draft. He attributed his dynamic body to his weight-lifting regimen and a seven-meal-a-day, 15,000-calorie diet. Packers general manager Tom Braatz wasn't concerned. "Our trainer talked to their trainer, our doctor talked to their doctor and I talked to George Perles...Our information is good that for the last two years he has not been on it," he said.

And that was that. When the draft came around in late April, the Packers wasted no time in selecting Mandarich at No. 2. Aikman and the three players selected directly after Mandarich— Barry Sanders, Derrick Thomas, and Deion Sanders—are all now in the Pro Football Hall of Fame.

"THE INCREDIBLE BUST" (1992)

Mandarich's tenure in Green Bay was a disaster from the outset. He spent the entire summer after the draft in a very public contract dispute. Five days before the Packers' regular-season opener, he signed a four-year, $4.43 million contract. At the time, it was the biggest contract signed by an offensive lineman in NFL history.

When Mandarich finally reported to camp, he was down from his 315-pound, pre-draft weight to under 300 pounds. His rookie season was a disappointment. He rarely played, and there were significant questions about his body. Rumors were rampant that his drastic weight loss was a result of the fact that he was no longer using steroids.

The speculation heated up even more in March 1990 when a *Detroit News* report alleged, among other things, that numerous players on the 1987 Michigan State team, with Mandarich front and center, injected each other with steroids the entire season, which they openly discussed together in the locker room and at the training table. It also alleged that up to 15 players used pre-brought, clean urine to pass NCAA drug tests. MSU officials denied knowledge of any of this.

During the 1990 season, his second year in the league, Mandarich started all 16 games for the Packers at right tackle. His performance was less than stellar. During a 31–0 mid-December blowout by the Eagles in Philadelphia, Mandarich was thoroughly embarrassed by eventual Hall of Fame defensive end Reggie White. In 1991, Mandarich started 15 games and wasn't much better. In 1992, he missed the entire season, landing on the non-football injury and illness list with hyperthyroidism.

By the end of September 1992, Tony found himself on the cover of *Sports Illustrated* again. This time, however, the package was much less flattering. Above a picture of a dejected Mandarich on one knee in his Packers uniform ran the headline THE INCREDIBLE BUST. The accompanying article read like a postmortem on his dwindling career.

Mandarich's four-year contract expired at the end of the 1992 season and the Packers did not renew it. He didn't play again for four years. Instead, he moved back to Michigan, during which time he was fully addicted to drugs and alcohol. After spending time in rehab, he got sober and was given a second chance with the Indianapolis Colts, who were coached by his former Packers' head coach Lindy Infante. He started all 16 games for the Colts in 1997 and was a serviceable lineman. After suffering a shoulder injury during the 1998 season, Mandarich hung up his cleats for good.

"I WAS TAKING WINSTROL B, FINIJEC, EQUIPOIS, ANADROL 50S, ANAVAR, TESTOSTERONE . . ." (2008)

In October 2008, after many years of vehement denials, Mandarich appeared on Showtime's *Inside the NFL* and came clean, admitting to using steroids throughout his career at Michigan State. He also wrote a tell-all book, further elaborating on his experiences. Six months later, in an interview that appeared in an "Outside the Lines" piece on ESPN's *SportsCenter*, he described some of the steroids he used regularly during college:

> I was taking Winstrol B, Finijec, Equipois, Anadrol 50s, Anavar, Testosterone, Dynobol. . . . At times, I would take half an Anadrol 50, and the results that I got from that drug was tremendous. I could take that for three days and be 10–15 percent stronger than I was three days prior.

According to Mandarich, once he was drafted, he stopped using steroids because the NFL's new testing program was significantly harder to beat than the NCAA's. The effect was drastic. He lost 20 pounds, and his edge along with it. However, he doesn't believe that quitting steroids was the most debilitating factor in sinking his NFL career. After coming clean in 2008, Mandarich also revealed that, during his entire Packers career, he was a habitual drinker and addicted to painkillers. He claimed he was not sober for a single day during the four years he was with Green Bay. The effect on his play was substantial. "Playing half in the bag, being on painkillers in the middle of games, is brutal," he said in a 2015 interview. "You think it's helping you, but you become lethargic, slow and non-aggressive because alcohol's a downer, as are painkillers."

After the Showtime interview aired, Telander revealed in an article in the *Chicago Sun-Times* that, during the days he was with Mandarich for his 1989 *Sports Illustrated* piece, he repeatedly asked Mandarich if he was using, to which Mandarich said, "Never." A couple of months later, Mandarich apologized for the 1989 interview. "I was wrong. I conned you...I was a jackass," Mandarich told him.

"THE WORST-KEPT SECRET AT [MICHIGAN STATE]"

As soon as Mandarich made his admission, other writers immediately professed to believing that Mandarich had been using during his college career. Jack Ebling, who covered Michigan State during the Mandarich years for the *Lansing State Journal*, called the lineman's steroid use "the worst-kept secret at MSU." It was a phrase that Mandarich told the *Detroit News* in 2008 he "had to laugh at because it's true." According to (Appleton, Wisconsin) *Post-Crescent* writer Tim Froberg, "Back then just about everyone in the Wisconsin media guessed that a balding, acne-orine Mandarich was, or had been, on the juice..."

In a blog post, titled "Tony Mandarich fails to stun the world with head-slappingly obvious admission of steroid abuse at Michigan State," Matt Hinton of *Yahoo Sports!* didn't hide his sarcasm. "Collegiate steroid abuse in the late eighties? Who could have possibly imagined?" "Boy, there's a real shocker," a *Philadelphia Daily News* blurb asked ironically. "What next? An admission from a former altar boy that he snuck in a few sips of wine." *Kenosha News* writer Mike Larsen simply wrote, "Ya think," in response to Mandarich's confession.

Despite his massive steroid abuse, Mandarich somehow made it through college and the draft process in a blaze of glory. When he was at Michigan State, steroids were a banned substance. However, the NCAA never tested for them until his second year there. Even then, it only tested players playing in late December or January bowl games. So as soon as the Michigan State players learned they were going to play in a bowl game, steroid users, including Mandarich, would stay clean for a certain period before the test to ensure the steroids were out of their system. They didn't even have to cheat on the test.

The NCAA did throw one curveball that almost exposed Mandarich well before 2008. In December 1987, two days before the Michigan State football team flew to Pasadena, California for its Rose Bowl game against USC, the NCAA announced there would be a surprise drug test administered to the MSU players upon their arrival. Also, unlike previous tests, the testing folks planned to watch each player urinate in the cup. This was a huge problem for Mandarich and any steroid-using teammates, as they had begun using again immediately after passing the test they took in East Lansing weeks earlier.

As a result, they had no time to flush out their systems and had to cheat on the test. During his 2009 ESPN "Outside the Lines" feature, Mandarich explained the innovative maneuver his teammates and he used to test negative:

I basically had strapped something to my back, a little... doggy toy, and took the squeakers out of it, hooked up a little hose to it, and left the top of it with a hole so it had air. Put in clean urine, ran a tube, you know, underneath, and um, put a piece of bubbalicious gum to cap it.

Mandarich also admitted to using a similar method to cheat on the drug test given just prior to his final college game, the Gator Bowl, against Georgia on New Year's Day in 1989.

So, even though he was a habitual steroid abuser of the highest order, Mandarich passed all five drug tests he was given. (He passed the fifth test, given by the NFL at the combine, because at that point, he had stopped juicing.)

In 2008, Mandarich said he never told the Michigan State coaches that he was using steroids, and he does not believe they knew. But given his later admissions about how rampant and out in the open it was in the program, it is clear the coaching staff didn't investigate very rigorously.

"WITHIN THE FIRST FIVE YEARS IN THE LEAGUE, I WANT TO BE THE BEST LINEMAN EVER TO PLAY IN THE NFL"

Mandarich played the part of a cocky, overpowering, generational offensive lineman. He was like a more outspoken version of villain Ivan Drago from *Rocky IV.* "I'm big, I'm strong, I'm smart, and I like knocking people on their [butts]," he said before the draft. After the draft, he told reporters that "Within the first five years in the league, I want to be the best lineman ever to play in the NFL." Before his final college game, the Gator Bowl, Georgia defensive end Wycliffe Lovelace had called him overrated. "I called [Lovelace]

'Linda,'" Mandarich told *Sports Illustrated*. "I ripped his helmet off twice in the game. I abused him. I punished him."

When Mandarich confessed, few were surprised. But if so many people in the college football world had suspicions at the time, why did so few voice their concerns? For one thing, and most importantly, those who were suspicious had no verifiable evidence that he was using. Without that, making a serious accusation that a player is cheating would not go very far. "I knew he was on juice," Telander wrote in *Sports Illustrated* in 2008. "There was nothing I could do... I hinted in my story, but I could not say what I was sure of."

Some may also wonder why *Sports Illustrated* was aggressively covering a player like Mandarich and helping raise the profile of a someone who was suspected by many to be a big fraud. In 2020, Telander explained:

> You write what you write... You write about people that are at the top of their game... We knew at *Sports Illustrated* that Tony Mandarich was going to be drafted very high; [his] statistics in college were off the charts. He was playing, he had been allowed to play. He hadn't been found guilty of anything, and in America you're innocent until found guilty, and to not write about this guy would have been to miss the highest offensive lineman draft pick in I don't know how long.

The NCAA played a key role (unintentionally) in providing a cover for Michigan State, the Packers, and anybody else who wanted to keep their eyes and ears at a distance. Until the NCAA began random testing in 1990, the number of student-athletes who tested positive for steroids never exceeded 1 percent. NCAA Executive Director Richard Schultz said that the low percentage was not because so few people were using the banned substances, but because the tests were so easy to beat. "Unfortunately, I think we only catch the dumb users."

When Mandarich came clean, numerous journalists started writing articles expressing their disappointment in Mandarich's lying. One suggested that Braatz and some others write a formal apology, since "They're the ones who couldn't see through Mandarich's snow job." But these critics may have been underestimating Braatz's intelligence. Did Braatz really fail to see through Mandarich? Was he that naïve? It could be that the Packers' front office didn't "fail to see" anything.

They might have just chosen not to look.

Braatz always claimed he never discovered any explicit evidence of Mandarich's steroid use. That's probably true. But given the way the team investigated the issue, it is easy to see why nothing turned up. The Packers' vetting process into Mandarich's strength-training practices was hardly thorough. According to Braatz in 1989, his due diligence into the issue consisted of the Packers' doctors and him having various discussions with Michigan State's trainers, doctors, and Michigan State football head coach George Perles and his staff. Not exactly objective parties.

The Packers likely didn't jump through hoops to find out the truth about Mandarich's muscle-building methods because, frankly, they didn't really care. Braatz essentially admitted as much. In comments to the media during the weeks leading up to the draft, he made it pretty clear that the Packers' front office believed Mandarich, without the assistance of steroids, would be just as effective as Mandarich using steroids, as long as he maintained a competitive offensive lineman weight. Braatz said, "The point is moot in this case... [Mandarich] is a 305-pound man. If he was on them and had to get off, he wouldn't go down to 240. He'd be 280, 285, and be big enough. The risk comes in the case of somebody that's 250 and might go to 210." This rationale was shared by a few others around the league. Bob McGinn, who covered the Packers for almost 40 years, wrote in 2019 in *The Athletic* that pro people thought that Mandarich's destructive power would carry him over to the NFL, regardless of whether or not he was on steroids. According to McGinn, shortly before the 1989 Draft, a personnel director for an AFC team said that "[Even] if he comes down to 280 or 290 pounds when he gets off the 'roids, he's still going to be outstanding."

The weight loss and loss of strength from being clean had a major effect on Mandarich's game. The Packers also didn't expect that he would come in with serious drug addiction issues that would further compromise his potential. Nevertheless, the message from the Packers seemed clear: Whether or not Mandarich was a steroid user at Michigan State was not the Packers' problem. And with the assurances from the Michigan State coaching staff, along with the drug tests he passed during his college career, Green Bay had all the plausible deniability it needed to select Mandarich No. 2 overall with a clear conscience.

BLINDED BY THE MYTH

When Washington general manager Bobby Beathard was raving about Mandarich before the 1989 Draft, he proclaimed that he was "so good it's almost like he's not real." Turns out, he wasn't. But like so many draft busts before and after him, the team who selected him was the one left holding the bag. Braatz, who was fired by the Packers a few years later, admitted that he bought into the mythological figure. "The hype was bigger than what he really was," he said. "There isn't anybody that good."

"WHEN IT COMES
TO WINNING THAT
ONE CRITICAL GAME,
BILL COWHER
CAN'T DO IT"

(1992–2005 PITTSBURGH STEELERS)

B y the end of the 1997 season, Bill Cowher had already led the Pittsburgh Steelers to three AFC Championship Games. But the rest of the decade wasn't as kind. Pittsburgh failed to make the playoffs the next three seasons and finished 1998 and 1999 with losing records. By the turn of the 21st century, they had lost 19 out of their last 32 games. In the mostly unstable world of NFL coaching, that kind of two-year stretch has frequently resulted in the coach losing his job. But the Steelers are different. Through 2021, the franchise has only had three head coaches in the previous 52 years.

The Pittsburgh Steelers were founded by Art Rooney in 1933. Art ran the team until his son, Dan, began managing the day-to-day operations in 1969 and was given full control of the team in 1975. During the 1970s, Dan Rooney presided over the greatest run of success in the franchise's history. Under his leadership, and that of legendary head coach Chuck Noll, the Steelers won four Super Bowls and became one of the most well-known and respected brands in the league. But the team fell on tough times in the 1980s, and by the end of 1991, they had made the playoffs only once in the previous seven seasons.

COWHER REVITALIZES THE STEELERS (1992–1996)

Chuck Noll retired after the 1991 season. To replace him, Dan Rooney hired Cowher, then a 34-year-old defensive coordinator with the Kansas City Chiefs. Cowher immediately turned the Steelers' fortunes around. In his first season, he led the Steelers to an 11–5 record and their first division title in eight years. For his efforts, Cowher was named the NFL's coach of the year by the *Sporting News* and the Associated Press. In 1995, the Steelers were one game shy of a championship, but lost to the Dallas Cowboys in the Super Bowl.

Initially, Cowher's coaching style, demeanor, and personality were a hit in Pittsburgh. With his famous long double-jointed jaw, he had a confrontational and intense style. He would snarl around the sidelines, get in his players' faces, and spew spit-laced tirades when upset. While some opponents found him annoying, fans thought he was infectious, and the players raved about him. The media touted him as an excellent communicator and motivator.

"CAN YOU THINK OF ANY OTHER REASONS COWHER SHOULD [NOT BE FIRED]? I CAN'T" (1997–2000)

The Steelers made the playoffs in each of Cowher's first six seasons as head coach. However, by 1998, things started to get rocky. Free agency was chipping away at the Steelers' roster. Many of the Steelers' Pro Bowlers or future Hall of Famers, like Rod Woodson, Kevin Greene, Leon Searcy, Greg Lloyd, and Chad Brown, who were all integral to the team's success, were either deemed too expensive and released or signed by other teams for more money upon free agency. Essential members of the coaching staff also started to move on.

As the Steelers started to lose more, Cowher's passion and emotion began to be viewed much less sympathetically. His coaching acumen was drawing questions. His teams sometimes looked unprepared and his late game decision making and clock management were shaky. The Steelers were also stuck with a long-term contract with inconsistent-but-promising quarterback Kordell Stewart after giving him an extension in 1999 that bound him to the team until 2003.

In mid-December 1999, after Pittsburgh's fifth consecutive loss dropped them to a 5–8 record, Dan Rooney sent a message: "You guys talk about all the free agents we lost, but we signed everybody this year that we really went after," he said after the game. "The talent should be there." The knock was viewed as a subtle jab at Cowher, and, at the same time, appeared to be an endorsement of general manager Tom Donahoe. "It's safe to say Tom Donahoe's job isn't in jeopardy," wrote local columnist Ron Cook in the *Pittsburgh Post-Gazette*.

During the 1998 season, the previously strong relationship between Cowher and Donahoe, who both joined the team around the same time, began to deteriorate behind the scenes. The tension between the two came to a head at the end of the 1999 campaign. "Tom and Bill disagreed over many things, especially who had the greater say—the coaches or the scouts—over player personnel," Dan Rooney recalled years later. "Bill didn't want Donahoe in coaches' meetings because he thought Tom was a spy. Tom thought Bill was finished as an NFL coach."

It became apparent that one of the two was going to have to go. "We were beyond mediation or a conversation to clear the air," Cowher wrote in his 2021 memoir *Heart and Steel*. "I could not and did not want to work with Tom anymore." According to team vice-president Art Rooney II, the tension between the two became so heated that the organization could not function. From the outside, the bet was on Donahoe surviving. "It would be an upset if Bill Cowher remains in Pittsburgh," wrote Thomas George in the *New York Times*. In the *Los Angeles Times*, writer Houston Mitchell wrote that it "might be wise" for Cowher to move on from Pittsburgh and take a step back.

In the *Post-Gazette*, Cook wrote that he thought Cowher should go:

> Think of the reasons Bill Cowher should be fired
> as Steelers coach: A 6–10 record. Two consecutive

seasons out of the playoffs. A team that has grown stale after six successful seasons. A team that lacks discipline. A lousy working relationship with his general manager. Then think of the reasons Cowher should be retained: Those six successful seasons a lifetime ago. A contract that has three years left and will pay him $2 million per season... Can you think of any other reasons Cowher should stay? I can't, either. Shouldn't this be an easy call for Dan Rooney?

The growing theory among Steelers fans and the NFL media was that Cowher was immovable for the Rooneys. If the Steelers terminated Cowher, they would have to absorb the remaining three years of his contract, which had been extended in 1998 after the Steelers made the 1997 AFC Championship Game. The *Post-Gazette*'s Mark Madden agreed. He wrote: "The Steelers won't fire Cowher and eat the last three seasons of his [contract]... But Rooney and Donahoe would probably be happy if Cowher quit. And maybe it is time for Cowher to move on. Cowher is still an excellent coach, but the team isn't responding to him."

On January 12, 2000, a "league source" told the *Green Bay Press-Gazette* that "the Steelers are going to fire Cowher today." That never happened. A few days later, both Cowher and Donahoe offered their resignations. Rooney only accepted Donahoe's. Not long thereafter, the Steelers announced that Donahoe had "resigned." Donahoe's departure was described as Cowher winning a long-standing "power struggle" between the two. However, Cowher insists a power struggle never existed, and that he didn't want to be the general manager's boss. "I just wanted a collaborative and transparent approach to the job," he recently insisted.

"THE STEELERS SIGNED THE FRANCHISE'S DEATH WARRANT MONTHS AGO" (2000)

The reactions among fans about Cowher coming back were mixed, but many were upset. "I am writing to express disappointment and disgust with the Rooneys' decision to accept Tom Donahoe's 'resignation' and to keep that foul-mouthed, in-your-face, spitting, childish Bill Cowher," a fan wrote to the *Post-Gazette*. "Giving more power to Bill Cowher is like giving a Ferrari to a teenager with his learner's permit," wrote another.

Fans weren't the only ones who disapproved of Rooney's decision. Bob Smizik of the *Post-Gazette* thought Cowher should have been given the ax. "This stunning decision is potentially disastrous for the Steelers," he wrote. "The chances of the Steelers hiring someone of similar competence to replace Donahoe are minuscule." Smizik believed the Rooneys shared some responsibility for letting Donahoe and Cowher's relationship become so tenuous that one had to leave. "They had two men who were at the top of their fields," Smizik added. "It was their job to make certain they worked together." The *Los Angeles Times*'s T. J. Simers was even more critical. "The Steelers signed the franchise's death warrant months ago," he wrote a few months later. "Choosing between personnel whiz Tom Donahoe and tyrant Bill Cowher, owner Dan Rooney went with the fixed jaw."

"[COWHER] HAS PROVEN HIS INEPTNESS TIME AND TIME AGAIN AND HIS CONTRACT MUST BE TERMINATED IMMEDIATELY" (2000-2002)

The Steelers lost their first three games of the 2000 season. After the second game, a 23–20 road loss to the lowly Cleveland Browns in which Cowher made numerous questionable coaching decisions, Smizik wrote "an 0–16 season isn't likely, but how can anyone rule it out?" In the *Californian*, writer Jay Paris contemplated whether the Steelers' final regular-season game, a Christmas Eve showdown against the also-struggling San Diego Chargers would be between two 0–15 teams. During the CBS broadcast of Game 3, a loss to the Titans, play-by-play commentator Ian Eagle remarked that "It's funny how much can change in two years. [Cowher] was thought of as the players' coach, the great motivator...Things have certainly taken a turn." Former Washington Pro Bowl offensive tackle Mark May, Eagle's partner on the broadcast, added that if Cowher were stock, people would've wanted to "dump him in '97." At least a few people thought Cowher's firing was inevitable. The following day, a blurb in the *Los Angeles Times* suggested that Cowher should give baseball manager Davey Johnson, who was on the brink of being fired by the Los Angeles Dodgers, "a call to plan a joint vacation." Paris also thought Cowher had reached the end of the road in Pittsburgh. "Cowher is toast," he wrote. "The only question is if he can last a year."

Cowher's tenuous predicament didn't last long. The Steelers quickly turned it around. They fired off five straight wins, including back-to-back shutouts, led by their powerful defense, which gave up a minuscule 22 points total during the streak. The team finished the season at a respectable 9–7. Although it wasn't enough to make the playoffs, the improvement was promising.

By the time the 2000 season began, Cowher and new Steelers general manager Kevin Colbert had already developed a positive working relationship. As for Donahoe, after the 2000 season, the declining Buffalo Bills hired him as their general manager. Cook was bullish about Donahoe's future, but not as optimistic about Cowher's. "The guess here is the Bills will be a bigger winner over the long haul than the Steelers, and that Donahoe still will be working in Buffalo long after Cowher has moved on to his next job." Cook was wrong. Donahoe's tenure with the Bills was inglorious. He was fired after five seasons, during which the franchise posted a 31–49 record. Only three players Donahoe drafted were selected to a Pro Bowl while with the Bills. As for the Steelers, in 2001, they finished 13–3 and won the AFC Central. But after polishing off the Ravens in the Divisional Round, they were upset at home by the eventual Super Bowl champion Patriots in the AFC Championship Game.

Despite the Steelers' tremendous bounce-back year in 2001, by the time the following season started, it didn't take long for the fans to start moaning and groaning again. After Pittsburgh lost its first two games in 2002, a group of Steelers fans created a petition on the web, addressed to Dan Rooney and the rest of the Steelers owners:

> Finally, after 10 years of agony living through the un-imaginable [sic] a Super-bowl [sic] loss, 0–3 at home for AFC championship games, I have come to the realization that Bill Cowher is incapable of coaching this championship caliber team. I can or will no longer put up with his childish tirades on the sidelines when the obvious problem begins at the top.
>
> Pittsburgh, a town so-enriched with football talent and tradition, can no longer be the place where Bill Cowher can coach. He has proven his ineptness time and time again and his contract must be terminated immediately.

It could have gotten ugly, but the team again bounced back, closing the regular season with wins in five out of its next six games. The Steelers finished 2002 with a 10–5–1 record. But once again they failed to get to the Super Bowl, eliminated by Tennessee in the Divisional Round of the playoffs in a heartbreaking 34–31 overtime loss.

"WHEN IT COMES TO WINNING THAT ONE CRITICAL GAME, COWHER CAN'T DO IT" (2003)

The great success from the 2001 and 2002 seasons didn't last long. Cowher's roller coaster with the Steelers continued in 2003, when the team ended the season at 6–10, causing the complaints about his personality to resurface. For years, Cowher had been criticized for the substantial turnover within his coaching staff, but this time reports of incidents of verbal abuse toward his assistants surfaced, and his relationships with a few of them were falling apart.

Would Cowher be able to survive another disappointing season? If it were up to *Beaver County Times* reporter Chuck Curti, the answer would be no. Curti wrote that other coaches around the league, like Dennis Green, Marty Schottenheimer, and Tony Dungy, all were eventually fired after years of big-game failures, "yet, Cowher continues to get a free pass. And contract extensions." He added: "When it comes to winning that one critical game, [Cowher] can't do it. His record bears that out…"

"I HAVE A SOLUTION TO THE STEELERS DEBACLE … GET A NEW HEAD COACH" (2004–2005)

In 2004, the Steelers drafted Miami (Ohio) quarterback Ben Roethlisberger with the 11th pick in the draft. He started the final 13 games of the regular season, and the Steelers won all of them.

However, after finishing 15–1, the best regular-season record in team history, the Steelers couldn't get past their nemesis, the Patriots, losing to New England 41–27 in the AFC Championship Game.

The 2005 season got off to a rocky start. In early December, the Steelers fell to 7–5 when they lost at home, their third loss in a row, to the Bengals. With the win, the Bengals essentially clinched the division for the first time in 15 years, while the Steelers were in grave danger of missing the playoffs. The fan mail wasn't pretty. "The Steelers will never get to [another] Super Bowl as long as Bill Cowher is their coach," wrote one fan to the local paper. Another wrote, "I have a solution to the Steelers debacle…Get a new head coach."

The Steelers likely had to win their final four games to even make the playoffs. "Is the season over?" read the headline on the front page of the NFL Xtra section of the *Post-Gazette* on the Monday after the Bengals loss. The answer to that question was a resounding no. The Steelers didn't lose another game that season. In the playoffs, they avenged regular-season losses to the Bengals and Colts and beat the Broncos in the AFC Championship Game, all on the road. Then, in future Hall of Fame running back Jerome Bettis's final NFL game, the Steelers beat the Seahawks 21–10 to win Super Bowl XL in Detroit. Cowher had finally thrown the monkey off his back.

Right before the Steelers' Super Bowl XL triumph, Dan Rooney asserted that he was never tempted to fire Cowher at any point. He said he trusted his instincts about how cyclical the NFL is. It is impossible to gauge whether that is the complete truth, but it's quite clear that Rooney did not want to have to let Cowher go. "We're about stability—having good people and keeping them," he said in 2002. "We know what we've got here."

THE TOMLIN ERA AND THE PHILOSOPHY OF PATIENCE

The 2006 season was Cowher's 15th and final season as an NFL head coach. Despite coming off a Super Bowl win, the Steelers failed to make the playoffs. Cowher immediately retired upon season's end. His replacement, Mike Tomlin, was a 34-year-old defensive coordinator, just as Cowher had been when he was hired.

Dan Rooney's son, Art Rooney II, took control of the day-to-day operations of the franchise around 2003. The family philosophy about coaching stability still hasn't changed. As of 2022, after 15 seasons, Tomlin is still the head coach. He has yet to have a losing season. Nevertheless, during his tenure, he has endured turbulence and success, much as Cowher did. During the 2008 season, Tomlin coached the Steelers to a Super Bowl title, and in 2010 he led them to another Super Bowl appearance. Since then, the team has made the playoffs 7 out of 11 seasons. However, during that time, the Steelers have only been to one AFC Championship Game and no Super Bowls. Tomlin has often been the target of the same type of criticism Cowher received during his tenure. At times, he is berated by the press and the fans about issues such as clock management, team preparation, and his way of dealing with star players. Almost every off-season, there is gossip and rumors about Tomlin's job security. Despite that, Art Rooney II has stuck with him.

To the Steelers, firing a head coach means starting over and dismantling the stability they believe is critical for the continued success of their franchise. Cowher wasn't perfect. He had issues with his coaching staff and front office. He lost many big games. Nonetheless, Dan Rooney never lost enough confidence in Cowher to terminate him. It's the kind of patience and loyalty that is rare in the NFL, but can sometimes bear fruit—and rings.

"THE 49ERS SHOULD DO EVERYONE A FAVOR. TRADE STEVE YOUNG. THE MYTH. AND THE MAN"

(1987–1994 SAN FRANCISCO 49ERS)

These days, no team would be able to afford to have two of the most talented quarterbacks in the NFL on its roster for five straight years. Even if a team was somehow able to procure two quarterbacks of that caliber, it would be lucky to be able to keep both of them for even two seasons. Once unrestricted free agency began in 1993 and the salary cap went into effect a year later, in order to keep two top-tier quarterbacks, a team would have to sign both to big money, long-term deals. Thus, practically speaking, if a team has two star signal-callers, it could only sign one to a huge extension. As a result, the other player is almost always traded or signs a handsome contract somewhere else.

From 1987 to 1992, the San Francisco 49ers, in the middle of the best decade in the team's history, enjoyed the luxury of having Joe Montana and Steve Young, two Hall of Fame quarterbacks, on their roster at the same time. Although, back then, few viewed it as much of a luxury. Niners head coach Bill Walsh, who was responsible for bringing both players to San Francisco, found it difficult to navigate a roster of two great quarterbacks who desperately wanted to play but despised their predicament and resented each other for it. It became the longest and most contentious quarterback rivalry the NFL has ever seen.

The way in which the 49ers' coaching staff and front office handled the situation is still fodder for debate. But while it may not have looked like it at the time, Montana and Young's rivalry arguably may have been the best thing to happen to the two players, and the franchise.

By the end of the '80s, most were certain that the intense and combustible pairing would eventually leave a messy legacy. But, somehow, it didn't. And while few foresaw the actual end result, at some point during the five years the two quarterbacks were on the roster, countless journalists and commentators throughout the Bay Area and the country, levied just about every possible criticism and predicted just about every type of conclusion to the story. The commentary left many Freezing Cold Takes in its wake—a treasure trove waiting to be dug up decades later.

"THEY BELIEVE THE ROSTER CONSISTS OF ONE MAN, MONTANA"

To categorize Joe Montana, the iconic San Francisco 49ers quarterback, as a hero in the Bay Area is an understatement. Before Montana came along, this same town saw Willie Mays and Willie McCovey play baseball for the Giants. But Montana was even bigger and more beloved than either of those baseball legends. In San Francisco, Montana was the idol of all idols.

Fiercely competitive, handsome, with a winsome personality, the city quickly developed an attachment to its star quarterback. Simply put, in the 1980s, Montana *was* San Francisco sports. For a town that had never seen a professional team win a title (only Oakland-based franchises had produced championships), when Montana came along and started leading the 49ers to Super Bowls, the reality shifted for its fans. He was a household name, even for residents who only watched the NFL casually, or not at all. As one local columnist described it in 1993, "Most of the people who cheer for the 49ers know as much about football as Madonna knows about San Andreas Fault. They believe the roster consists of one man, Montana."

WALSH, MONTANA, AND THE "TEAM OF THE '80S"

Now recognized as the "team of the '80s," the San Francisco 49ers hadn't achieved anything notable before that breakout decade. By the end of the 1978 season, the Niners had suffered six straight losing seasons, during which time they had gone through five different head coaches. But their fortunes changed in 1979 when owner Eddie DeBartolo Jr. hired Stanford head coach Bill Walsh. Walsh immediately pushed the team to draft Montana, who had just graduated from Notre Dame, in the third round of the NFL Draft. Montana didn't look like a superstar. Listed at 6-foot-2, which was considered small for a quarterback at the time, his physical frame was considered slight, average at best. His arm strength was sufficient but not amazing. Nevertheless, he and Walsh ended up being a match made in heaven.

An offensive pioneer, Walsh immediately implemented his complex, innovative, pass-heavy offense in San Francisco. Later coined the "West Coast Offense," Walsh's system emphasized short horizontal routes by wide receivers instead of a heavy running game. It also prioritized ball control and favored the mentally strong quarterback who could, with perfect timing, quickly decipher what the defense was showing and then determine who to throw to. The quarterback needed to think quickly and be precise, and an extraordinary arm was not a prerequisite.

Montana fit right in to Walsh's system and quickly mastered it. He had a natural ability to process a significant amount of information just before and after the snap and understand who would be the open receiver, then make a perfect throw. While not noticeably fast, Montana had quick feet and glided through the pocket to avoid sacks. He possessed the sharp improvisational skills to make a play when needed.

Perhaps Montana's most important win came during the 1981 season, his third, in the 1981 NFC Championship game against the Dallas Cowboys at Candlestick Park in San Francisco. It is, at the very least, the one for which he is best known. By that point in the season, the Cowboys had established themselves as the biggest brand in football. Down 27–21 with 0:58 left, it was 3rd and 3 with the ball at the Cowboys' 6-yard line. Montana rolled right toward the boundary, pump-faked once, and threw an off-balance ball toward the back of the end zone, where Niners wide receiver Dwight Clark leapt up and snared it. Clark's game-winning touchdown catch capped a four-minute-plus, 14-play, 83-yard drive, led by Montana. The 49ers won 28–27. Now known as "the Catch," it is universally considered one of the most memorable plays in the history of the NFL.

A few weeks later, Montana led the 49ers to a 26–21 win over the Cincinnati Bengals in Super Bowl XVI for the franchise's first Super Bowl title. The win made Montana a bona fide national sports star and a hero in San Francisco. After falling short in 1982 and failing to make the playoffs, Montana and the 49ers kicked it into high gear offensively in 1983. Having developed a productive running game with rookie Roger Craig and veteran Wendell Tyler, Montana had his best regular season yet. However, it was cut short when the Niners lost to eventual Super Bowl XVII Champions Washington 24–21 in the NFC Championship game. The 1984 season would have a much happier ending, as the Niners they bounced back, going 18–1 and destroying the Dolphins and their young superstar quarterback Dan Marino in Super Bowl XIX, winning 38–16.

By 1985, Montana, who had a reputation as being one of the most durable players in the league, started to show cracks in his armor. During training camp, a CT scan of his back showed an inflamed disk that was causing spasms, forcing him to miss two preseason games. In June 1986, he underwent shoulder surgery, as he had been hampered with persistent pain in his throwing shoulder when he was throwing.

Montana faced even more medical issues at the beginning of the 1986 season. In the first game, he suffered an injury that required surgery for a ruptured disk in his back. The procedure cost him half the season. But, against all odds, he was back on the field by Game 10. Sadly, however, the season ended with a thud when the 49ers ended up getting blown out by the Giants 49–3 in an NFC Wild Card game. The Giants' defense was relentless. Montana spent much of the day on his back as the Giants' defense delivered ferocious hit after hit, including one by Giants defensive tackle Jim Burt that knocked Montana out of the game near the end of the first half.

The playoff drubbing by the Giants, who would go on to win the franchise's first Super Bowl title, was a reality check for the 49ers. They had lost in the NFC Playoffs to the Giants in two straight seasons and didn't score a touchdown in either game. Local papers immediately started harping on the "major rebuilding job" Walsh faced. Some of the Niners players even conceded that the rest of the NFL finally had caught up with them.

"JOE MIGHT WANDER AROUND A LITTLE BIT. BUT THERE'S NO WAY HE'S GOING TO BE ABLE [PLAY FOOTBALL] ANYMORE" (1987)

Walsh was beginning to believe that Montana was just about nearing the end of his run. Montana had no interest in quitting. But the veteran coach wasn't the type to rest on his laurels. He needed not just a suitable backup, but an heir apparent. A capable quarterback to take over when Montana hung up his cleats. He quickly focused on Steve Young.

Young, a left-hander, was ahead of his time. Not only did he have a quality arm but he possessed great speed, and was, at the time, one of the few quarterbacks in the NFL who was a threat with his arm and his legs. After a stellar career at Brigham Young University, he was the top-rated quarterback in the country coming out of college and was projected to be the first pick in the 1984 NFL Draft. Instead, he chose to sign a contract with the Los Angeles Express of the upstart United States Football League (USFL). Announced as a four-year deal worth $40 million, the contract was, at the time, the richest for any professional athlete. But by the time the Express's second season ended in June 1985, the team and the league were on the brink of collapse. As a result, the USFL let Young out of his Express contract, paving the way for him to play in the NFL. He signed with the Tampa Bay Buccaneers, who owned his rights after they selected him No. 1 in a supplemental draft of USFL players in June 1984.

The Bucs were terrible before Young came in, and they weren't any better with him. In each of the two seasons Young was with the team, they finished with a 2–14 record. Young started 19 of those 32 games, and won only 3. He threw 11 touchdowns and 21 interceptions. Young felt he didn't have a great foundation to work with in Tampa. He later recalled, "The football I played at the LA Express, the coaching I had, and the teammates that I had were much, much better in every situation, and every way, than in Tampa Bay in the NFL." After Tampa Bay used its first pick in the 1987 Draft to select University of Miami quarterback Vinny Testaverde, the Buccaneers agreed to allow Young to look for a team with whom Tampa Bay could seek a trade.

Walsh couldn't understand why a guy who was so athletic and threw with such sharpness and accuracy could be discarded so quickly. He was convinced that Tampa didn't use him properly. The 49ers' offensive coordinator, Mike Holmgren, was keenly aware of Young's talent, as he had been Young's quarterbacks coach at BYU.

In discussions with Walsh, Young naturally expressed concerns about Montana, but Walsh assured him that wouldn't be a problem. "Steve, you don't come back from a second back surgery," he told Young. "Joe might wander around a little bit. But there's no way he's going to be able to do it anymore." The trade for Young was consummated on April 24, 1987. The Niners didn't even have to give up a first-round pick. Throughout the previous six years, Montana had faced no competition within the franchise—the quarterbacks on the depth chart behind him had been wholly inferior. That was about to change.

When Young arrived at the 49ers minicamp a month later, he quickly realized that Montana had not gotten the memo about his career being over. On his first day of camp, Young saw Montana come onto the field, move around normally, and throw perfect passes. He looked healthy. Contrary to what Walsh had been telling Young, Montana had no interest in hanging up his cleats any time soon.

Montana possessed an unmatched competitive spirit that was borderline maniacal, and was not happy with Walsh's recent acquisition. He referred to Young as the "opposition," and considered him a threat. According to Young's agent, Leigh Steinberg, if Young and he knew that Montana would be up and throwing when training camp started, Young would never have accepted the trade to San Francisco.

In 1987, Montana remained the starter. He had the best statistical season of his career up to that point, and the 49ers finished the regular season with the best record in the NFL. Young didn't see his first regular-season action until late October. In December, Montana pulled a hamstring, forcing Young to take the majority of the snaps for San Francisco's final three weeks of the regular season. In the three games with Young at quarterback, the 49ers outscored their opponents 124–7. Young threw nine touchdowns and zero interceptions. Not long after, legendary Hall of Fame head coach and CBS radio commenter Hank Stram gave Young the highest of praises. "Steve Young is a clone of Joe Montana," he said. "He does the same things Montana has been doing for the 49ers all these years, except that Steve is faster than Joe." The 49ers destroyed the Rams 48–0 in the final regular-season game to finish 13–2 for the year. Young played the first half, Montana took over in the second. Both played great. But Young's play in December turned some heads. "In the present tense," wrote Dave Albee in *USA Today*, "Young is the 49ers' quarterback of the future."

Going into the 1987 Playoffs, San Francisco was the odds-on favorite to represent the NFC in the Super Bowl. The consensus was that the one team in the conference that even posed a threat to the 49ers in the NFC was the Saints, who had beaten them in San Francisco two months earlier. But when the Minnesota Vikings took out New Orleans in the first round, San Francisco was essentially declared, by much of the media, Super Bowl champions.

Montana was reinstalled as starter for the Divisional Round game against Minnesota. The Niners were expected to win easily. However, Montana struggled to handle the pressure from the Vikings' defensive line, particularly Minnesota's young defensive end Chris Doleman. With the 49ers down 27–10 in the third quarter, Walsh threw everyone for a loop when he benched Montana for Young. It was his first playoff game appearance. He almost led the 49ers to a comeback victory but fell short at the end and the Niners lost 36–24. It was the 49ers' third consecutive postseason loss and the third consecutive postseason start where Montana did not lead the 49ers to a single touchdown. Soon after, Walsh said that there would be an "open competition" at the quarterback position the next season.

"MONTANA MIGHT NOT HAVE LASTED MORE THAN A COUPLE OF YEARS IN THE NFL WITH SOME TEAMS"

By the time 1988 rolled around, some were starting to wonder about the effect the previous three seasons' playoff failures would have on Montana's legacy. One journalist started writing about that before the 1987 season ended. In November 1987, *San Francisco Chronicle* columnist Glenn Dickey wrote that, essentially, the many local folks who thought that Montana was the greatest quarterback of all time couldn't see the forest from the trees, and chalked up their jaded minds to the "provincialism" of the Bay Area.

Dickey added that he didn't even think Montana was the best in his own era and hinted that Dan Marino and John Elway had surpassed him. "Montana's local reputation rests entirely on the four years, 1981–84, when he took the 49ers to two Super Bowl wins," he wrote, explaining that, up to that point, other quarterbacks had more Super Bowl wins, and Montana had never led the league in passing.

Dickey also essentially labeled Montana a "system quarterback." "Montana has been, indisputably . . . the right man in the right system," he wrote. He then added that quarterbacks always prospered under Bill Walsh, and, while he admitted that without Montana the 49ers wouldn't have won two Super Bowls, it was Walsh's offense that "could take advantage of Montana's strengths and minimize his weaknesses." Dickey also believed that "Montana might not have lasted more than a couple of years in the NFL with some teams."

"QUARTERBACK CONTROVERSY" (1988)

Montana had elbow surgery a month after the playoff loss, but he was ready to play in time for the start of the 1988 season. Despite Walsh's declaring an open quarterback competition eight months earlier, Montana's job never really appeared to be in any jeopardy. There was little doubt around the 49ers organization that Montana was still the team's No. 1 quarterback. However, possibly feeling that Montana was too comfortable, Walsh stirred the pot. He told NBC's Merlin Olsen, during a taped interview that aired before the 49ers' preseason opener, that the team had "a quarterback controversy, and we're going to have to select between Steve Young and Joe Montana." It momentarily caused a stir, and Walsh eventually tried to walk back his words. But whether or not it was intentional, it had an effect on Montana.

During the 1988 regular season, Young saw more action than he did the year before. He was even given a chance to start some games. However, he didn't perform as consistently as he did in 1987. In one 49ers loss, Young threw crucial interceptions in the fourth quarter. In another, which Young played from start to finish, the 49ers blew a 23–0 third-quarter lead. In yet another one, Walsh replaced him at halftime with Montana who led the 49ers to a thrilling fourth-quarter win, courtesy of a late 78-yard game-winning touchdown pass to Jerry Rice. Young's best game was in Week 9, where, as the starter, he led the Niners to a 24–21 home win against the Vikings, which included him scoring on a 49-yard, game-winning touchdown run that is now considered perhaps the most exciting play of his career.

By Week 12, the Niners were 6–5 and on the ropes. On *Monday Night Football*, Joe Montana started and led the 49ers to a 37–21 win over Washington, the defending Super Bowl champions. San Francisco never looked back after that. Montana became the permanent starter, and the 49ers won six out of their last seven games to finish 10–6 and win the NFC West.

The Niners' near-dominance in the last half of the regular season carried over to the playoffs. They made it to Super Bowl XXIII, facing off against the Cincinnati Bengals once again. Down three with 3:10 left in the fourth quarter, a cool, calm, and collected Montana led one of the most famous drives in NFL history, a methodical 11-play, 92-yard march, culminating in a game-winning 10-yard touchdown pass to wide receiver John Taylor. The 49ers won 20–16, and, once again, Montana was the hero.

After Montana's heroics in Miami, any confidence or ground gained by Young from the previous postseason was essentially lost. He never really had much support, if any, among the fans or the locker room in the first place, so by this time Montana had a firm grip on the job.

"[I]T SEEMS INEVITABLE THAT [YOUNG'S] UNEASY RELATIONSHIP WITH THE 49ERS WILL BE OVER" (1990)

Bill Walsh retired after the Super Bowl. Defensive coordinator George Seifert was elevated to head coach and he immediately named Montana the permanent starter. However, when Montana suffered more injuries, Young clocked significant time as a backup. This time, he played very well, starting three games, and winning all of them. But Montana played even better and picked up his first league MVP award. With the best record in the NFL, the 49ers again breezed through the playoffs with Montana leading the way. In Super Bowl XXIV, a 55–10 Niners romp over the Broncos, Montana threw five touchdowns and was voted MVP. It was his fourth Super Bowl ring.

Young played in the final four minutes of the Super Bowl. To him, it was bittersweet. His contributions to the team's success were, once again, minimal. Young was 28. He did not want to wait until he was 33 or 34 to again become a permanent NFL starter. But with a year left on his contract, there was nothing he could do.

If that wasn't ominous enough, during training camp, Montana signed a four-year, $13 million contract extension.

In late August 1990, writer Tom Jackson, in the *Sacramento Bee*, suggested that Young demand a trade. "He's running out of time," Jackson wrote. "And he darn well ought to be running out of patience." Also, Jackson surmised that "it seems inevitable that [Young's] uneasy relationship with the 49ers will be over" at the end of the 1990 season.

Young languished on the sidelines for almost the entire 1990 season as the 49ers rolled to a 14–2 record, while Montana won his second straight league MVP. As the Niners were nearing another Super Bowl appearance, a vicious fourth-quarter hit by the Giants' Leonard Marshall knocked Montana out of the NFC Championship game. Young came in, but with under three minutes left in the game, the Niners up 13–12 and trying to run out the clock, running back Roger Craig fumbled. The Giants recovered on their own 43-yard line, and they eventually drove downfield and converted a field goal to win 15–13 with no time left.

STEVE YOUNG GETS HIS SHOT AS THE STARTER (1991)

Young's contract with the 49ers expired after the 1990 season. Against the advice of many, he signed a two-year contract to remain with San Francisco. He thought that the 49ers' offense fit him well, and that he was getting close to becoming the full-time starter. It was a gamble, but it paid off immediately. Due to a nagging elbow injury, Montana was physically unable to play for most of the 1991 and 1992 seasons.

With Young at quarterback in 1991, the 49ers started 2–4. In the fifth game of the season, the Niners lost an ugly game 12–6 to the Raiders at the Los Angeles Memorial Coliseum. Young threw two terrible interceptions and he could not capitalize on numerous red zone opportunities. After the game, fiery 49ers defensive end Charles Haley went berserk. According to a witness, he shouted, "I don't want anyone from this losing team touching me!" It became so bad, he took a swing at George Seifert, which luckily didn't connect. Niners reps had to ask former 49ers safety (and Raiders offseason acquisition) Ronnie Lott to calm Haley down.

Haley wasn't shy about his disdain for Young. "He was such a whiner," Haley recalled years later. "He was always moping around the locker room, bad-mouthing Joe, stabbing him in the back."

Haley wasn't the only one clamoring for Montana's return. After the game, former 49ers receiver and Montana's close friend Dwight Clark, then a 49ers executive assistant, said on TV that "Joe Montana could have won this game in his sleep."

In the following game against Atlanta, Young threw for 348 yards, ran for two touchdowns, and played brilliantly for three-and-a-half quarters. But on the team's final two drives he threw two interceptions, both to former 49ers cornerback Tim McKyer, and the 49ers lost 39–34.

The loss to the Falcons further raised speculation, perpetuated by many, that Young would never win a Super Bowl because he was not "a winner," and he buckled under pressure in the fourth quarter. This was in contrast to Montana, whose most famous trait was his ability to thrive in the most pressure-packed situations and lead the 49ers to victories at the end of games. In his NFL career, Montana led San Francisco to 31 fourth-quarter comeback victories. By 1991, Young made mistakes in quite a few games, costing the team in the fourth quarter.

After the game, not only did Young's teammates have to answer questions about his capability in late-game situations, but Atlanta players had to field a few, too. "I'm just glad Joe Montana didn't come on the field at the end," said Falcons safety Scott Case.

"JUST IMAGINE THE NUMBER 16 ON [STEVE BONO'S] JERSEY AND YOU WOULD THINK YOU WERE WATCHING MONTANA" (1991)

If Montana's shadow wasn't large enough, another quarterback was about to join the fray. In 1989, the 49ers signed Steve Bono, a six-year veteran with little experience, as their third-string quarterback. During the 1987 players' strike, he crossed the picket line and started three games for the Steelers, but that was almost all the NFL experience he had. A 6-foot-4, pure pocket passer out of UCLA, Bono wasn't as talented or athletic as Montana or Young, but he had a strong arm.

In Atlanta, during the 49ers' ninth game, Young was hurt. Bono came on and threw a 31-yard, go-ahead touchdown pass to John Taylor on 3rd and 21 with 53 seconds left (though the Falcons completed a miracle Hail Mary touchdown with 1 second left to win the game 17–14).

With Young injured, Bono started the next six games. After getting swallowed whole in his first start by the 49ers' division rival New Orleans Saints in a 10–3 loss, he led the Niners to five straight wins. His best game came in the Saints rematch at Candlestick Park. In a 38–24 Niners win, Bono threw for 347 yards and three touchdowns, including the go-ahead score with under two minutes left. That evening, while narrating the highlights on ESPN's weekly Sunday night staple *NFL Primetime*, host Chris Berman exclaimed, "It looks like [Bono] has been running this offense for six years." Bono's performance also spawned a media narrative that Bono, like Montana, and unlike Young, could execute in the fourth quarter.

Bono's apparent composure under pressure, willingness to stay in the pocket, and fourth-quarter calmness started to remind people of Montana. It was as if he were a Montana clone (albeit a less talented and taller one). San Francisco was a Montana town, and Bono seemed to most closely resemble the real thing. Bono had become yet another barrier in Young's journey. Now he wasn't just trying to surpass Montana; Young was going to have to shake off Bono as well.

The Montana body-double theory started to take hold. "[Bono] is quickly becoming a poor man's Montana," wrote Joe Santoro in the *Reno Gazette-Journal*. "He's right handed . . . he throws 15-yard passes that turn into 47-yard touchdowns, and he wins games in the fourth quarter." Hall of Fame quarterback Dan Fouts went even further, "Just imagine the number 16 on that jersey and you would think you were watching Montana," he said.

There was more. "Bono is Montana's surrogate," wrote Larry Minner in the *Modesto (California) Bee*. "He runs the system the same. He stands firm against the rush, and he passes—dink, dink, boom!—Montana style." The following week, as the Seattle Seahawks were preparing to play the 49ers, their assistant coach Joe Vitt scouted Bono. "Believe me," Vitt said. "If you didn't know the [jersey] numbers, this guy looks like Montana."

"[STEVE YOUNG'S STOCK] HAS BECOME SO DEVALUED THE POOR GUY VIRTUALLY DROPPED OFF THE EXCHANGE" (1991)

In a *Chronicle* column, Lowell Cohn became one of the first to truly advocate for Bono to permanently start over Young. "[Steve Young's stock] has become so devalued the poor guy virtually dropped off the exchange," Cohn wrote. "The brutal truth is that Bono could do what Young couldn't—win." He continued, "It is a fact that Bono seems more of the 49ers' type of quarterback...The 49ers should consider trading Young after this season for a good running back."

Not all journalists felt this way. A few days later, (Santa Rosa, California) *Press Democrat* columnist Mike Silver staunchly defended Young:

> The Bay Area has officially gone insane...Make
> Bono the 49ers' quarterback of the future? You
> people have all gone stark, raving mad...It's really
> very basic. Steve Young is a better quarterback than
> Steve Bono. He's better than almost anybody in the
> league. He's big, strong, fast, and intelligent, a threat
> to throw short, throw deep or run at any moment.
> He's one of the few players in the league opponents
> actually dread facing, and if he hadn't spent the last
> four years toiling behind the greatest football player
> in history, he'd be a superstar.

It wasn't so much that Silver was down on Bono, he just couldn't fathom how people were willing to toss aside a talent like Young. "I definitely wasn't anti-Bono. I loved him. He was a good dude," he said in 2020, "and I thought he played tremendously. I just didn't think people were getting it."

Bono started the next game and led the 49ers to a win over the 5–8 Seahawks in Seattle. Despite San Francisco turning the ball over five times, including two interceptions by Bono in the last four minutes, the Niners were able to get one more chance. With 1:08 remaining in the game, Bono hit John Taylor in the end zone from 15 yards out. It was the go-ahead score, and the 49ers held on to win 24–22. "Get ready for the Montana/Bono comparisons now, Tim," commentator Irv Cross told play-by-play man Tim Ryan after the touchdown on the CBS game broadcast. He was right. Various scribes likened Bono's heroics to Montana's iconic Super Bowl XXIII–winning touchdown pass to Taylor in Miami three years earlier.

As Bono's stock continued to rise, he started to receive more and more media endorsements. Dan Fouts thought that with Bono, the Niners didn't need Young. "Steve Bono can play in the NFL and is perfect for San Francisco's system—better than Young," Fouts explained. "Bono has the obvious physical traits of height and a strong arm but can also put touch on a pass. He's studied Montana so well that he copied some of Joe's characteristics. He's become a Montana clone."

The 49ers won their final two games in 1991. Young recovered from his injury in time to start the final game, a 52–14 shellacking over the Bears. But the Niners missed the playoffs. Young finished the season only 5–5 as a starter, but he led the NFL in passing efficiency.

The following off-season was tough for Young. With Joe Montana expected to be ready to go by training camp, Young was in a precarious position. If Montana was cleared to play, Young would almost certainly revert back to his backup role. As the *San Francisco Examiner*'s Ray Ratto put it, "If Montana is healthy, he starts. It is as immutable as a law of gravity in these parts." In addition, because of the emergence of Bono, who, at that time, had no problem playing second fiddle behind Montana, there was a sense that Young was expendable.

"TIME TO SAY SO LONG TO STEVE YOUNG" (1992)

Young was almost shipped out of San Francisco before the 1992 season. Near the end of the 1991 season, rumors were spreading that Young might be traded. One plugged-in writer, *Chronicle* scribe Ira Miller, wrote in December about his "inescapable" conclusion that the 49ers needed to trade Steve Young so that they could fill needs at safety and running back.

Four months later, the Niners almost heeded Miller's advice. "There was a lot of pressure to trade Steve," team president Carmen Policy said later in the year. "There were many factors, including the friction between Joe and Steve as superstar quarterbacks and the belief that the 1992 Draft was critical to our franchise...Even Bill Walsh said he thought it would be best to trade Steve." The morning of the 1992 NFL Draft, the Niners were set to trade Young to the Los Angeles Raiders. They wanted two first-round draft picks in return, but Raiders owner Al Davis only agreed to two second-rounders. No deal was made.

That off-season, Young's frustration began to mount, so much so that he made some uncharacteristic remarks at the opening of minicamp. "I'm not going to accept No. 2 status," he told reporters. "That would be like running the Kentucky Derby and then going back to run with the trotters at Yonkers. It's illogical in my mind. There would be no fulfillment in that. No way."

Young's rant didn't go over well with much of the media, to whom he came across as a whiner. "Time to say so long to Steve Young," wrote Bruce Jenkins in the *Chronicle*. "It doesn't look that complicated from here." (San Jose, California) *Mercury News* columnist Mark Purdy wrote, "Barring a Montana setback, the 49ers must trade Young. Period." In his column in the (Santa Rosa, California) *Press Democrat*, Bob Padecky agreed. "Steve Young is not a winning quarterback," he wrote. "The 49ers should do everyone a favor. Trade Young. The myth. And the man."

"STEVE YOUNG HAS A BETTER ARM ... STEVE YOUNG IS A BETTER ATHLETE ... IT DOESN'T MATTER ... BECAUSE STEVE BONO IS A BETTER PRO QUARTERBACK (1992)"

At the start of training camp in 1992, Seifert designated Montana the 49ers' starting quarterback. But persistent soreness in his elbow caused him to miss the preseason. While it seemed to be a minor issue at first, it turned out to be a significant problem. Montana ultimately ended up sidelined for most of the regular season. The 49ers won their first two preseason games. Young started the first, but sat out the second with a sore back. In Game 3, a 17–15 win over Washington in London, Young played the entire first half, but San Francisco scored all of its 17 points in the second half with Bono at the helm. In each of the three games, Bono led the Niners on fourth-quarter, game-winning scoring drives. Young started the next pre-season game in San Diego, and played the whole first half, but once again, the Niners were unproductive with him while Bono thrived in the second half. He led San Francisco on two touchdown drives in the final 3:43 to win 20–14. While Bono was making a great impression with his preseason play, Young failed to move the offense into the red zone in any of the drives in which he was playing.

A growing faction in the media was starting to endorse Bono as the starter. Padecky once again threw his support behind Bono. In a column, he declared himself to be "pro-Bono." Although he admitted that Young had a better arm and was a better athlete, he believed that Bono was the better quarterback. He theorized that the 49ers' offensive system was tailor-made for Bono, and that Bono gave them a better chance of making the Super Bowl. Padecky wasn't alone in these beliefs. On CBS, Randy Cross explained that "If you took a poll of 49ers, they'd have much more confidence in Steve Bono than in Steve Young." In an interview with Cross that aired prime time on CBS, Montana told Cross that he should start ahead of Young if he was able to play.

Despite some of the media backing Bono, in late August, before the final preseason game, Seifert formally announced that Steve Young would be the 49ers quarterback for the 1992 season. It wasn't without drama. Even though Montana had missed the entire preseason and most had written him off, he started throwing passes in practice the week prior to the opening game and felt he was close to being ready. When Seifert made the announcement that Young would start, Bono, who was close friends with Montana, relayed that Montana was angry. "To put it mildly," said Bono, "I think he has a right to be…A healthy Joe Montana—if that's the case—is kind of hard to put on the bench."

The 49ers won their final preseason game 24–17 over the Seahawks at Candlestick Park. This time it was Young leading the way with two touchdown passes and one rushing score. In the days leading up to the game, there were discussions by Seifert and others about the possibility that Montana could, and would, play. However, Seifert stuck with Young. When Montana heard that Young would be starting, he didn't even suit up. On the sidelines, he refused to recognize Young's existence.

Young started the first game of the regular season against the Giants and led the Niners on a touchdown drive on its opening possession. But he left the game with a concussion late in the first quarter after his second series of plays. Bono took over, threw two touchdowns, and led the Niners to a 31–14 win. "Steve Bono should still be the quarterback," wrote Chris Mortensen in the *Sporting News* a few days later.

Week 1 of the 1992 season was the last week that Steve Bono was ever associated with an active 49ers quarterback controversy. The following week, at Candlestick Park, the defending

AFC Champion Buffalo Bills beat the Niners 34–31 in one of the great offensive games of the decade. It was the first time in the history of the NFL in which neither team punted. Both Steve Young and future Hall of Famer Jim Kelly threw for more than 400 yards.

Although the 49ers lost to Buffalo, it was truly a breakout game for the 49ers offense, and a preview of what was to come under Mike Shanahan, the 49ers new offensive coordinator. Shanahan was hired by Seifert after Holmgren left in January 1992 to become the head coach of the Green Bay Packers.

One of the common criticisms of Young early in his career was that he was too eager to take the ball, leave the pocket, and run. Many felt he should stay in the pocket longer and focus on his progressions. Shanahan worked with him on keeping his options open as he began to scramble, to focus on throwing on the run, and to maintain the ability to pass until the moment he got to the line of scrimmage. Young loved Shanahan's aggressive play-calling and truly began to shine. After the Buffalo loss, the rest of the 1992 regular season went near perfectly. The 49ers won 13 out of their final 14 games and finished with a 14–2 regular-season record, the best in the NFL. They also finished with the league's No. 1 offense. Young won his first league MVP and led the NFL in passer rating and touchdown passes.

"I HOPE STEVE YOUNG BREAKS HIS LEG" (1992)

In the 1992 regular season, Young proved he was truly one of the NFL's elite signal-callers. But even an MVP season wasn't going to catapult him over Joe Montana in terms of popularity. Soon, Montana would be ready to return, and his presence would serve as a reminder that Young's future remained unresolved.

Montana was back at practice on November 25 and was cleared to play three days later. That was a big deal. Soon, for the first time in almost two years, Joe Cool would join the 49ers' active roster. There was one major caveat: He was no longer the team's starting quarterback. Young had been fantastic. He was the NFL's top-rated passer and its leader in throwing yards for a 49ers team that was No. 1 in the NFL in total offense. Seifert was not going to permanently bench Young. At least not for the remainder of the '92 season.

Young may have remained the starter, but for one week, he lost the spotlight. Going into the last week of the regular season, Montana was gearing up for some action. The 49ers had a home game on *Monday Night Football* against the Lions, and had already clinched home-field advantage throughout the playoffs. There was much talk during the week about whether Montana would play. People were desperately hoping to see Montana at least one more time. "I hope Steve Young breaks his leg," said one caller to KGO-AM Radio in San Francisco.

"A LEGEND BECAME LARGER MONDAY NIGHT" (1992)

It was a cold and rainy Monday night at Candlestick Park. Just prior to the game, Seifert told Young that he would start but that Montana would play the second half. The scene was set as a tribute for Montana. Signs were plastered everywhere welcoming him.

In an uninspiring, sloppy first half, Young led the 49ers to a 7–6 lead. Montana entered the game for the 49ers' first drive of the second half, and the crowd thunderously roared. Up in the broadcasting booth, Dan Dierdorf, calling the game for ABC along with play-by-play man Al Michaels and Frank Gifford, felt the energy. "And all is right with the world once again," Dierdorf said. After a slow third quarter, Montana picked it up in the fourth. With under

12 minutes remaining, he threw a 9-yard touchdown to tight end Brent Jones, and the crowd went wild. "It might be raining, but, for this crowd, the sun just came out," said Michaels. When the Niners got the ball back with 6:31 remaining, Montana led them on a surgical 10-play, 74-yard drive, capped off by an 8-yard touchdown pass to running back Amp Lee. "Now. All is well," said Gifford, echoing Deirdorf's earlier comments. Montana completed his final six passes in the 49ers 24–6 win. He finished the game 15-of-21 for 126 yards and two touchdowns.

The Montana adulation was apparent in the papers the next day. "Yes, if it is possible, The Legend became larger Monday night," wrote Padecky. The performance also spawned another discussion: whether he had done enough to supplant Bono as Young's backup for the playoffs. "You hate to say it but now we can tell what the difference is between Montana and Young," Padecky noted. "Montana moves his team smoothly through a defense; in comparison, Young's offense looks like it struggles."

If the fans had it their way, Montana would be taking the snaps. According to the 49ers' play-by-play radio voice Joe Starkey, some fans thought that "Montana is the greatest quarterback [and the] greatest human being in the world and no matter what, he should be starting." A few days before Montana's return to the field, (New York) *Newsday* columnist Bob Glauber reported that at a Golden State Warriors NBA home game in Oakland, Steve Young, who was in attendance, was booed by the Bay Area crowd. Fans were fighting over Montana versus Young at bars. "Last week, these guys started throwing punches and we had to break it up," a bartender at Ricky's, a popular sports bar in San Leandro, told the *Los Angeles Daily News* in early January 1993. "I asked someone what they were fighting about and they said, 'Montana and Young.' It's getting crazy."

Michael Wilbon, in his *Washington Post* column a few days before the game, expressed his desire to see Montana play against Washington. Despite acknowledging that it was "unjustifiable, and borders on irresponsible," he wished for an unserious ailment to fall upon Young during the game. "What would be the harm in Young coming down with a three-hour virus, right around 4 p.m. Eastern on Saturday," Wilbon wrote. "Something that would leave him temporarily congested and stuff just long enough to see The Man in one more playoff game."

In the 49ers' first playoff game, a Divisional Round matchup against Washington, Young and the 49ers were victorious 20–13 on a rain-soaked, muddy field at Candlestick Park. Young tossed two touchdown passes, but also threw an interception and fumbled three times. The Niners won, but it didn't make anyone forget about Montana.

The NFC Championship game was a major disappointment for Young and the 49ers. In what launched one of the great rivalries of the '90s, the Dallas Cowboys, led by Troy Aikman, beat the Niners 30–20 in San Francisco. The 49ers had four turnovers. Young had 313 yards passing but threw two interceptions in the fourth quarter. The Cowboys were clinical. In the first 23 minutes of the second half, the 49ers only ran 12 plays from scrimmage. It was another disappointing loss for Steve Young. From Lowell Cohn's next day *Chronicle* column: "Someone from the cleanup crew watched Young walk through the parking lot. 'One day you can fill Joe's shoes,' the cleanup man said."

The loss paved the way for another off-season of great speculation. Within a few hours after the game ended, KGO-AM had already received 1,300 calls responding to the question "Should the 49ers trade Joe Montana?" A whopping 59 percent said no.

After the game, Seifert told the media that "right now" Steve Young is the quarterback and "at this particular moment I don't foresee any change." Young's agent, Leigh Steinberg, immediately stirred the pot and said that he was going to push for Young to "consider someplace else where he can be recognized for himself." Young countered those statements two days later, and said that he wanted to stay. His contract was about to expire, but the Niners were poised to put a franchise tag on him, which would restrict him from becoming a free agent.

Joe versus Steve was, once again, the top topic of conversation in the city. The day after the loss, *Sacramento Bee* writer R. E. Graswich wrote a column titled "1993 will be the Joe show," where he confidently predicted that the quarterback job would go back to Montana. Frank Cooney, in the *San Francisco Examiner*, suggested that the Niners trade Young because they could get more in return for him, as opposed to Montana, and the team could use the compensation to improve the defense.

It didn't end quietly. The resolution to the San Francisco Montana/Young saga was as dramatic as it was bizarre. Montana wanted a fair shot at the quarterback job he felt he lost by default, but made it clear that he would rather be somewhere else as a starter than in San Francisco as a backup. At the end of March, the 49ers signed Steve Bono to a multi-year deal to be Young's backup, and Seifert reassured Young he would be the starter moving forward. They told Montana to look for teams to whom they could trade him.

Almost a month later, Montana agreed to a three-year deal for more than $10 million with the Kansas City Chiefs. However, the 49ers and Chiefs reached an impasse on the terms of a trade. Then, a plot twist: The day after Montana flew to Ohio to say goodbye to his pal, owner Ed DeBartolo Jr., Seifert announced that Montana would be the "designated starter" going into the season, a decision that Seifert said was solely his.

None of this made any sense. Young was known to be Seifert's guy. Ray Ratto, in the *Examiner,* called it "one big silly charade." "I think it was meant for it to go this way," he speculated. "Joe Montana gets offered the world, turns it down, and the 49ers get to say, 'Well, we did everything we could.'" The *Sacramento Bee*'s Mark Kreidler was suspicious as well, "Are we being taken for a ride?" he asked. "Listen, does Mr. Toad live at Disneyland?" In the *New York Daily News,* Gary Myers had a theory:

> Either DeBartolo was getting so weepy over losing
> Montana or the 49ers were scared of the public
> backlash if they traded Montana solely because he
> wanted a chance to start... The 49ers orchestrated
> the whole thing knowing they had nothing to lose: if
> Montana left, he was walking out on them, not the other
> way around... They used Montana to get off the hook.

"Moe, Larry and Curly would be proud of this bunch," wrote Graswich in another column. "The 49ers insist they are doing what is best for the franchise. If that is true, they should think about trading Young, firing [team president and GM Carmen] Policy and Seifert and rebuilding."

"[SEIFERT] JUST LOST HIS LAST CHANCE FOR GLORY ... NOW HE'S STUCK WITH A DOOMED TEAM" (1993)

A day after Seifert's surprise reversal, Montana, tired of all the drama, declined the offer to be the 49ers' starter. He said it was in his "best interest and that of my family to play for the Kansas City Chiefs." DeBartolo and Seifert came off looking bad. Shortly thereafter, the 49ers traded Montana, a third-round pick in the 1994 NFL Draft, and safety David Whitmore to the Chiefs for their first-round pick (No. 18) in the upcoming 1993 Draft. The saga was over. In May 1994, Bono joined his pal in Kansas City, when the 49ers traded him to the Chiefs. There, he backed up Montana for a year before becoming the Chiefs' full-time starting quarterback in 1995.

The reaction to the trade was mixed, but the backlash from the detractors was sharp. Bruce Jenkins in the *Chronicle* called it the darkest day in the history of the 49ers. "[Seifert] just lost his last chance for glory," he wrote. "Now he's stuck with a doomed team." He continued: "The fans might be the biggest losers of all... [Joe is] gone, and they don't understand why. They've been hurt, scorned, and violated." The *New York Times* summed up some of the reactions from 49ers' fans: "A 14-year-old boy sobbed for 15 seconds on live television, grown men vowed to shred their season tickets and a somewhat militant crowd gathered outside the San Francisco 49ers training complex this morning to echo 'We want Joe. We want Joe.'"

The 1993 season, Young's first year without Montana hovering over his shoulder, didn't go as well as the year before. The Niners went 10–6 in the regular season and made it to the NFC Championship game, but again were defeated by the Cowboys. It was a disappointing end to the season. Once again, Young led the league in passer rating and touchdown passes.

The losing quarterback in the AFC Championship game was a familiar one: Joe Montana. His Chiefs lost 30–13 to Buffalo. Montana, who missed five games during the season due to injury, was knocked out of the game in the third quarter with a concussion.

After their second straight championship game loss to Dallas, the 49ers made it clear that they were going to leave nothing to spare in an effort to improve their team enough to beat them. They addressed their biggest problems, starting with revamping their defense with many free agent signings, including superstar cornerback Deion Sanders and former Cowboys linebacker Ken Norton Jr.

"THIS WAS THE GAME THAT . . . EXPOSED THE 49ERS AS A TEAM THAT DOES NOT HAVE JOE MONTANA" (1994)

The second game of the 1994 season, the Niners traveled to Kansas City for a matchup with Joe Montana and the Chiefs. Predictably, the game was preceded by a sizable amount of hype. The Chiefs won 24–17. Young threw for 288 yards, one touchdown and two interceptions, but he was sacked four times (one for a safety) and fumbled once. Montana threw for 203 yards and two touchdowns. To *Chronicle* writer Scott Ostler, Montana's victory was appreciable and revealing:

> This was the game that made Joe Montana famous and exposed the 49ers as a team that does not have Joe Montana.
>
> This was the game that Joe fans will point to forever as proof that their man is superior to Steve Young, and probably to Zeus.
>
> This is a game that Montana will tell his grandchildren about some day. Maybe someday next week.
>
> Montana and Young had been right, after all. This game wasn't Joe vs. Steve. It was just Joe.

"IT'S TIME TO ADMIT IT: STEVE YOUNG IS AS GOOD AS JOE MONTANA AT HIS BEST" (1994)

After two straight wins to go to 3–1, the Niners were trounced at home by the Eagles. With the Eagles up 33–8 in the third quarter, Young suffered a brutal hit, one of many he incurred throughout the day. Siefert had seen enough. Before the next play, he sent in backup Elvis Grbac to take over. Young had been violently brought to the ground numerous times throughout the game, and Seifert felt, with the game out of the 49ers' reach, there was no reason for him to keep taking the punishment. Young threw a fit on the sidelines, directed at Seifert, and Seifert was criticized for embarrassing Young by giving him the hook mid-drive. Meanwhile, the 49ers' defense looked atrocious. Philadelphia amassed 437 yards of total offense and won the game 40–8. Eagles running back Charlie Garner had 16 rushes for 111 yards. "Management for the best defense money can buy may soon want a refund," wrote Kevin Lyons in the *Washington Times*.

Young's sideline tirade ended up being the turning point in the season. After the Eagles' debacle, the Niners won 10 of their next 11 games. Young had the best season of his career. He achieved what was then the NFL record for highest passer rating in a season, and was once again named league MVP. San Francisco finished with the best record in the NFL.

After leading the 49ers to a 44–15 win over the Bears in the Divisional Round of the playoffs, Young exorcised his Cowboys demons. In the third straight NFC Championship game between the two teams, the Niners jumped out to a 21–0 lead and never looked back. The Cowboys turned it over five times. Young led the 49ers to a 38–28 win, clinching a spot in Super Bowl XXIX in Miami. There, the Niners walloped the Chargers 49–26. Young threw six touchdowns, a Super Bowl record, eclipsing Joe Montana's five in 1990.

Stories in the papers the next day paid homage to Young. The Super Bowl triumph confirmed what Young and Seifert already knew: Parting ways with Montana was the right thing to do. "If you were watching carefully, you might have seen that spectral image [of Joe Montana's shadow] lifting off Young's shoulders Sunday evening," wrote *Washington Post* columnist Tony Kornheiser. Glenn Dickey saw enough to make the ultimate declaration: "It's time to admit it: Steve Young is as good as Joe Montana at his best," he wrote in the *Chronicle*. "Yesterday was the final proof."

The 49ers never made it back to the Super Bowl with Steve Young. They were always competitive, but they couldn't get over the hump. As with Montana, injuries started to catch up with Young, as well as many of the other Niners stars. Also, with free agency and the salary cap in full swing, the talent on 49ers rosters were nowhere near as dominant as they had been in the '80s. The 49ers ran into significant salary cap issues down the road, partly because of their decision to enter into incentive-laden contracts with free agents to stockpile talent for the 1994 season and go all-in to try to win it all. It paid off with a Super Bowl, but many of the players hit their incentives, giving the team salary cap issues for years to come.

Montana ended up missing seven games to injury in two seasons in Kansas City. After he led Kansas City to the AFC Championship game in 1993, the Chiefs quietly lost to the Dolphins in the Wild Card Round of the 1994 playoffs. Montana retired for good a few weeks later.

THE UNEXPECTEDLY, IMPERFECTLY, PERFECT PLAN

There was a time around 1988 where the transition from Montana to Steve Young seemed like it was going to come sooner rather than later. Montana's body appeared to be falling apart, Walsh was bringing in Young in important game-time situations, and Walsh was showing no deference to Montana's legacy. Few thought pitting the two against each other was a good idea.

As for Young, at some point, practically nobody believed he would ever become the 49ers' full-time starting quarterback. It is not what anyone around the Bay Area wanted. No matter what Young did, he couldn't hold a candle to Montana. Even after Young won the passing title two years in a row and was coming off an MVP season, and Montana was 37 and had missed almost the entire previous two seasons to injury, there were numerous reporters who were still convinced that the Niners should unload Young.

The quarterback competition with Young fueled the fire and altered the narrative for Montana, who enhanced his game at a time when he was operating in cruise control, and proved, with four championship rings, that he was more than just a "system QB." The same can be said for Young, who became stronger mentally and as a player, after grudgingly sticking out a frustrating situation before finally getting his chance and taking advantage of it. "What about all the people who have criticized you for not being Joe Montana?," someone asked Young after the Super Bowl win over the Chargers, "To hell with them," Young said, smiling.

"WHY WOULD WE GIVE UP A FIRST-ROUND PICK FOR [BRETT FAVRE]?"

(1992–1998 GREEN BAY PACKERS)

I t had been a slow, plodding, excruciating decline into irrelevancy. In the early 1960s, the Green Bay Packers were not just the best team in the NFL; they were one of the most dominant NFL dynasties in league history. Under legendary coach Vince Lombardi, they won five NFL championships and their first two Super Bowls. By the beginning of the '90s those days were long gone. The once-proud franchise was a shell of its former self. After the Packers won Super Bowl II in 1967, they had just five winning seasons throughout the next 24 years and made the playoffs only twice. The hallowed grounds of the Packers' stadium, Lambeau Field, had turned into the home of the downtrodden.

In November 1991, just over halfway through what would be another losing season, the Packers, in an attempt to revitalize the franchise, hired Ron Wolf as their new general manager. Wolf was known as one of the best talent evaluators in the game. A real "football man," he was well-respected and considered shrewd and creative. But the local press and the fans had no reason to be optimistic. The franchise had seen five head coaches since the Lombardi years, and around the same amount of people in charge of personnel. Each of these individuals, at one point, convinced the Packers faithful to believe in him, but, in the end, it was always the same—failure and mediocrity.

Wolf knew that, to turn the franchise around, he needed a championship-level coach, a difference-making franchise quarterback, and to upgrade talent on the roster using every possible means. Moreover, he wanted it all to be done as quickly as possible. Somehow, he accomplished his objectives in warp speed. In just five years, Wolf would help the Packers bring the Lombardi Trophy back to Green Bay.

The Packers' return to glory was set into motion by three seminal transactions, completed within a span of just over a year: (1) hiring head coach Mike Holmgren, (2) acquiring quarterback Brett Favre, and (3) signing free agent defensive end Reggie White. Each move was initially met with some skepticism, pushback, and derision.

"HIRING MIKE HOLMGREN LOOKS LIKE A LATERAL MOVE" (1991)

The Packers closed out their 1991 campaign with a 4–12 record, their ninth season in a row without making the playoffs. As soon as the season ended, Wolf immediately fired embattled coach Lindy Infante, who had only won 10 total games in the previous two seasons. To replace Infante, Wolf targeted San Francisco 49ers offensive coordinator Mike Holmgren.

A Bill Walsh disciple, Holmgren was known as an offensive and quarterback guru who ran Walsh's pass-heavy "West Coast Offense." As an assistant coach at BYU, he had worked with quarterback Steve Young, and then at San Francisco with Joe Montana and Young again. The "hot" candidate of the coaching hire cycle, Holmgren had been interviewed by five other teams. On January 10, 1992, Holmgren reached an agreement with Wolf to become the Packers' new head coach. The Packers gave a second-round pick to the 49ers to let him out of his contract with San Francisco.

The move was met with rave reviews by some. Others were underwhelmed. Joseph Dill, the sports editor of the *Oshkosh Northwestern*, thought Wolf shouldn't have hired an offensive coordinator because he believed that "defense wins championships." He also grumbled that Wolf should have interviewed the "two best candidates" for the job, defensive coordinators Richie Petitbon

(Washington) and Wade Phillips (Denver). Petitbon and Phillips were both promoted to head coach by their respective teams a year later. Petitbon ended up being let go after one season after Washington finished 4–12. He never coached again on any level. Phillips was fired after only two years in Denver.

Some critics were skeptical about Holmgren because, on paper, he looked like a carbon copy of Infante. One doubter, Tom Silverstein, writing in the *Milwaukee Sentinel*, pointed out that, like Holmgren, "Infante was also a highly successful offensive coordinator and directed a complicated passing offense." Former 49ers center Randy Cross, who played for Holmgren from 1986 to 1988, didn't seem impressed, either. "In a lot of ways this looks like a lateral move," he said. "They're going from one offensive coordinator and quarterback coach to another offensive coordinator and quarterback coach." Local columnist Tom Oates had similar reservations. "It was George Santayana who once said: 'Those who cannot remember the past are condemned to repeat it,'" he wrote in the *Wisconsin State Journal*. "It appears the Packers will attempt to change history. That's never an easy task."

It wasn't just that Holmgren and Infante's resumes were so similar. Infante's pass-heavy offenses didn't thrive in Green Bay, and some felt that, given the often-freezing conditions in northeast Wisconsin, there should have been more of a run-pass balance. Chris Mortensen, in the *Sporting News*, asked, "Can anyone explain the difference between the pass-oriented offenses of [Infante]...and Holmgren? Wasn't Infante fired because [Ron] Wolf believed the Packers must run the football to win crucial late-season games in those harsh Wisconsin conditions?" On that same note, an anonymous NFL official told the *Milwaukee Journal Sentinel* that, like Infante, Holmgen's pass-oriented West Coast Offense might hit snags in Green Bay. "In that division, you've got to play smash-mouth football," the official said. "You're not playing half your games indoors or in great weather...And it's not like they have a Joe Montana."

What Anonymous didn't know was that the Packers were about to get their version of Joe Montana, and that he would have a similar impact.

RON WOLF ZEROES IN ON HIS FRANCHISE QUARTERBACK (1991)

When Wolf said he wanted to move fast on the rebuild, he wasn't kidding. On December 1, 1991, five days after his introductory press conference and the first day he was officially on the job, Wolf had already homed in on his franchise quarterback. In the press box at Atlanta–Fulton County Stadium, while the Packers were warming up to play the Falcons, Wolf told team president Bob Harlan that he was going to find a way to trade for Atlanta's languishing third-string quarterback, Brett Favre.

Wolf had been smitten with Favre for almost a year. During the 1990 season, while he was a personnel director with the New York Jets, Wolf took a trip to the University of Southern Mississippi, where Favre was a senior in college, to scout and watch his films. He came back extremely impressed, especially with Favre's strong arm and overwhelming confidence.

Favre was relegated to third on the Falcons' depth chart during his rookie season in 1991. He only played in two games and had a grand total of four pass attempts. Much of that had to do with his off-the-field antics, which were kept under wraps by the team. His excessive drinking and partying put him in head coach Jerry Glanville's doghouse. "Favre was always late for meetings, drinking a lot," recalled then–Falcons general manager Ken Herock. "[He] couldn't even run the scout team, they were telling me."

A few days after the Atlanta game, Wolf met with the Packers' Executive Committee to explain his idea to pursue Favre. Since the Packers are a community-owned franchise, the team does not have an individual owner. Instead, it is owned by a publicly held, nonprofit corporation. A seven-member Executive Committee elected by the team's Board of Directors governs the corporation. "[The Executive Committee] had no idea who I was talking about," Wolf told author Rob Reischel in 2015. "But they were all for it." At least that's what they told Wolf. Who knows what they said when he left the room. "I sure would have liked to have been a fly on the wall when I walked out," Wolf said during a 2019 podcast interview. "Because I'm sure that those guys looked at each other and said, 'My word, what do we do here? We got an idiot in here.'"

"THE PACKERS SHOULD [DRAFT] DAVID KLINGLER. BUT FOR SOME REASON, THEY'RE SOLD ON BRETT FAVRE AS THE ANSWER" (1992)

Negotiations between Wolf and Herock about a deal for Favre went on for two months. On February 10, 1992, the teams settled on the Packers giving the Falcons one of the two first-round picks they held for the upcoming draft, the 17th overall selection. Favre was unknown to most NFL fans. Team president Harlan recalled that day in the press box in Atlanta, when Wolf told him about Favre: "I thought his name was Fav-ray." Wolf would sometimes have to clarify to reporters who were interviewing him that it "rhymes with Carve."

Packers fans weren't sold on Wolf or Favre. "Some of the worst mail I ever got was when Ron made that trade for Favre," Harlan remembered. "Who is this Wolf guy you hired? Giving up a [first-round pick] for a third-string quarterback?" People thought Wolf was nuts. "I'll never forget one seven-page letter I got from an attorney somewhere who said I killed the Packers franchise and I would be fired in three years," Wolf recalled. According to Mark Scheifelbein, who was the assistant PR director for the Packers at the time, another attorney sent Wolf a greeting card, "You open it up and there is a middle finger and the message 'What the fuck are you doing?'" Locals called in to the *Green Bay Press-Gazette* to voice their displeasure. "We...made a stupid trade for that Brent Favor!" said one.

The trade even had members of Holmgren's own coaching staff and players a bit puzzled. When Jon Gruden, Holmgren's new quality-control coach, heard about the deal, his first thought was, "Why would we give up a first-round pick for that guy?" Packers safety Chuck Cecil was also stunned. "Who the hell is [he]?" he said.

A faction of the local media was also skeptical. "What in the world are they doing?" thought Bill Jartz, a sports anchor at local Green Bay TV station WBAY-TV. The *Commonwealth Reporter*, a newspaper based in the town of Fond Du Lac, located about 70 miles from Green Bay, wasn't ready to give Wolf the benefit of the doubt. "Prove it to us," the paper wrote in an editorial. "Pardon our raised eyebrows...[but] Favre's credits are five passes thrown, none caught by his side and two by the other side."

Many other local writers also had their doubts. "So now we will find out if Ron Wolf is *really* the pro football genius we have been led to believe he is," wrote writer Len Wagner in the *Green Bay Press-Gazette*. John Lindsay, writing for the Scripps Howard News Service, was more blunt. Describing what he thought the Packers should do in the upcoming NFL Draft, where they held the fifth overall pick, Lindsay wrote that "The Packers should take [University of Houston senior star quarterback] David Klingler. But for some reason, they're sold on Brett Favre as the answer."

By the beginning of April, there were rumors that Klingler, a 1990 Heisman Trophy finalist, who broke passing records during his time in college at Houston, and who was initially pegged as a top-10 pick, was going to fall below his projection. Some writers, like the *Wausau (Wisconsin) Daily Herald*'s Jay Lillge, were frustrated that the Packers no longer had the 17th pick it gave to Atlanta as part of the trade:

> It's pronounced Farv, which comes all too close to Farce or Barf, but that's incidental . . . Now, just this past week, [*Rochester Democrat and Chronicle*] sportswriter Bob Matthews' column came across with a tidbit saying Houston quarterback David Klingler's stock has dropped to the point where he's going to be a late first-round pick. Like, maybe he would have been around No. 17?

Klingler didn't end up slipping to No. 17. He was drafted sixth overall by Cincinnati. His career, however, was forgettable. Now considered a huge draft bust, he had 24 total NFL starts (all for Cincinnati) and won four of them. He retired from the NFL before the 1998 season.

"A SECOND-YEAR OBSCURITY NAMED BRETT FAVRE REPLACED MAJKOWSKI, AND THE BENGALS MADE HIM LOOK LIKE BART STARR" (1992)

Favre wasn't supposed to play much in 1992. But that changed at Lambeau Field during the first quarter of the Packers' second game of the season. When starting quarterback Don Majkowski severely hurt his ankle, Holmgren replaced him with Favre. The rest is history. In his *Cincinnati Enquirer* game report, writer Tim Sullivan summed up how the day unfolded: "A second-year obscurity named Brett Favre replaced Majkowski, and the Bengals made him look like [former Packer, and Hall of Fame quarterback] Bart Starr."

Favre didn't look like Starr right away. In two-and-a-half quarters he was sacked five times and had four fumbles, three of them on consecutive plays. According to Favre's wife Deanna, who was in attendance that day, it got so bad that fans were chanting for third-string quarterback, 1990 Heisman Trophy winner Ty Detmer, to take over. But by the fourth quarter, Favre found his groove. He led the Packers back from a 17–3 deficit late in the third quarter to a 24–23 comeback win, guiding the team on an 88-yard touchdown drive at the beginning of the fourth and a 92-yard drive in the final minute that was capped by a 35-yard, game-winning touchdown pass with 13 seconds left to wide receiver Kitrick Taylor.

Majkowski never took another snap for the Packers. Favre started every game for the franchise for the next 16 years (253 consecutive games total). By the end of the 1992 season, he had thrown for over 3,200 yards and 18 touchdowns, and the Packers finished with a 9–7 record. Green Bay barely missed the playoffs. Favre made many mistakes that season and frustrated Holmgren at times, but he had shown that he might be the franchise quarterback for which the organization had been searching for years.

"THE PACKERS HAVE THREE PEOPLE TO TRADE OR RELEASE . . .: FIRST . . . RON WOLF; A CLOSE SECOND . . . MIKE HOLMGREN; . . . THIRD . . . BRETT FAVRE" (1993)

The 1993 season began with Favre fully entrenched as the Packers' starter, but as it went along, his on-field performance started to decline. He was inconsistent and ended up leading the league in both interceptions, with 24, and in turnovers, with 30. In some games, he was downright awful. Both Holmgren and Favre were subjected to intense criticism throughout the season.

After the Packers lost their third game in a row to start the season 1–4, the heat started to crank up. "A confused rattled shell of a quarterback," one writer wrote the next day. "The book on Favre appears to be simple: Put pressure on and he will fold." One fan, writing to the *Press-Gazette*, had seen enough:

> Unfortunately, once defenses figure out [Holmgren's offensive system], that system is too complex to adapt. Brett Favre looks completely lost (yes, it worked for San Francisco, but the 49ers had Joe Montana) . . . Ron Wolf has spent a fortune hiring a losing team. In the business world, he would be fired for nearly bankrupting his corporation with no results.

A month later, after Favre threw three interceptions and lost two fumbles during a loss to the Chiefs on *Monday Night Football* in Kansas City, the noise increased. It was a winnable game, and Favre couldn't get it done. Some fans wanted Detmer to replace him. "At least [Detmer is] a proven winner," said one fan in a call to a local paper's sports line. Another fan derided his local paper, the *Daily Herald*, for printing too many positive columns about Favre, who he believed was the worst quarterback in football. "Stick Ty Detmer in and they'll start winning," he added. Another wrote a letter to the *Wisconsin State Journal*, which listed a three-step plan to get the Packers on track: "The Green Bay Packers have three people to release or trade at the end of the season. The first to go should be Ron Wolf. A close second to go should be Mike Holmgren. Finally, the third to go should be Brett Favre."

Local scribe Chuck Carlson was also concerned about Favre's play. "[Favre] is struggling—badly—and his problems have dragged the Packers down with him," he wrote in his *Post-Crescent* column. "For the first time, there are more questions than answers about Brett Favre."

A little over a month later, the Packers saw their playoff hopes suffer. They lost 21–17 to Minnesota, failing to score the go-ahead touchdown after having first-and-goal on the 2-yard line with two minutes left. Later that week, Racine, Wisconsin–based columnist Gary Woelfel slammed Holmgren in the *Journal Times*. According to Woelfel, the second-year head coach's play-calling defied all logic. "Why are some members of the Wisconsin media so infatuated with Holmgren?" he asked. "Is it because some so-called objective reporters thoroughly despised...Infante?"

Green Bay still was able to win nine games and squeeze into the 1993 Playoffs. They won their first matchup, a road game in Detroit, 28–24, after Favre, with 55 seconds left, and the Packers down by 3, rolled left and threw a bomb to the opposite side of the field to a wide-open Sterling Sharpe in the end zone for a 40-yard game-winning touchdown. It was Favre's first playoff win and the first for the Packers in 11 years. The streak would end there though, as Green Bay was eliminated from the playoffs the following week in Dallas after losing 27–17 to the Cowboys.

TWO MVPS AND A SUPER BOWL (1993)

That summer, the Packers signed Favre to a five-year, $19 million contract extension. It was worth every penny. The following four seasons, Favre went on a run that ranks as one of the greatest stretches by a quarterback in league history. During that time, not including the playoffs, he threw for 145 touchdowns to only 56 interceptions. He developed a strong rapport with Holmgren and became more disciplined on and off the field. After 1993, the Packers made the playoffs again the following two seasons, but were eliminated by Dallas each time. Not all was lost, though. In 1995, Favre won his first MVP award.

Going into the 1996 season, Brett Favre was, in many people's eyes, the best player in the NFL. However, he had yet to reach a Super Bowl. That changed when the Packers strung together what was probably the franchise's best season in the post-Lombardi era. Finishing the regular season 13–3, Green Bay was dominant on both sides of the ball. Their offense led the league in points scored and the defense led in fewest points allowed. Favre won his second straight MVP. After dominating their first two playoff games, the Packers dispatched the Patriots 35–21 at Super Bowl XXXI in New Orleans and brought the Lombardi Trophy back to Green Bay. Favre threw two touchdown passes in the game, including a 54-yarder to Andre Rison on the second play of the game and an 81-yarder to Antonio Freeman in the second quarter. He also had one rushing touchdown.

The Packers once again finished 13–3 in 1997, and Favre claimed his third straight MVP title. They made it back to the Super Bowl and were heavily favored, but were upset by John Elway and the Broncos.

Favre never earned another Super Bowl trip, but he did continue to bring great success to the Packers organization. He played in Green Bay a total of 16 seasons before announcing his retirement in March 2008. At the time, he was the NFL leader in victories by a starting quarterback, touchdown passes, and passing yards. But after a few months, feeling like he had a little more gas in the tank, Favre reneged on his retirement plans. In August, the Packers, at Favre's request, sent him to the Jets.

After one year with the Jets, he signed with the Packers' rivals, the Minnesota Vikings, where he played two seasons. In 2009, he had one of the best seasons of his career, leading the Vikings to the NFC Championship game, where they lost a heartbreaker to the Saints in overtime. He retired for good after the 2010 campaign. In total, Favre played 20 seasons. He was inducted into the Pro Football Hall of Fame in 2016.

Favre's departure from Green Bay in 2008 was messy. It took seven years before he returned in a non-professional capacity. Time, however, heals a lot of wounds, and the Packers retired his jersey in a 2015 ceremony at Lambeau Field.

"WHY WOULD A PLAYER GO TO GREEN BAY UNLESS HE HAD TO GO?" (1993)

Mike Holmgren and Brett Favre didn't bring the Packers back all by themselves. While they were the foundation on which the revived teams were built, they still needed more talent, especially on defense. Fortunately, the spring of 1993 was the perfect time to get the ball rolling.

Prior to 1993, NFL players were, for the most part, confined to the same franchise for the entirety of their careers unless the team traded them or elected not to keep them around. Players had few avenues available to leave the team by which they were drafted. This changed dramatically in the first months of 1993, when a group of NFL players won a lawsuit that paved the way for unrestricted free agency. As a result, qualified veterans whose contracts had expired could freely talk to and sign new contracts with any other team in the league. The first period of unrestricted free agency began on March 1, 1993.

Free agency in the NFL had been years in the making. By the mid-1980s, players were becoming increasingly frustrated with their limited ability to be able to move to other teams. In 1989, feeling the pressure of an ongoing antitrust lawsuit by the National Football League Players Association (NFLPA), the owners adopted a "Plan B free agency" rule, where teams could protect 37 players (out of 47-man rosters) from becoming free agents. For a two-month period, beginning February 1 and ending April 1 of each year, the unprotected players were free to negotiate with, and sign with, any other team without the signing team owing any compensation.

The NFLPA did not believe the Plan B system was sufficient. Most of the top players on each team were still confined. In September 1992, after a group of players filed an antitrust lawsuit against the league, a jury in federal court struck down the Plan B system. A couple of weeks later, Philadelphia Eagles defensive lineman Reggie White and two other players filed a class-action lawsuit against the league seeking free agency for all NFL players whose contracts expired at the end of the 1992 season (around 280 players in total). This led to a compromise between the NFL and the NFLPA, memorialized in the collective-bargaining agreement that allowed players who had completed five years in the league to be eligible for unrestricted free agency when their contracts expired, except for one player that each franchise could protect.

Prior to the settlement, the owners' primary argument against free agency was that it would destroy the league's competitive balance. At first, the concern was that large-market teams with more money would just outspend the small-market franchises for free agents, causing player salaries to astronomically rise, creating a sizable talent gap. However, as part of the settlement, the parties agreed to the creation of a salary cap, which established a ceiling of how much a team could spend each season. Based on the mechanics of the agreement, it was a near certainty that the salary cap would kick in for the 1994 season. Thus, teams had no spending limits for free agents in 1993, but they had to be cognizant of how any multi-year deals would affect their cap the following season and beyond.

Even with the upcoming salary cap, many of the owners were concerned that the best free agents would only sign with franchises located in the most traditionally desirable, warm-weather, or otherwise glamorous cities, like Los Angeles or Miami. During any discussion about which teams would be most significantly disadvantaged by free agency, the Green Bay Packers were almost invariably the first team mentioned.

On paper, as a small town with brutally cold and snowy winters, Green Bay was seemingly Exhibit 1 in the argument for competitive balance. One general manager contended that there were only 8 to 10 teams that players found attractive as free agents, and that Green Bay was at the bottom of the pile. "Players will go to the large markets and glamorous cities, more than other places," said New York Giants general manager George Young in 1992. "Look at the dynasties, like Green Bay and Pittsburgh. Under a free agency system, those kinds of teams may not have a chance to flourish."

The cold-weather teams were never afraid to bring up this issue. In 1987, Buffalo Bills general manager Bill Polian said that free agency would be "a decided disadvantage to the northern snowbelt teams." That same year, Cleveland Browns general manager Ernie Accorsi mentioned that "The first words out of the mouths of a lot of players these days is 'I want to play in California or someplace where it's warm.'" Former Cowboys general manager Tex

Schramm agreed. "The players...will gravitate towards the cities that have more to offer outside of football," he said in 1991, "and that sure isn't Green Bay." Ironically, when Packers head coach Mike Holmgren was an assistant with the 49ers, he used to try to scare undisciplined or underperforming players by threatening to send them to Green Bay.

Some dismissed these concerns as hogwash. They argued that it made no logical sense to conclude that all the best quarterbacks, or all the best running backs, would gravitate to just a handful of teams. "Not everyone is going to break to the Rams or the Raiders or the 49ers," Eagles running back Keith Byars said in 1992. "You think all the running backs are going to go to the same team?"

Another issue frequently mentioned about Green Bay was that its lack of diversity could be a big negative for many players. "It was...the whitest community in the NFL," former Packers defensive line coach Greg Blache told *Sports Illustrated* in 2006. In 1989, Chicago Bears legendary Hall of Fame running back Gale Sayers wrote a newspaper column about the effect free agency would have on small-market teams. He asked, "Why would a player go to Green Bay unless he had to go? It's cold in Green Bay...and a minority player really wouldn't find many minorities in the town."

If players truly didn't want to play in Green Bay, they weren't showing it. From 1989 to 1992, the Packers signed more Plan B free agents than any other team in the league, and team executives had no problems getting players to visit.

"THE PACKERS NEED REGGIE WHITE LIKE A HORSE NEEDS FRENCH LESSONS" (1993)

Reggie White was the crown jewel of the inaugural NFL free agent class. White had spent his entire NFL career wreaking havoc on quarterbacks. In eight seasons with the Eagles, White totaled more sacks (124) than games played (121). At 6-foot-5 and 300 pounds, and incredibly strong and athletic, White overpowered offensive linemen and essentially controlled the game from the line of scrimmage. At 31 years old, he was still in his prime and one of the most dominant defensive players in the league. After his Eagles contract expired in January 1993, White was ready to test the free agent waters.

This was supposed to be a scary time for the Packers. They were now at risk of losing their best players to the wealthier, large-market teams, and they weren't supposed to be able to woo star free agents like White.

That theory would be debunked in short order.

Just before the free agency period began, Wolf decided that he was going to make an all-out effort to sign White, who was being courted by seven or eight teams. It seemed like a long shot, but if Wolf was willing to offer big money (he was), the Packers had a chance. They were a dark horse candidate: good enough to compete, but not a glamorous choice. Harlan and others thought Wolf was out of his mind. "I didn't think we had a prayer in the world," Harlan recalled. Defensive coordinator Ray Rhodes, who was on board with the pursuit of White from day one of free agency, said people laughed when he suggested it.

White immediately made clear his most important selling points. He wanted to play for a team that was going to contend for a championship soon (he had yet to win a championship at any level), and he wanted to establish a Christian ministry in his new city and serve as a role model for inner-city youth.

The Reggie White free agency competition became a 37-day marathon courtship which included a seven-city tour, where he was wined and dined and treated like royalty at almost every stop. Cleveland Browns owner Art Modell gave Reggie's wife Sara an expensive leather coat and had both the mayor of Cleveland and Browns legend Jim Brown call White to recruit him. In Atlanta, the Falcons set up a meeting between White and the Georgia governor. Falcons cornerback Deion Sanders told him (in a tongue-in-cheek manner) that he'd buy Reggie his own church if White signed with the Falcons. When White visited the Jets, he realized that their current quarterback situation was suspect at best and told management that the franchise would be more attractive if veteran Bengals quarterback Boomer Esiason was there. A day later, the Jets completed a trade with Cincinnati for Esiason.

When he first visited the Packers, Green Bay was the furthest city from his mind. But his agent Jimmy Sexton suggested that he talk to them. The Packers were only finally able to arrange a visit because White had been in Detroit visiting the Lions, and Green Bay was close enough to make a stop on his way home to Knoxville, Tennessee. When he arrived in Green Bay, there were four inches of snow on the ground. His recruitment meal was a lunch at Red Lobster with Holmgren, Rhodes, and Wolf.

Wolf and Holmgren didn't really have a strong case in terms of Reggie's plan for his inner-city ministry. White pointed out that Green Bay didn't have inner-city problems, or even an inner city at all. But Holmgren and Wolf told Reggie that Milwaukee was 100 miles away and it had the highest teen pregnancy rate in the country. They assured him that the organization would support his plan to open a ministry there.

After Reggie's visit to Green Bay, he had great things to say about the organization and the town. As a result, a small case of Reggie fever started to develop in Green Bay. But not everyone's temperature was high. Chuck Carlson, a columnist for the (Appleton, Wisconsin) *Post-Crescent* didn't get why a team would make such an investment. "It shouldn't happen," he wrote. "The Packers need Reggie White like a horse needs French lessons." Carlson continued: "[Of course] Reggie White likes Green Bay...It's a nice, quiet inoffensive little town...What other town lists Chuck E. Cheese's as a four-star restaurant?" In Carlson's mind, the real question was whether it was worth it for the Packers to mortgage their future for one player whose skills, he believed, would soon decline. He didn't think it was. He thought they could use the same amount of money to sign several young players. "For the good of the Packers and their delicate uncertain future," he pled, "let Reggie go somewhere else."

Ed Meyer, a columnist covering the Cleveland Browns for the *Akron Beacon Journal*, thought along the same lines as Carlson when he wrote about why he thought the Browns should pass on White. Like Carlson, he thought that the money allocated to White could be used on five or six good players. "It would not make much sense," Meyer wrote, "for the Browns to blow a wad on [him]."

New York Daily News columnist Mike Lupica was incredulous at the amount of attention teams were giving to White. "When exactly did Reggie White become the greatest and most essential living football player?" he asked. "This silliness...is over the top, even for New York." Also, like others, Lupica thought White was too old for this type of long-term financial commitment. "I do not believe Reggie White, at his age, with the mileage he has on him, is some kind of franchise-altering defensive presence," he wrote.

Reflecting on it in 2020, Carlson remembers thinking that he didn't believe White would sign with Green Bay. When all the writers on the Packers beat heard that White was visiting, they all kind of laughed about it. But when it started to leak about how much money was involved, it seemed crazy, which triggered his column. "To spend that kind of money," he said, "at that point, it just didn't make sense… There was no salary cap [yet], and free agency was brand-new." Surprisingly he didn't face much fan backlash for his negativity about White. It was actually the comment about residents considering Chuck E. Cheese a four-star restaurant that set off some people. "Taking shots at the city—I got more response on that."

San Francisco became involved in the Reggie sweepstakes about halfway through the process. At one point, it appeared that the 49ers were a perfect fit. They were perennial contenders, located in a big city. White said one day near the end of that March that if he had to pick at that moment, he would pick San Francisco. However, he added that it wasn't up to him. "I've got to go where God wants me to go," he said. Upon reading about those comments, Holmgren left a message on White's answering machine. "Reggie," Holmgren said. "This is God. You ought to go to Green Bay."

Messages from God aside, Wolf and Holmgren did an admirable job selling White on Green Bay. He came away impressed with the organization and felt the Packers were seriously committed to winning. White was attracted to a quiet, peaceful community like Green Bay. Rhodes and Holmgren even flew to Knoxville and visited White at his home there, a gesture that touched him. All of it played a role in bringing him to the Packers. But, ultimately, when it came down to brass tacks, the deciding factor was the financial package the Packers offered.

If it was mainly a championship White wanted, the 49ers were in the best position. They were coming off a 14–2 season in 1992 and had the reigning league MVP Steve Young at quarterback. A game changer like White could have been just the guy to put them over the top. The 49ers offered him a five-year contract worth $19.5 million. At that point, White recalled, "I was 99 percent sure that

God was calling me to San Francisco." However, the deal gave San Francisco an opt-out clause after three years. That, to Reggie, was a deal-breaker. He wanted a full commitment.

The Packers sealed the deal with a four-year, $17.6 million offer, which, at the time, was the largest contract ever given to a defensive player in NFL history. No opt-outs. The total amount was nice, but the clincher was the guaranteed money, and that he would receive a substantial amount up front, as soon as he signed the deal. The Packers gave White a $4.5 million signing bonus and $4.5 million in salary his first year. His second year, he would get a salary of $3.1 million. White was getting $9 million total in his first year, and $12 million total by the end of his second year.

"I HEARD THE LORD SAY ... REGGIE, I WANT YOU TO GO TO GREEN BAY" (1993)

Even though Green Bay was known to be very much in the running for White, the announcement that he had signed with the Packers still came as a surprise to many. "It was an amazing day," Carlson remembered. "Everybody who covered the Packers was just dumbfounded that that actually happened."

And what about God, who, according to White, at first, clearly told him to go to San Francisco? Four years later, in his autobiography, he explained that it was all a misunderstanding:

> As I listened for the Lord's voice, I heard a question
> in my thoughts: Reggie, where did the head coach,
> defensive coordinator, and the offensive coordinator
> of the Packers come from before they went to Green
> Bay? Instantly, I remembered ... San Francisco,
> from the 49ers.

In my mind, I heard the Lord say, And what do the reporters call Green Bay? . . . and Green Bay's offense? And it came to me: They kept calling Green Bay 'the San Francisco of the East,' and the offense 'the West Coast Offense.'

Then aloud I said, 'Huh! So that's the 'San Francisco' that You have been talking about!' And again, in my thoughts, I heard, That's right. Reggie, I want you to go to Green Bay. That's the 'San Francisco' I was talking about.

"[THE [EAGLES] WERE RIGHT IN THE SENSE THAT [REGGIE WHITE'S] BEST DAYS ARE BEHIND HIM" (1993)

After seeing how much the Packers paid, some thought the teams that passed on him had made the right play. "From a business point of view, [the Eagles letting White go] was a shrewd and calculating move," wrote the *Philadelphia Inquirer*'s Bill Lyon. "They felt he did not have four good years left, and they were right in the sense that his best days are behind him."

After Reggie signed, the Packers would continue, each season, to sign more key players from free agency. Standout defensive end Sean Jones signed the following year. In his three seasons with Green Bay, Jones had 24.5 sacks. In the summer of 1996, they brought in wide receiver and return man Desmond Howard, and in mid-season the same year signed wide receiver Andre Rison. Both Howard and Rison, along with defensive tackle Santana Dotson, another free agent signee, were key factors in Green Bay's Super Bowl triumph over the Patriots in 1997. Rison scored a touchdown and Howard had 244 combined punt and kick return yards, including a kick return for a touchdown that thwarted New England's gaining momentum after the Patriots had scored a touchdown to cut the Packers' lead to six late in the third quarter. Howard was named the Super Bowl MVP. White's former Eagles teammate, linebacker Seth Joyner, joined White for the 1997 season.

On the field, White didn't just live up to his billing—he was better than advertised. Including the playoffs, he had 76.5 sacks in six seasons in Green Bay, including 15 sacks in 1993. It was in October of the '93 season, during a must-win game in Denver, when he truly announced his presence as a Packer. Green Bay had lost three out of their first four games and, up to that point, White had made minimal impact. In the fourth quarter, he sacked John Elway twice on back-to-back plays to preserve a 30–27 Packers win. In Green Bay's XXXI Super Bowl victory over the Patriots, Reggie sacked Patriots quarterback Drew Bledsoe three times, still a Super Bowl record.

In 1993, many were sure that White didn't have much mileage left and that his best days were behind him. They were wrong. In 1998, his final season in Green Bay, Reggie White, at age 36, had a whopping 16 sacks and was named the Associated Press NFL Defensive Player of the Year. He passed away in 2004 at the age of 43 after succumbing to cardiac arrhythmia. His legacy still lives on.

White is still considered by most as the best free-agent signing in NFL history, not only because of his on-field impact, but because it instantly weakened the owners' long-standing position that quality free agents would avoid signing with cold-weather and small-market teams.

In 1992, while the free agency issue was still being heard by the US District Court in Minneapolis, Kansas City Chiefs president Carl Peterson ironically posed a rhetorical question: "You ask a guy whether he wants to play in Green Bay, Wisconsin, or Los Angeles, where do you think he's going to choose?" A year later, he had his answer.

"THE VIKINGS FLEECED THE COWBOYS TO GET HERSCHEL WALKER"

(1989–1995 DALLAS COWBOYS)

We didn't have enough players." Jimmy Johnson recently recalled, bluntly describing the state of the Dallas Cowboys when he became the head coach in 1989. The franchise was, indeed, a mess, and he had his work cut out for him. The Cowboys, known as "America's Team" since they became perennial championship contenders in the '70s, had fallen on hard times. Johnson was brought in to turn things around. But he and his new boss, the owner of the Cowboys (and his college pal) Jerry Jones, were, for a time, collectively, public enemy number one in Dallas.

THE JERRY JONES ERA BEGINS IN DALLAS (1989)

On Thursday evening, February 23, 1989, Cowboys head coach Tom Landry and general manager Tex Schramm became aware that the sale of the Dallas Cowboys was imminent. They learned about it in the same manner as hundreds of thousands of Cowboys fans and Dallas-area residents: through local TV, via a breaking report that aired during KXTV Channel 5's 10 p.m. newscast. Earlier that evening, Arkansas oil tycoon Jerry Jones and Cowboys owner Bum Bright quietly shook hands on a deal for Jones to buy the team.

The big news didn't deter Landry, still the team's head coach, from going to the team offices the next morning and performing his head coaching duties as if it were any other day. However, if he knew the conversations that were taking place while he was there, he probably would have made different plans. While Landry was in his office watching game film, Miami Dolphins head coach Don Shula called Schramm and told him about a conversation his son, David Shula, just had with University of Miami head coach Jimmy Johnson. At the time, David was the Dolphins' quarterbacks coach.

According to Don, Johnson told David that Johnson was the new head coach of the Dallas Cowboys. Johnson then offered David a job as an assistant coach on his Cowboys staff.

On Saturday morning, the front page of the *Dallas Morning News* included a photo of Johnson and Jones, taken the night before, at Mia's Tex-Mex Restaurant in Dallas, one of Landry's favorite eateries (and where scads of pictures of Landry decorate the walls). The image depicts Johnson and Jones sitting in a booth, with their significant others, smiling contentedly and enjoying their Friday night dinner. On that Saturday afternoon, Jones finalized the purchase of the team.

"[TOM LANDRY] IS, A LEGEND, AND THEY TREATED HIM LIKE DIRT" (1989)

Jones's next order of business was to push Landry, the only coach the Dallas Cowboys had ever had, out the door. Landry was hired before the franchise's inaugural season in 1960. He led the Cowboys to a 270–178–6 all-time record and two Super Bowl championships. During one stretch under Landry, the Cowboys had 20 straight winning seasons. However, the team had just suffered through a 3–13 season, their third straight losing campaign.

All of the losing was affecting the Cowboys' brand, and the fans were getting restless. According to sportswriter Gary Myers, who covered the Cowboys for the *Dallas Morning News* during the last eight years of the Landry era, an overwhelming number of Cowboy fans wanted to see Landry gone. "If you would have taken a poll in 1988," of Cowboy fans, Myers said in 2021, "it would have run about 90 percent [in favor] of firing [Landry]."

Once the sale of the team was official, Jones hopped on his Learjet with Schramm, and headed to a resort west of Austin to visit Landry, who was playing golf. In what Jones described as a very awkward conversation, particularly for Schramm, who had been Landry's right-hand man all of his 29 years as head coach, Landry was relieved of his duties.

The coaching shakeup was hardly a surprise. Throughout the previous month, Landry had been seeing rumors in the press about a potential team sale and his possible dismissal. The reaction to his firing, however, was dramatic. Landry was a beloved and legendary figure in Dallas, and many thought Jones failed to treat him with the deference he deserved during his firing. "They didn't show Tom any respect at all," said Cowboys offensive line coach Jim Erkenbeck. "Here he is, a legend, and they treated him like dirt." Dave "Kidd" Kraddick, a disc jockey at Dallas radio station KEGL wrote a song, "The Landry Years" using the melody from the Mike and the Mechanics hit song "The Living Years." Some of the lyrics:

> The Landry Generation, is stepping out the door.
> He goes with some frustration, but he's seen it all
> before.
> He's been a Dallas hero for 29 long years
> He gave us all the good times, and now it gives us
> tears
> I just wish we could have told him . . . in the Landry
> Years . . .
> . . . We've all felt the magic, as we watched him from
> the stands.
> And now it seems so tragic.
> The way they treated this great man.

"To see the man who pioneered the whole thing be thrown away like yesterday's paper. It really hurts," Kraddick told a Fort

Worth TV reporter at the time. Landry's friends and backers are still, to this day, angry about what went down. Longtime sports broadcaster Verne Lundquist, who worked in Dallas for WFAA-TV for many years and was the Cowboys' radio play-by-play voice from 1967 to 1984, thought Landry deserved better. "Firings are hard, I know," he later recalled, "but they can be handled with class, and Tom's wasn't." In late April 1989, the city held a parade called "Tom Landry Day." Fifty thousand people showed up in downtown Dallas to celebrate Landry's career. There were 86 floats.

"THEY'RE TAKING AIKMAN TO SELL TICKETS . . . BUT [HE'S] NOT AN IMPACT PLAYER" (1989)

The same day Jones fired Landry, Jimmy Johnson was announced as the Cowboys' head coach. Jones's teammate at the University of Arkansas, Johnson was a successful college coach who led the University of Miami to a National Championship in 1987. However, in over 20 years of coaching, he had never even been on an NFL coaching staff. Jones had played football in college but had never been involved with an NFL franchise. And yet, he did not hire a general manager.

As soon as Johnson reviewed his roster, he knew that he had to immediately address the quarterback position. The Cowboys' quarterback room was in desperate need of a revamp. In 1988, the team was led by veteran Steve Pelleur, who was 8–19 as a starter in his Cowboys career. Fortunately, Dallas had the No. 1 overall pick in the 1989 NFL Draft, where Troy Aikman was waiting in the wings.

Most draft experts thought Aikman should be the top choice in the draft. A 6-foot-4, 200-plus-pound All-American out of UCLA, Aikman had just led the Bruins to a 10–2 season and a 20–4 record in his two seasons as starting quarterback. He had all the tools scouts desired in a quarterback: a rocket arm, great size, and intelligence. "[He] could be the closest thing to a franchise quarterback since Denver drafted John Elway out of Stanford," wrote Robert Sansevere in the (Minneapolis) *Star Tribune*. "Even Broncos personnel are saying that."

Not all draft experts thought Aikman was the best choice. NFL Draft guru Mel Kiper Jr. loved Aikman but said he would have chosen Michigan State offensive lineman Tony Mandarich with the first pick and that the Cowboys' division rivals were hoping Dallas would pick Aikman. "If [the Cowboys] took Tony Mandarich, he'd give Dallas a virtual 300-pound line for [the Cowboys' superstar running back] Herschel Walker to run behind," Kiper said. (The Packers ended up selecting Mandarich at No. 2, and he turned out to be one of the biggest draft busts in NFL history—read more about this in chapter 10.)

Dallas didn't even wait until they were on the clock to lock up Aikman. They signed him to a six-year, $11.037 million contract three days before the draft. ESPN's Joe Theismann thought it was a silly move. "They're taking Aikman to sell tickets," he said. "But Aikman's not an impact player like [former Cowboys quarterback] Randy White or [Hall of Fame former Cowboys running back] Tony Dorsett." *Houston Chronicle* columnist Al Carter had the same opinion, and he didn't mince words. "The Cowboys blew it," Carter wrote. He thought they went for the "quick fix" by choosing a quarterback instead of trying to improve their defense. "Had the Cowboys been able to live with Steve Pelleur, they could have drafted Tony Mandarich."

A few months later, despite having signed their new franchise quarterback, the Cowboys shocked everyone and acquired another quarterback, Steve Walsh, through the NFL's Supplemental Draft.

Walsh was one of Johnson's quarterbacks at the University of Miami, where he had a 23–1 record as a starter. He was the Hurricanes' quarterback during the 1987 National Championship season. At the time, college underclassmen could choose to skip the college entry draft and enter a supplemental draft along with players who were barred, for whatever reason, from entering the NFL Draft. By rule, after picking Walsh in the supplemental draft, the Cowboys had to surrender a first-round pick in the 1990 entry draft.

Aikman wasn't thrilled when Johnson acquired Walsh. It triggered an uneasy relationship between the two that lasted a couple of years. According to Aikman's agent, Leigh Steinberg, leading up to the draft he and Aikman had multiple conversations with Jimmy and Jerry about their plans to build a team around Aikman. Upon learning that the Cowboys had drafted Walsh, Steinberg wondered, "How could we believe another word now?" Jones assured him that they would eventually trade Walsh.

"THE VIKINGS GOT HERSCHEL WALKER. THE COWBOYS GOT NOTHING MORE THAN A HUGE HANDFUL OF MINNESOTA SMOKE" (1989)

The Cowboys weren't completely devoid of talent when Jones and Johnson took over. Their first two picks in the 1988 Draft, wide receiver Michael Irvin and linebacker Ken Norton Jr., each had solid rookie seasons. Their roster also included a reliable tackle in Mark Tuinei, a young guard in Nate Newton, and veteran defensive lineman Jim Jeffcoat.

At the time, the Cowboys' most valuable asset was running back Herschel Walker. One of the game's best-known stars and a former Heisman Trophy winner, Walker rushed for 1,514 yards in 1988. But, despite his obvious talent, he was more of a power runner, and Johnson thought his system favored a more elusive, more agile running back. Johnson considered Walker expendable.

Minnesota Vikings general manager Mike Lynn thought that his team had Pro-Bowl talent at almost every position except running back, and the lack of production from their running game was the one thing holding them back. He believed Walker was the Vikings' "missing Super Bowl link." Five games into the 1989 season, Johnson and Lynn agreed on a trade to send Walker to Minnesota. It turned out to be one of the most impactful transactions in NFL history and would change the fortunes of both franchises for years to come.

The deal involved many players and many moving parts. Minnesota, in return for Walker, sent Dallas a bevy of draft picks, along with linebackers Jesse Solomon and David Howard, cornerback Isaac Holt, running back Darrin Nelson, and defensive end Alex Stewart. While the group of players were unspectacular, the draft picks were the cornerstone of the deal. The Cowboys a received a first-, second-, and sixth-round pick in 1990 and five conditional picks over the next three years that included two first-rounders, two second-rounders, and one third-rounder.

Since the players coming to Dallas from the trade weren't difference makers, the Cowboys' haul didn't look overwhelming on the surface. However, many—especially people with front-office experience who knew the power of draft picks—understood the need to rebuild. Former Washington general manager Bobby Beathard thought that the Cowboys "did the right thing" because they were going nowhere, even with Walker. For the same reason, *Sports Illustrated*'s Peter King wrote that "trading Walker was the smartest move Dallas could make."

The next day, Johnson gloated and boasted that one "NFL voice" told him that he had just pulled off "the great train robbery."

Not everyone agreed. Randy Galloway, a prominent Dallas journalist and radio personality, thought Johnson was digging his own grave with the deal. He wrote a scathing column in the *Dallas Morning News* ripping the coach. "Yes, we have a prime suspect in this heist," he wrote. "The Vikings got Herschel Walker. The Cowboys got nothing more than a huge handful of Minnesota smoke. And who knows if there will be any fire. Love that steal for Minnesota." He went on to lament about the unexceptional players the Cowboys received in return and claimed the draft picks were a mystery. To him, relying on the draft as a major part of the rebuild was unwise.

Conversely, while he ripped Johnson, Galloway heaped praise on the Vikings. "[They] gave up nothing they could not afford to lose," he wrote. "It's a textbook example of how the strong fleece the weak in a blockbuster trade. All they had to do is find somebody dumb enough to fall for it."

Galloway wasn't alone. Longtime Dallas scribe Frank Luksa called the package the Cowboys received "a bag of beans and a cow to be named later." Skip Miller, a writer for the (Newport News, Virginia) *Daily Press*, also had a laugh. "It's a lot like giving up four Bob Uecker baseball cards for one vintage Mickey Mantle," he wrote. "The Dallas rebuilding job seemed so simple a week ago. Build the offense around Walker...Any football coach will tell you once in a career a lucky coach will get a player like Herschel Walker. He then builds around that player."

"THEY'RE PITIFUL. THEY HAVE NO CLUE. WITH HERSCHEL TRADED, THIS IS A SUB-EXPANSION TEAM" (1989)

Before the trade, the Cowboys were 0–5; by the end of October they were 0–8. They weren't just losing, they were getting blown out, losing by an average of 16 points a game. They were also last or close to last in many offensive and defensive categories. "The town is just about ready to dump them," Luksa told the (Oklahoma City) *Oklahoman*. "It's sad to see what a wretched piece of business they've become. They're awful. They're pitiful. They have no clue. With Herschel traded, this is a sub-expansion team."

Based solely on the team's on-field performance, Luksa wasn't wrong. But that should have been expected. When he made the deal with the Vikings, Johnson had not only given up Walker, he essentially gave up on being even remotely competitive for the remainder of the 1989 season. The team was bad with Walker. Without him, they were a complete Dumpster fire. A few days after the trade, Johnson foreshadowed how the rest of the year would pan out when he was asked about any possible alterations to their game plan without Herschel, and he simply said he would plug in the next man up: some running back named Darryl Clack. "Darryl Clack is our guy and he'll jump right in there and play," Johnson replied. "We'll have the same offense, only Darryl Clack will be carrying the ball rather than Herschel Walker." Clack didn't last two months. He was released near the end of November.

Looking back on it, Galloway, now retired, remembers being caught off guard by Johnson's markedly different approach to the rebuild. "To build a team through the draft," he said in 2020, "was very unusual in those days…It was…considered a six-, seven-, eight-, nine-year process." Johnson was trying to vastly accelerate that process, and Galloway was not convinced that Johnson and Jones would be able to execute such an ambitious plan. "I just didn't respect Johnson's ability to draft," he said. Not because he didn't think Johnson and Jones were smart, but because they were NFL rookies who had yet to prove they had the chops to do it. "I didn't have a sample size."

Turns out, Galloway said, if he would have known how good many of the players Johnson drafted in the 1989 Draft (months before the Walker trade) would become, he would have judged Johnson differently. Four of the Cowboys' first six picks in that draft: Aikman, fullback Daryl Johnston, offensive lineman Mark Stepnoski, and defensive end Tony Tolbert were all integral contributors to the team's forthcoming dynasty run.

HERSCHEL'S DAZZLING MINNESOTA DEBUT (1989)

While the Cowboys floundered during the first few weeks after the big trade, the Vikings were on cloud nine. Walker roared off to a booming start in Minnesota. Four days after the trade, Walker was dressed and ready to go for the Vikings' home game against Green Bay. It was, up to that point, the largest crowd in Metrodome history.

Walker was on the sidelines for most of the Vikings' first drive. But after the Packers scored to make the game 7–0 with 6:27 left in the first quarter, he was sent out to receive the Packers' kickoff. On the CBS broadcast, Herschel appeared on the screen in the end zone standing alone, preparing for the kick. Play-by-play announcer Verne Lundquist, with the deep, soothing voice that helped make him one of the top voices in sports broadcasting for over 40 years, officially announced Walker's arrival in Minnesota.

"He's here."

Moments later, Herschel returned the kickoff 51 yards down the sideline. The crowd went berserk. Unfortunately, an illegal block-in-the-back penalty nullified it. But it got the crowd going. A few drives later, Walker came in on second down to a huge ovation. Soon thereafter, he took a handoff from Vikings quarterback Tommy Kramer and scampered to a 47-yard run, losing a shoe in the process.

By the fourth quarter, the Vikings were leading comfortably 26–7. The Vikings' defense, considered one of the best in the NFL at the time, swarmed Packers quarterback Don Majkowski on every play. At one point during the game broadcast, former Vikings running back Chuck Foreman was shown sitting among the Metrodome crowd. Foreman was (at the time) the Vikings all-time leader in rushing yards, and two-time NFL All-Pro. "That is Chuck Foreman," Lundquist told viewers. *Until this afternoon*, perhaps the greatest running back in Vikings history."

Walker finished the game, a 26–14 Vikings win, with 148 yards rushing on 18 carries.

"MAYBE THE MINNESOTA VIKINGS DIDN'T GIVE UP ENOUGH FOR HERSCHEL . . . WHAT A BARGAIN"

After his debut, the Twin Cities were already hooked on Herschel. According to Peter King, who covered the game for *Sports Illustrated*, during a time-out in the third quarter, the Metrodome crowd broke out into spontaneous applause for the Vikings' new running back. "Maybe the Minnesota Vikings didn't give up enough for Herschel Walker," pondered Michael Wilbon in the *Washington Post*. "What a bargain. The Cowboys ought to get on the phone pronto and demand that the Vikings send a couple more of those high draft picks south." NBC commentator Paul Maguire felt similarly. "The Vikings just found the missing ingredient for the Super Bowl," he said.

Later in the evening, after the Vikings' triumph over Green Bay, KARE-11 Minneapolis 10:00 p.m. news reporter Mark Daly's game story introduced viewers "to the phenomenon called 'Herschelmania.'" During his report from the Metrodome, numerous Vikings fans yelled "Super Bowl!" in the background. Daly also spoke with famed Minneapolis sportswriter Sid Hartman, who said on camera that the trade is "going to mean a Super Bowl, in my opinion." During another segment later in the 10:00 hour, KARE sports anchor Tom Ryther said, "I don't know if I've ever attended a more satisfying Vikings game than today."

After Herschel's first two games in Minnesota, the Vikings were 5–2 and riding a four-game win streak. The community was riding the Herschel wave. A deli at the Riverplace Market in Minneapolis renamed its Veggie Supreme Sandwich the "Healthy Herschel." At a St. Paul elementary school's Halloween party, half the boys dressed as Herschel.

"THINGS JUST DIDN'T WORK OUT REAL WELL" (1989)

The Herschel hype train would fizzle quickly. Walker never came close to duplicating that first game. As the season progressed, his carries were dramatically reduced. Turns out, just as Jimmy Johnson didn't think Walker was a good fit for the Cowboys' system, Vikings head coach Jerry Burns began to realize that Herschel didn't work for the Vikings offense, either. It partly stemmed from Walker's preference to run out of the I-formation. The Vikings, who had used the "I" about 20 percent of the time before they acquired Walker, added more "I" plays once Herschel joined the team, but it wasn't very effective. "We were a two-back, sweeping, trapping team," Burns recalled 20 years later. "Things just didn't work out real well ... You know how it is in pro football, your team reaches a peak then levels off and goes down the tubes."

According to Vikings defensive lineman Chris Doleman, Mike Lynn just outsmarted himself with the Herschel trade. "Sometimes you think that you are smarter than you really are," Doleman said in 2017. "I think that's what happened ... Mike Lynn looked at it and said, 'Hey, look, you know, I thought [Walker] could do x, y, and z, and he was limited.'"

The Vikings would go on to lose in the first round of the 1989 playoffs, and Walker lasted only two more seasons in Minnesota, both of them unspectacular.

When Minnesota acquired Walker, there were concerns about whether they would be able to keep him on the roster after his contract expired a few years later. But when that day came, in early 1992, the Vikings had no interest in retaining him. The following season, Herschel signed with Philadelphia. Ironically, he finished his career with the Cowboys.

On that glorious October afternoon when Herschel made his Vikings debut, after he officially gained over 100 yards, Lundquist casually remarked, "It won't be his last 100-yard game," implying that there would be countless others. Unfortunately, there weren't many more. Walker played 41 more games for the Vikings after that first one, and only rushed for 100 yards in three of them. All three occurred two years later, during the 1991 season. By then, Herschelmania was a distant memory.

"TRADE AIKMAN, GET A GUY LIKE PELLEUR BACK, AND YOU'LL WIN SOME BALLGAMES" (1989)

Meanwhile, in Dallas, by the middle of the 1989 season, the Cowboys' quarterback situation hadn't looked any better than it had in previous years. Before the season, Johnson had pitted Walsh and Aikman against each other in a training camp battle for the starting job. Aikman won, but he struggled playing on a Cowboys team that had very little talent. "The team I left at UCLA had more talent than this professional team I was playing for," he would later say about his rookie season.

After an 0–4 start, Aikman broke his finger and Walsh took over for the next five games. He led the Cowboys to their lone victory that season, a Week 9 triumph in Washington, but otherwise he wasn't very good. Even in the win, he completed only 10 of 30 passes. As for Aikman, he finished the season 0–11 as a starter and had only nine touchdowns, while being picked off 18 times.

The Cowboys finished the 1989 season with a 1–15 record, and by its end, fans were predictably angry. Johnson, Jones, and Aikman received the bulk of the criticism. "I distribute liquor in Grand Prairie and make $12,000 a year, and I have to make decisions," one fan wrote to the *Fort Worth Star-Telegram*. "These high-paid guys in the Cowboys organization should be able to make the same decisions. Trade Aikman, get a guy like Pelleur back, and you'll win some ballgames." Another fan wrote, "So [Jones and Johnson] thought they couldn't do any worse. One-and-15 sounds pretty bad to me."

Aikman was an easy target for derision. He had an up-and-down year. But during the season, it became clear who was the better quarterback—him or Walsh. Walsh was skinny, slow, and had a below-average NFL arm. Aikman was the prototypical NFL quarterback with the ability to make any throw. But Johnson had given up a first-round pick in the upcoming draft to acquire Walsh, and he wanted to get it back in a trade. He had been trying to trade Walsh throughout the 1989 season, to no avail.

Despite the appearances throughout the season of a legitimate quarterback competition, it was clear that Walsh didn't have much of a chance to be the full-time starter because Aikman, unless injured, would ultimately always get the start no matter how badly he played. Johnson later admitted that he never publicly gave Aikman the full-time job because he wanted Walsh's trade value to be as high as possible so he could soon unload him for another first-round pick. The whole charade wore on Aikman, who felt that his coach lacked faith in him.

SKIP BAYLESS: PRESIDENT OF "TEAM STEVE WALSH"

Few people actually believed Walsh was a worthy starter over Aikman. But there were a few exceptions. One of them: Local radio personality and *Dallas Times Herald* columnist Skip Bayless. These days, Bayless is a boisterous, brash TV personality. For almost two decades, has appeared (and, as of 2022, continues to appear) on shows on ESPN and, since 2016, Fox Sports 1, earning handsome paychecks for engaging in "debates" with other TV personalities about relevant sports issues. In 1989, he was in his 15th year as a sports columnist at a major-market newspaper and in his ninth year in Dallas, where he once had a column in the *Dallas Morning News* at 26 years old. He was also a local radio show host and appeared on local and national TV shows. Eventually, he started working for ESPN.

From the moment Aikman came to Dallas, Bayless was relentlessly and aggressively critical of him. "It's almost like a vendetta," Aikman said in 1992. "There's very few days where I've picked up his column and he hasn't taken a shot at me. It's gotten to the point that it's funny because it's so absurd."

Aikman's disdain for Skip Bayless is well documented. He categorically detests the man. But that has less to do with Bayless's lifelong criticism about his play, and more to do with what Aikman feels was irresponsible journalism in Bayless's 1996 book *Hell-Bent: The Crazy Truth about the "Win-or-Else" Dallas Cowboys*.

In early 1996, after the Cowboys won their third Super Bowl in four years, Cowboys second-year head coach Barry Switzer (Jimmy Johnson's successor) and many of his right-hand men on the coaching staff spoke with Bayless for *Hell-Bent*. Aikman had been embroiled in a bitter feud with Switzer during the 1995 Playoffs. Despite the tumultuous relationship between quarterback and coach, the Cowboys still managed to earn a trip to the Super Bowl. But the animosity between the two hit peak level just before the big game. There had been leaks to the media (Switzer's staff was suspected) that Aikman hadn't spoken to Switzer in months because Aikman found out that Switzer didn't defend him when an assistant coach told Switzer that Aikman was perceived by many as racist, and that he chastised Black players during games using racial slurs. Further, staff members told Bayless that they had heard a rumor that Aikman was gay and that the media in Dallas had ignored it to protect his image.

Aikman steadfastly denied all the rumors and accusations, including the allegations of racist treatment of teammates. None of the rumors were supported by any credible corroborating evidence.

When Bayless published *Hell-Bent*, he included what the Switzer camp had heard about Aikman's sexuality. Some folks in the media described it as Bayless accusing Aikman of being gay, and using the book to essentially out him, which is inaccurate. The information wasn't even based on a first-person account. It was merely a rumor that some people in the Switzer camp told Bayless they *had heard*. But many, especially Aikman, thought that publishing those rumors with absolutely no corroboration was tabloid-like junk and irresponsible, as they resulted in Aikman having to answer personal questions from the media about his sexuality. *Boston Globe* columnist Dan Shaughnessy elaborated on this in a 1996 column. "It's not fair to print the residue of 'word on the street,'" he wrote. "It's unattributed gossip of the worst kind."

It should not surprise anyone that Bayless was on Team Walsh in the Aikman/Walsh QB "controversy," and, at least a few times, advocated for the Cowboys to ditch Aikman for Walsh. To Skip, Walsh was the "un-Troy." "[Aikman] didn't have Walsh's eye for speed reading defenses or Walsh's feel for finding second or third receiving options," Bayless wrote in 2006. Bayless also wrote that Cowboys coaches anonymously criticized Aikman and has repeatedly written that the majority of the players on his Cowboy teams could not stand him. Also, according to Bayless, "Jimmy [Johnson] didn't think Aikman was all that football smart and didn't love his intangibles."

In a September 1992 profile of Aikman, *D Magazine* summed up Bayless's criticisms of Aikman during his first four seasons in the NFL: "At one time or another, Bayless has written, said or implied that Aikman can't throw long passes, isn't a smart quarterback, is not a team leader (too reserved to fire up a team) and could never lead Dallas to a Super Bowl victory." It wouldn't take long for Aikman to disprove each of those theories.

"JIMMY JOHNSON, YOU'RE NO TOM LANDRY" (1989)

Johnson and Jones didn't make many friends during the 1989 season. Adding to their frustrations, probably, was Tom Landry's ascent back into Dallas popularity. All season long, Jimmy and Jerry were the targets of the Landry faithful. Losing did not make it better. Fans sometimes brought signs to the game expressing how they felt, like one a week after the Walker trade that read:

> RIP DALLAS COWBOYS. RIP TOM LANDRY.
> RIP HERSCHEL WALKER.

Or the one with a 1988 Vice Presidential Debate reference:

> WE KNEW TOM LANDRY; WE PLAYED TOM LANDRY; JIMMY
> JOHNSON, YOU'RE NO TOM LANDRY.

Throughout the 1989 season, Landry made public appearances across the country, including a commercial for the hotel chain Quality Inn that was aired during the Super Bowl. Post-retirement Landry was not shy about talking to the press. In one interview with ESPN, he expressed disappointment at how Jones had handled his dismissal. At a speech in Virginia, he told the attendees, who were mostly fans of Cowboys division rival Washington, "[You] ought to love me now." After the Walker trade, Landry said he never would have traded a player like Herschel and questioned the value of the draft picks Johnson got in return.

The only Cowboys game Landry saw in person in 1989 was a road game in December against the New York Giants, after receiving a personal invite from Giants owner Wellington Mara. Landry told the media he promised he wouldn't root for either team, although, right after, he admitted that he'd like to see the Giants get into the playoffs.

If that wasn't tiring enough for Johnson and Jones, in mid-January, Landry was selected into the Pro Football Hall of Fame on the first ballot. "It shows they haven't forgotten me," he said shortly after he heard the news.

Each appearance would serve as a reminder to all the loyal Landry backers of how Jerry Jones ended the relationship. Some fans showed up to one game wearing T-shirts that simply said I HATE JERRY JONES. In January 1990, Galloway wrote, "[Landry] is more popular now in exile than he ever was as head coach."

EMMITT SMITH: JUST THE ELUSIVE RUNNING BACK JIMMY JOHNSON WANTED (1990)

It was hard to find people who were optimistic about the new Cowboys, but there were a few who saw the bigger picture. Kevin Lyttle, a sportswriter for the *Austin American-Statesman,* understood what Johnson was trying to accomplish with all of his roster maneuvering. "Johnson could have kept Landry's veterans and at least matched his 3–13 record [in 1988]," he wrote in February 1990. "Big deal. Instead he made a move for the future and discarded them."

In the 1990 Draft, Johnson used the first-round pick the Cowboys received from the Vikings and traded up to pick University of Florida running back Emmitt Smith at No. 17. Although he was just 5-foot-9 and not an overwhelmingly fast sprinter, Smith was just the elusive running back that Jimmy wanted. Most experts thought selecting him that low was a steal at the time. They were right. He was an immediate game changer. Despite holding out the entire preseason in a contract dispute, he ran for 937 yards and 11 touchdowns in his rookie season in 1990, was named Offensive Rookie of the Year, and was a selection to the Pro Bowl. Emmitt ended up becoming the NFL's all-time leading rusher (a title he still holds as of 2022) and is in the Hall of Fame.

Johnson made other pivotal moves during the 1990 Draft besides drafting his franchise running back. He also made trades to accumulate more draft picks for the 1991 Draft, and acquired additional unprotected players from what was then known as "Plan B" free agency (the system the NFL briefly used before unrestricted free agency was implemented in 1993). One of them was Phoenix Cardinals tight end Jay Novacek, who would become a crucial part of the Cowboys a few years later.

"THE SAINTS FOUND A WAY TO REMEDY THOUGHTS OF A SINKING FRANCHISE—TRADE FOR STEVE WALSH." (1990)

The Cowboys' 1990 season didn't start off much better than the year before. With 10 minutes left in the Cowboys' second game, a home blowout loss to the Giants at Texas Stadium, Johnson pulled Aikman in favor of Walsh. Aikman did not take it well, and after the game, he admitted that he was not comfortable being on the same team as Walsh.

Eventually, the quarterback room became untenable. Johnson knew he had to unload Walsh. In late September 1990, in what may have been one of the most lopsided trades in NFL history that nobody talks about, the Cowboys traded Walsh to the New Orleans Saints. In return, the Saints gave Dallas a *first-* and *third*-round draft choice in 1991 *and* a second-round choice in 1992. The Saints were desperate. Their regular starter, Bobby Hebert, was embroiled in a season-long holdout for more money. Hebert expected to be traded. But Saints general manager Jim Finks, on principle, refused any and all offers for him and doubled down, deciding he would neither pay Hebert nor trade him. After the Saints began the season floundering with an overmatched John Fourcade at quarterback, Finks tripled down on his Hebert stance and gave up a boatload of picks for Walsh.

Walsh's first appearance for the Saints, and the reaction that followed, was similar to the one after Herschel's debut in Minnesota. In mid-October, a few weeks after the Walsh trade, the Saints were 1–3, facing the Browns at home in the Superdome. Head coach Jim Mora benched Fourcade after two series and brought on Walsh, who proceeded to complete 15 of 26 passes for 243 yards and three touchdowns. The Saints won 25–20.

The reactions to Walsh's New Orleans debut were predictable. The headline of the sports page in the *Lafayette Daily Advertiser* the next day read, WALSH JUST WHAT THE DOCTOR ORDERED FOR THE SAINTS. In his game report, *Daily Advertiser* sportswriter Kevin Foote wrote, "The Saints found a way to remedy thoughts of a sinking franchise—trade for Steve Walsh." Another area writer, the

Hattiesburg American's Stan Caldwell, surmised that Saints fans may be thanking Hebert's agent, Greg Campbell, because his "bad advice" to Hebert for him to hold out, ultimately led to the Saints trading for "a 23-year-old prodigy [Walsh] who can win Super Bowls for New Orleans."

Further igniting the flames was the fact that Walsh's Saints debut came on the same day as rock bottom for Aikman and the Cowboys. At the same time Walsh was leading the Saints over the Browns and endearing himself to New Orleans, Aikman's squad lost 20–3 on the road to the lowly Cardinals. In the loss, Dallas managed to produce a franchise record–low 100 yards of offense. Aikman completed only 9-of-25 passes, finished with a paltry 61 yards passing, was sacked four times, and threw two interceptions. "This was one of Troy Aikman's least memorable days as a pro, collegian or anything," wrote Tim Cowlishaw in the *Dallas Morning News*. "Even Troy will tell you he didn't justify his salary." The next day, writers from the *Los Angeles Times* and the *New York Daily News* pondered whether the Cowboys had traded the wrong quarterback.

The remainder of Steve Walsh's career in New Orleans never lived up to the promise of his first start. The Saints were able to sneak into the 1990 playoffs, but Walsh wasn't particularly impressive. New Orleans scored 20 or fewer points in the eight games that Walsh started and lost 16–6 to the Bears in the Wild Card Round. That summer, Finks caved and signed Hebert. Walsh lost his starting job and only started eight games in his remaining three seasons in New Orleans before signing with Chicago.

Aikman was inconsistent for most of 1990, but found his groove near the end of the season and, for one stretch of the final two months, led the team on a four-game winning streak. He was playing some of his best football and the Cowboys were in playoff contention, when, unfortunately, he separated his shoulder early in the team's 15th game. The offense sputtered without him and the Cowboys lost their final two games to finish 7–9 and miss the postseason.

"DID SOMEONE MENTION PLAYOFFS? . . . CERTAINLY NOT IN THE COWBOYS' LOCKER ROOM" (1991)

The 1991 off-season was the most impactful of Jimmy Johnson's tenure as head coach. First, finding the offense too inconsistent and Aikman not developing fast enough, he demoted offensive coordinator David Shula. He initially wanted Miami Dolphins offensive coordinator Gary Stevens, who was on Johnson's staff at the University of Miami, to replace him, but Stevens declined. He settled on Norv Turner, the Rams' wide receivers coach, who some say was Johnson's fourth choice.

Johnson and Jones also made some moves before the draft. They traded up from the 11th pick of the 1991 Draft to the first overall pick. Also, through various trades and using the vast array of picks they had in their arsenal, the Cowboys were able to acquire additional first- and second-round picks in the same draft.

After all of Johnson's maneuvering, including many of the picks they acquired the year before, the Cowboys made *18* picks in total in 1991, significantly increasing their chances of accumulating quality talent. The strategy worked: The Cowboys were able to acquire a slew of players who were key to the team's eventual success. With the first overall pick, they selected Miami defensive tackle Russell Maryland, who had played for Johnson a few years earlier with the Hurricanes. Among the Cowboys' other selections:

wide receiver Alvin Harper (12th overall), Dixon Edwards (second round), linebacker Godfrey Miles and offensive tackle Erik Williams (third round), and offensive tackle Leon Lett and cornerback Larry Brown (seventh round). The picks all proved strong. Maryland, Williams, and Lett were Pro Bowlers. Harper was the Cowboys' number-two receiver and was a perfect complement to Michael Irvin. Brown later became a Super Bowl MVP.

The 1991 season began about as well as the previous two. After splitting their first two games, the Cowboys were clobbered by the Eagles, who were playing without quarterback Randall Cunningham, 24–0. Aikman was sacked 11 times, threw three interceptions, and lost a fumble. The Eagles held the Cowboys to only 90 total yards. "Did someone mention playoffs?" wrote Rick Gosselin in the *Dallas Morning News* the next day. "Not this Sunday, and certainly not in the Cowboys' locker room." "The look on the face of...Norv Turner...was hauntingly similar to the one that sat on David Shula's brow before Johnson ushered him out of town," wrote Jim Reeves in the *Star-Telegram*.

Aikman eventually found his stride in Turner's offense. The previous two seasons, he was getting pounded every game. Under Turner, Aikman started releasing the ball more quickly, taking less punishment. Also, Aikman developed a friendship with Turner that helped make him more comfortable with the staff.

Despite all the progress, the Cowboys had a rough November, losing three out of five games. In a late-November contest at Washington, Aikman suffered a partial knee tear and was replaced by veteran backup Steve Beuerlein. The injury would cost Aikman the rest of the regular season. His statistics up until his injury were stellar. He had a 65 percent completion percentage and threw for a total of 2,754 yards. By the time the regular season ended, Aikman had already been selected to his first Pro Bowl.

"NOW ... YOU WONDER WHETHER JOHNSON MIGHT CONSIDER TRADING [AIKMAN]" (1991)

In the market all summer for a capable backup quarterback, Johnson acquired Beuerlein in a trade with the Los Angeles Raiders just before the 1991 season started. Beuerlein, a Notre Dame product, was a four-year league veteran with a solid arm who was a respected thrower but had little mobility. He was a productive part-time starter in LA for two seasons, and was the Raiders' best quarterback in 1989, but was unceremoniously discarded after a lengthy holdout before the 1990 season. The Raiders eventually put him on the inactive list, where he remained the entire year.

In Aikman's absence, Beuerlein led Dallas to five consecutive wins, including four as the starting quarterback. Three of those wins came against eventual playoff teams. Beuerlein didn't blow anyone away; he threw only five touchdowns in those five games and completed less than 50 percent of his total passes. But he was able to lead the team to victories by not making mistakes. The Cowboys didn't commit a single turnover for the first 15 quarters after Beuerlein took over for Aikman.

Aikman wanted to start the Cowboys' first-round playoff game against the Bears in Chicago. His knee wasn't 100 percent, but he swore he was perfectly capable of playing. After Aikman made clear to reporters that he expected to start, Johnson said he wasn't ready.

Johnson's decision to start Beuerlein worked out. With cameras often cutting throughout the CBS broadcast to a sullen-looking Aikman standing on the sidelines, Beuerlein led the Cowboys to a 17–13 win over the Bears.

A few days later, Johnson announced that he would ride the "hot hand" and start Beuerlein for their upcoming Divisional

Round game in Detroit. Aikman wasn't quiet with his frustration. "To say it doesn't bother me would not be accurate," he told reporters. "I feel like I should be playing right now."

Despite Beuerlein's success, as far as most were concerned, Aikman was still the Cowboys' quarterback of the future. Beuerlein always understood his role. However, Aikman was getting restless, and his insecurity and uneasiness about the Cowboys' faith in him were starting to come to a head. With Aikman noticeably unhappy, there were rumblings about what might be in store for the following season. Ed Werder, the *Orlando Sentinel*'s NFL beat writer, wrote, "During Aikman's rookie season, the Cowboys were losing all the time, and Aikman wanted to be traded. Now they are winning all the time, and you wonder whether Johnson might consider trading him."

Any thoughts of Beuerlein becoming the permanent starter were quickly quashed after the Cowboys were annihilated by the Lions. After trailing at halftime 17–6, Johnson benched starter Beuerlein for Aikman. It didn't do any good, and Detroit won 38–6.

After the game, Randy Galloway ran into Aikman in the locker room, where the quarterback told him, "I'm gone. I'm asking for a trade. This is not going to work." However, the next day, Aikman called Galloway after a meeting with Jimmy Johnson where Johnson told him, "This is your team. You are my guy. No more fooling around.'" From that point forward, there wouldn't be another quarterback controversy in Dallas for the rest of the decade.

The Cowboys only had four total picks in the 1992 Draft, and essentially went 4-of-4. Cornerback Kevin Smith (first round), linebacker Robert Jones (first round), and cornerback Darren Woodson (second round) all turned out to be Pro Bowl players. Even wide receiver Jimmy Smith, also picked by the Cowboys in the second round, turned out to be a five-time Pro Bowler, though all those seasons came after his stint with the Cowboys, who cut him after the 1993 season.

In addition to the draft, Johnson was also able to pull off a tremendous coup when he traded San Francisco for eventual Hall of Fame defensive end Charles Haley. Haley and 49ers head coach George Seifert's relationship had deteriorated so badly that the Cowboys only had to give up a second- and third-round pick to get him.

The 1992 Cowboys set a franchise record with 13 wins. Aikman had a breakout year. He hit career highs in yards and touchdowns. He also completed 64 percent of his passes. Emmitt Smith set the franchise record with over 1,700 rushing yards and won the league rushing title. Michael Irvin had almost 1,400 yards receiving. These gaudy statistics were partly made possible by what many feel was the best offensive line in the history of the NFL—"The Great Wall of Dallas." In addition, the Cowboys' defense was flat-out swarming. They finished first in the NFL in total defense, fewest first downs allowed, and preventing third-down conversions.

Aikman's performance in the NFC Championship game against the 49ers was particularly memorable. It put him on the map as a big-game quarterback. The 49ers had boasted the best record in the NFL and MVP quarterback Steve Young. The Cowboys were heavy underdogs. At a muddy Candlestick Park in San Francisco, Aikman threw for 322 yards in a 30–20 Dallas triumph, including a crucial 70-yard pass to Alvin Harper after the Niners had cut the Cowboys' lead to four. The defense also forced four turnovers. A few weeks later, Dallas destroyed the Buffalo Bills at the Rose Bowl to win Super Bowl XXVII.

For both Jerry Jones and Jimmy Johnson, the Super Bowl win was nothing short of vindication. During that first season in

1989, Johnson was taken to task at every turn, especially after he shipped off Herschel Walker, and the team labored to a 1–15 record. As *Hartford Courant* columnist Alan Greenberg put it: "[The Cowboys'] new management was about as popular as bubonic plague." It was no walk in the park for Jones, either. The first couple of seasons, Jones was put through the ringer by many Cowboys fans and the local media for the manner in which he fired Tom Landry. After the Super Bowl triumph, Cowboys radio voice Brad Sham tried to put in perspective just how acrimonious it was for Jones during his first few years in Dallas. "[Jones has] taken more abuse than any person I've ever known," he said.

Upon winning Super Bowl XXVII, expectations for the Cowboys skyrocketed. They had star players who were set to remain in Dallas for a while, alongside the youngest roster in the league, with average age of 26. America's Team was poised to win for a long time. A long time that included 1993, the very next season, when the Cowboys won Super Bowl XXVIII 30–13 in a rematch over the Bills. Not even halfway through the '90s, the Cowboys should have just been starting toward a decade of dominance. However, after that second Super Bowl win, the team slowly began to deteriorate. Jones and Johnson had a falling-out. It got so bad that Jones showed Johnson the door just weeks after the Super Bowl XXVIII win. He replaced Johnson with another of his buddies, former University of Arkansas teammate Barry Switzer. After a few years off, Johnson eventually moved on to the Miami Dolphins.

Switzer, like Johnson back in 1989, was a college coaching legend who had no NFL experience. In his 16 seasons as head coach at the University of Oklahoma, the Sooners won three National Championships; however, he had been retired from coaching for five years when he was called in by Jones to take over the most high-profile team in the NFL. He held the fort down as best he could, but he was often criticized as being in over his head and bailed out by all of the Cowboys' talent. He also had a terrible relationship with Troy Aikman.

By the end of the 1994 regular season, confidence in Switzer was waning. "The Dallas Cowboys are not going to win the Super Bowl with Barry Switzer coaching," wrote Tony Kornheiser in the *Washington Post*. Somehow, the team persevered and did manage to win another one—Super Bowl XXX—in the 1995 season. It was downhill from there. The following year, the Cowboys began to decline substantially, and after suffering through a 6–10 season in 1997, Jones fired Switzer.

FORWARD-THINKING STRATEGY

After the Cowboys traded Herschel Walker, and were losing every game, an editorial in a small publication, the *Longview News-Journal*, expressed befuddlement at how a team could favor its system over its best talent. The column offered this fateful analogy: "The new Cowboys are beginning to take on the look of a company acquired through a leveraged buyout that now finds it must sell off its assets to stay afloat." It was, in their eyes, a "losing strategy." But Jimmy Johnson knew he needed significantly more good players than he had, and the best way to accumulate them was through the draft.

Essentially, beginning with the Herschel Walker trade, the Cowboys chose to tank in the short-term in order to set themselves up for long-term success. In 2022, this isn't out of the ordinary. While many teams that use this strategy are condemned for disrupting the competitive balance of their respective leagues, the approach is not criticized as being unintelligent. In 1989, however, it was taboo, and so unconventional that people couldn't completely comprehend it. The *Longview News-Journal* seems to have been in that boat. They just did not understand the plan. The Cowboys were not "selling off assets to stay afloat"; they were selling off their biggest asset in order to accumulate a substantial amount of future assets to be used to rebuild. They were just ahead of their time.

"TURNS OUT, THE PATRIOTS' UNLIKELY 2001 SEASON JOURNEY SEEMS MORE AND MORE LIKE AN ABERRATION"

(2000–2005 NEW ENGLAND PATRIOTS)

In 2000, the New England Patriots were largely irrelevant outside of the Northeast and the fourth most important professional team in Greater Boston. Then, in short order, they hired a new head coach, hit the quarterback jackpot, and won a Super Bowl. It was only the beginning.

For most of the 21st century, the Patriots achieved and maintained an NFL "dynasty," in which, as of 2022, they've won almost 300 games; appeared in nine Super Bowls; won six Super Bowls; won 31 playoff games; and won their division, the AFC East, 18 times. Many have pegged February 6, 2005, the night New England defeated Philadelphia 24–21 in Super Bowl XXXIX, as the date the Patriots were recognized by the sports world as a dynasty. It was the Patriots' second straight Super Bowl championship and their third in four years.

From 2000 to 2005, there were many important moments that were integral to winning those first three championships. Many of them were unexpected and involved the franchise being critically panned by commentators, experts, journalists, and the like. This chapter describes some of those moments, and reviews some of that commentary.

It all began with a coach nobody liked and a quarterback nobody knew.

"BELICHICK . . . YOU STILL STINK" (2000)

By the end of the 2000 season, the Patriots looked like a lost cause. Four years removed from a Super Bowl appearance, the franchise had sunk back into the mediocrity that had plagued them for most of their previous years. A year earlier, owner Robert Kraft fired head coach Pete Carroll after New England finished the 1999 season with a disappointing 8–8 record and failed to make the playoffs. Kraft replaced him with longtime Bill Parcells assistant Bill Belichick. Belichick had a stellar reputation as a defensive mastermind, but his ability and temperament to lead a franchise were in dispute.

From 1991 to 1995, Belichick had a 37–45 record as the head coach of the Cleveland Browns and was fired in early 1996 just before the franchise moved to Baltimore. After leaving Cleveland, he became the defensive coordinator for Bill Parcells, first with the Patriots for one season, and then with the Jets for three seasons. When Parcells retired in early January 2000, Belichick contractually took over as the Jets' head coach before abruptly quitting the next day. After much legal wrangling, and despite Kraft receiving a substantial amount of criticism, Belichick was introduced as the Patriots' new head coach near the end of the month. Along with becoming head coach, Belichick was given a substantial amount of administrative control, including being in charge of all personnel.

The early results on Kraft's investment were not promising. By mid-November 2000, the Patriots had won only 2 of their first 10 games. The 10th was a road game in Cleveland against the Browns, where Belichick had coached five years earlier. A large sign in the corner of Browns Stadium read BELICHICK 2-7. YOU STILL STINK.

The sign wasn't really wrong. Belichick's team did stink. That day, they lost 19–11 to an awful Browns team that had previously lost seven straight games and hadn't scored a touchdown in almost a month. The next day, veteran *Boston Globe* columnist Dan Shaughnessy wrote that "It's been 10 painful weekends and there is nothing left to say other than a once un-thinkable refrain: 'Bring back Pete Carroll.'" He added, "Bill Belichick is in charge of bringing respectability back to New England football, but right now, fans would settle for a little dignity, which was in short supply on Bloody Sunday in Ohio."

Shaughnessy never actually thought there was a possibility they would bring back Carroll. "I was just having fun there," he said in 2020. To him, it was more a dig directed at Robert Kraft than one directed at Belichick. Shaughnessy had been hard on Kraft since Bill Parcells left the Patriots after the 1996 season. Parcells had brought the franchise from the bottom, when he took over in 1993, to the playoffs in 1994 and then to the Super Bowl in 1996. But when Kraft bought the team in 1994, he and Parcells instantly became embroiled in a power struggle and consistently butted heads until Parcells eventually left.

During the final few years of Pete Carroll's run as Patriots head coach, Shaughnessy had been critical of Kraft for chasing off Parcells and hiring Carroll, under whose leadership the Patriots just got worse and worse each season. After the Patriots started off poorly under Belichick, Shaughnessy began to revive his digs about letting Parcells walk away. "It was a little bit of a nudge at the Krafts," he said. "Like, alright smarty pants...nice job getting Parcells out of here."

The Patriots finished the 2000 season, Belichick's first with the club, with a 5–11 record. From the *Boston Herald*'s Year in Review:

> The price for Belichick was an exchange of draft picks with the Jets that included the Pats' 2000 first-round selection. Now, nearly a year later Kraft has to be wondering if it was worth the price. The perceived catalyst of Kraft's "momentum change," has not only failed to arrest the Pats' downward spiral, he has accelerated it ... The future is not

exactly bright... There are also questions as to
whether Belichick, who fired former personnel
director Bobby Grier in May, is the right man to be
shopping for the groceries.

That off-season, New England signed its veteran quarterback
Drew Bledsoe to a 10-year, $103 million contract extension, even
though he still had two years remaining on his existing deal. At the
time, it was hailed as the richest contract in NFL history. Bledsoe
was the face of the franchise, owned almost all of its passing
records, was actively involved in the community, and had a great
relationship with Kraft, who felt that the 29-year-old quarterback
was going to be the Patriots' leader for years to come. "I saw this as
an opportunity to sign one of the great Patriots for the rest of his
career," Kraft said at the press conference announcing the Bledsoe
deal.

THE NEW ENGLAND PATRIOTS: "LEAST LIKELY" TO MAKE THE PLAYOFFS WITHIN THE NEXT FIVE YEARS (2001)

In March 2001, a month before the NFL Draft, the magazine *Pro
Football Weekly* polled "NFL Insiders" and asked which team
had the least chance of making the playoffs or going to the Super
Bowl in the next five years, and "The Patriots were the unanimous
choice." The publication also added:

When [the Boston media] have a bad team to cover,
they will blame everyone, especially the coaches
and management team. In the past, Bill Belichick
had a hard time coping with a very negative press
that treated him unfairly, and it remains to be seen

if he has reached the point where he can overcome the negative assault he will be hit with. It also remains to be seen how much time owner Robert Kraft will give the coach once the vultures start swooping around."

"THEY REACHED ON EVERY PICK" (2001)

During the 2001 NFL Draft, instead of using picks on skill position players to get "weapons" for Bledsoe, Belichick spent his top picks on University of Georgia defensive tackle Richard Seymour (6th overall) and offensive tackle Matt Light (second round, 48th overall). Local columnist Ron Borges did not agree with the strategy. On MSNBC.com, he torched Belichick for passing on top receiver prospects David Terrell and Koren Robinson. He wrote that Seymour "had one sack last season in the pass happy [Southeastern Conference] and is too tall to play tackle at 6-foot-6 and too slow to play defensive end." Additionally, Borges thought the Patriots "settled [in the second round] for Light, who will not help any time soon." But Belichick wasn't concerned. "[Receiver] was a low priority," he said. "We just didn't feel comfortable reaching."

During the beginning of the Belichick era in New England, Borges, who then primarily wrote for the *Globe*, was probably the least liked Patriots writer on the beat. To fans, he was the posterchild of Belichick-era contrarianism. He constantly took jabs at the coach, to a point where it almost seemed personal.

With regard to the 2001 Draft, some of the media's NFL Draft "report cards" agreed with Borges's view. The (Fort Lauderdale) *Sun Sentinel*'s Chris Perkins called the Seymour pick a "bit of a reach" and gave the Patriots' draft a "C." Alan Greenberg of the

Hartford Courant handed them a "C-plus." Jason Cole, in the *Miami Herald*, slapped them with a "D" and wrote that "They reached on every pick." *Boston Herald* writer Kevin Mannix was critical as well. By taking Seymour, he concluded, New England passed on "legitimate playmaker" David Terrell.

Seymour and Light turned out to be home-run draft selections. Seymour played 8 seasons with the Patriots and was one of the best defensive linemen in the league when he was active. He was inducted into the Hall of Fame in 2022. Light played 11 seasons, all with New England, and made three Pro Bowls. David Terrell was drafted by the Bears with the eighth pick in the first round. He didn't live up to his billing. He was released after his fourth season with the Bears, and never played another regular-season game.

On Twitter, Borges is frequently reminded about his comments about Seymour and Terrell. According to him, he's now good friends with Seymour and they "laugh a lot" about how people love to continue to bring up the same 2001 Draft comments year in, year out.

"IT'S GOING TO BE ANOTHER BLEAK NEW ENGLAND AUTUMN" (2001)

Before the 2001 season, New England was almost universally predicted to finish under .500. *Sports Illustrated* projected the Patriots would finish dead last in the AFC East. Other notable forecasts:

> I would be very surprised if they don't find
> themselves in the same place as they were in 2000—
> last in the division.
>
> —Mel Kiper Jr.

It's going to be another bleak New England
autumn...And wasn't Belichick supposed to be a
better coach than Pete Carroll?
                              —Ron Reid, *Philadelphia Inquirer*

The Patriots have been in reverse the last five
seasons, with no relief in sight.
                    —Bob Matthews, (Rochester, New York) *Democrat
                                                        and Chronicle*

What neither the *Democrat and Chronicle*, nor almost anyone else, knew, was that relief would come much sooner than expected. In the form of Tom Brady.

No one knew what Tom Brady would become when he graduated from the University of Michigan in 2000. But the Patriots brass saw at least something they liked, and drafted Brady in the sixth round (199th overall). It was a decision that puzzled some who felt New England didn't really need a quarterback. "So, what's with that? Why another quarterback?" asked Kevin Mannix in the *Boston Herald* the next day. "The Patriots have their franchise starter in Drew Bledsoe, a proven veteran backup in John Friesz, and a young developmental player in Michael Bishop." Alan Greenberg, in the *Hartford Courant*, wrote about Brady: "Obviously [he] has a great future in New England—as a practice squad quarterback."

Brady possessed some of the qualities NFL teams looked for in a quarterback. He was tall, smart, a natural leader, accurate, and good at reading defenses. The problem was, his negative attributes stood out like a sore thumb. He was skinny and didn't have a quarterback build. He was slow on foot and immobile. His scouting report didn't scream "greatest of all time" potential, but he impressed enough in training camp to win a roster spot for the

2000 season. Friesz was released, and Brady spent his rookie year as the Patriots' third quarterback behind Bishop. In 2001, Brady had a fantastic off-season and training camp. The coaches noticed his work ethic, his sharpness, and how good he was at executing reads. By the start of the regular season, Brady had surpassed both Bishop, who was cut in August, and Damon Huard to take the number two spot on the depth chart. Huard, an experienced veteran, was signed by New England before the 2001 season to be the Patriots' primary backup, but he couldn't thwart Brady's rapid ascent and was relegated to third string.

"WITHOUT DREW BLEDSOE . . . THE PATRIOTS ARE HOPELESS" (2001)

As the backup situation sorted itself out during training camp in 2001, Bledsoe was firmly entrenched as the Patriots' starting quarterback. That would change within weeks. The second season of the Belichick era continued where it left off. New England lost to a low-tier Cincinnati team to open the season. The team was on its way to a second loss in their second game as they were down 10–3 in the fourth quarter to the Jets. That is when Jets linebacker Mo Lewis hit Bledsoe so hard that Bledsoe sheared a blood vessel and was rushed to the hospital. Brady took over but couldn't salvage the game. The Patriots dropped to 0–2.

The injury ruled out Bledsoe indefinitely. While it seemed like a disaster, it couldn't get much worse. The offense was already struggling at the time Bledsoe was hurt. In his previous 26 starts, the Patriots had a 7–19 record and Bledsoe threw 32 interceptions. But according to Borges, who has long been considered to be an ally and friend of Bledsoe, the Patriots fans who had been critical of the franchise quarterback were about to see that the grass isn't always greener on the other side. "The New England Alliance of Drew Bledsoe Bashers now will get its wish," Borges wrote in the *Boston Globe* a few days after the Jets loss. "It will get to see firsthand what life without Bledsoe will be like... [It will be] a problem for this team... and will show a lot of people what he means to the Patriots. It's a big price to pay to make people finally understand his value." Other outlooks for the remainder of the Patriots' season:

> Without Drew Bledsoe... the Patriots are hopeless.
> —Terry Bannon, *Chicago Tribune*

> [The Patriots are] even more dismal without Bledsoe.
> —Jason Schaumberg, (Woodstock, Illinois)
> *Northwest Herald*

> New England's fortunes after a humbling 0–2 start would be bleak even with a healthy Drew Bledsoe.
> —Phillip B. Wilson, *Indianapolis Star*

> Honestly, I don't know what weapons they have with which to win a game.
> —Paul Zimmerman (aka "Dr. Z"), CNNSI.com

In Week 3, Brady led the 12-point underdog Patriots to a win over Indianapolis 44–13. Afterwards, rumblings started to be heard about a possible quarterback controversy upon Bledsoe's eventual return. That talk was tabled the next week after Brady and New England were throttled 30–10 by the Miami Dolphins in the sweltering South Florida heat. Brady was 12-of-24 for only 86 yards passing. In his next-day *Globe* column, Borges wrote: "The

New England Patriots' 'quarterback controversy' ended at 3:18 p.m. yesterday." He continued:

> The fact of the matter is, Brady is a young player who does not have the arm or a reputation earned of performances against tight defenses like Miami's over the years. He did a good job against the Colts and as good as he could against the Dolphins. What he did not do—and won't do any time soon—is replace Drew Bledsoe.

In the *Boston Herald*, George Kimball rubbed it in the face of the "idiots" who "were out in full force" a week earlier after the Pats beat the Colts, "suggesting that the Patsies might be a better team [with Brady]."

The next Sunday, Brady led the Patriots to a 29–26 overtime win over the Chargers in Foxboro. He was 33-of-54 for 365 yards and two touchdowns. On the CBS game broadcast, with over five minutes left in the fourth quarter and the Patriots down 26–16 with the ball, the camera cut to Bledsoe on the sidelines donning a headset and jacket before play-by-play man Ian Eagle reminded viewers that "There is no Drew Bledsoe to come in and save the day."

They didn't need Drew. New England scored 10 unanswered points to tie it in regulation. The comeback was highlighted by a 60-yard touchdown drive led by Brady in the final 2:10 to tie the game and send it to overtime.

Brady led the Patriots to wins in eight of their last nine games, including a six-game winning streak to close out the season to win the AFC East and earn a first-round playoff bye. By mid-November, Bledsoe was healthy and cleared to play, but he didn't get minutes the rest of the regular season. Belichick did not seem to even entertain the idea of giving the starting job back to Bledsoe. Bledsoe saw it differently. He has always maintained that Belichick promised him an opportunity to compete to win his job back when he became healthy, but Belichick changed his mind when that time came.

In the Patriots' first game of the 2001 Playoffs, an AFC Divisional Round matchup against the Raiders during a Foxborough snowstorm, the Patriots again scored 10 unanswered points in the fourth quarter to send the game to overtime, where they would win 16–13. The game will be remembered for the controversial play where a Raiders game-sealing fumble recovery from a Charles Woodson strip sack of Brady was, to the Patriots' great fortune, overruled by an NFL regulation called the "tuck rule." The rule provided that Brady did not actually fumble but threw an incomplete pass because he was trying to tuck the ball away when it was lost.

During the AFC Championship game in Pittsburgh, with the Patriots leading 7–3 with under two minutes left in the second quarter, New England was forced to call on a familiar face when Brady was knocked out of the game with an injury to his ankle.

The last time Drew Bledsoe had taken a snap from center was Week 2. But there didn't appear to be any rust. Bledsoe immediately led the Patriots offense down the field for a touchdown on his first drive. Brady never returned to that game, but Bledsoe kept the ship together and the Patriots went on to win 24–17, clinching a spot in Super Bowl XXXVI against the Rams.

Brady's injury wasn't serious, and he would be cleared to play in the Super Bowl. While some gave the impression that the team was considering having Bledsoe start the big game against the Rams, Belichick clarified that Brady was his guy. "The only reason it was up in the air was because [of] Brady's ankle," former Patriots center Damien Woody (1999–2003) said years later. "This was

Brady's team... If Brady was healthy, he was gonna play. Period." It was the right call, as the team completed its Cinderella season and won the Super Bowl by defeating the heavily favored Rams 20–17 on an Adam Vinatieri field goal in the final seconds.

After the Super Bowl, the Patriots fully committed to Tom Brady at quarterback and traded Bledsoe to division rival Buffalo. In August 2002, the Patriots rewarded Brady with a four-year, $28 million contract extension.

"THE NEW ENGLAND PATRIOTS GOT VERY BENEVOLENT OR VERY COCKY OR VERY STUPID" (2002)

With the Super Bowl champion label planted squarely on their backs, the 2002 Patriots season started with a bang. New England shot out to a 3–0 record and Brady continued where he left off, looking every bit the championship quarterback. That changed quickly. Beginning Week 4, the Patriots took a nosedive, and they lost four straight games. During that stretch, the offense struggled mightily, averaging only 13 points per game. Brady threw seven interceptions.

Some critics thought New England was relying on Brady to throw the ball significantly more than the previous year. In 2001, the Patriots' offense maintained a close to even balance of running and passing plays, and were able to control the pace of the game. In 2002, the team saw less balance and became more predictable. Brady's pass attempt numbers skyrocketed, though most of throws were short passes and screens. Defenses wised up and used different zone coverages, which forced Brady into more downfield throws with smaller windows.

During the losing streak, fans didn't hold back their discontent. After Brady threw three interceptions during a Week 6 loss to Green Bay in Foxboro, he was booed off the field by the home crowd. The critics started to dig in. "Tom Brady looks nothing like the man who took [the Patriots] to the Super Bowl," wrote Charles Bricker in the (Fort Lauderdale) *Sun-Sentinel*.

His coach wasn't coming off so great, either. The Patriots' defense, which was Belichick's specialty, couldn't stop anybody. Particularly the run defense. It was porous. By early October, New England's defense was allowing 5.6 yards per play. In Weeks 3 and 4, against Kansas City and San Diego, respectively, the Pats gave up a combined 459 yards on the ground. As the team struggled to maintain their winning ways from the Super Bowl, some of the local media spent much of the season wondering if Belichick was as smart as he was given credit for in February when he hoisted the Lombardi Trophy in New Orleans. "How could Belichick, the widely proclaimed defensive genius, have a team that can't do the most basic thing in football stop the run?" asked Jim Donaldson in the *Providence Journal*. In the *Boston Herald*, Kevin Mannix wondered if "there is a statute of limitations regarding genius."

Of all the Patriots' fodder in 2002, the most popular topic was whether the Patriots made the right decision trading Bledsoe and committing to Brady. The subject was particularly interesting during the first half of the season, because Brady was struggling and Bledsoe was prospering. During the same period where the Patriots suffered four losses in a row, Bledsoe's Buffalo Bills team had a 3–1 record. By the end of Week 8, Buffalo had more wins (five) than they did in all of 2001 (three). Halfway through the season, Bledsoe had thrown 16 touchdowns, had only five interceptions, and was leading the NFL in passing yards. The national media began to take notice. On NFL.com, former NFL coach and administrator Pat Kirwan gave out "Midseason Awards," and tabbed Bledsoe as Offensive MVP. He also awarded the Best Offseason Trade to the Bills for its trade for Bledsoe.

Bledsoe's play was all the rage. In late September, on Boston-area channel WBZ-TV's Sunday evening show *Sports Final*, local radio personality Scott Zolak, a former Patriots quarterback and Bledsoe teammate, said that he was twice as impressed about how Bledsoe had been playing with Buffalo as he was at how Brady was playing with New England. A week later, veteran *Globe* columnist Nick Cafardo said on local TV that Bledsoe (1) was clearly a superior quarterback to Brady, (2) was much more clutch than Brady, and (3) would have already replaced Brady as the starter if he were still on the Patriots. Even players on rival teams chimed in. Miami Dolphins all-pro defensive end Jason Taylor was annoyed that the Patriots helped another AFC East team improve. "I don't understand why New England traded [Bledsoe] to Buffalo," Taylor said. "It was kind of a stupid move on their part. Now we're stuck playing against him again. He's playing unbelievably."

Buffalo-area writers weren't shy, either. (Rochester, New York) *Democrat and Chronicle* Bills writer Sal Maiorana wrote that the Patriots made the wrong choice. "I just think that he is a better quarterback than Brady," he wrote. "Bledsoe is only 30, he's going to be around for quite a while, and I know the Bills are happy the way things turned out." At the end of October, (Syracuse, New York) *Post-Standard* columnist Bud Poliquin gleefully wrote about the Bills rebirth. If not for the Patriots shipping Bledsoe off to Buffalo, the 2002 season, Poliquin believed, would have seen the Bills continue descending to the bottom of the NFL barrel. "The New England Patriots got very benevolent or very cocky or very stupid," he wrote. *Buffalo News* columnist Bucky Gleason was also very thankful to the Patriots. "We knew Bledsoe was a wonderful quarterback, but we had no idea he was this great," Gleason wrote. "Lucky for us . . . Belichick was arrogant enough to trade him inside the AFC East and rationalize playing against him twice a year."

"JUST LIKE THAT . . . [THE PATRIOTS] WERE JUST ANOTHER TEAM AGAIN" (2002)

The Bledsoe/Brady debate fizzled a bit during the second half of the 2002 season, mostly because Bledsoe played poorly. His passing statistics decreased dramatically. Beginning Week 9, the Bills only won two games during a six-game stretch where Bledsoe threw seven touchdowns and eight interceptions. Teams had seen enough film on the Bills' offense and started to figure out ways to slow it down. Bledsoe had a hard time making reads, started making poorer decisions, and forced more throws.

Brady played better in the second half of the 2002 season and, at one point, New England won 5 out of 6 games. However, near season's end, the third-year QB reverted back to the poor form he showed during New England's winless October. His low point was when he threw for less than 150 yards and only one touchdown in back-to-back December games, both crucial losses, which practically destroyed the Patriots' playoff chances.

By season's end, despite a few rough December performances, Brady was starting to show that the Patriots' decision to keep him around in 2002 was the right one. Brady's biggest selling point was that the Patriots dominated Buffalo twice during the season. Collectively, during the two games, the Patriots outscored the Bills 65–24. Bledsoe played poorly in both. In the games, the Bills' offense only scored a combined four times in 20 possessions and turned the ball over six times. Four were Bledsoe interceptions during the second game. Meanwhile, Brady threw for a combined five touchdowns and zero interceptions in the two contests.

New England finished the 2002 season with a 9–7 record, while the Bills closed at 8–8. Both teams missed the playoffs. Despite the poor second half, Buffalo saw a five-win improvement from 2001.

Bledsoe set team single-season records in passing (4,359) and completions (375). Most around the league believed that the franchise was on a positive path. As for the Patriots, going from a Super Bowl victory to missing the playoffs altogether triggered some more negative commentary. Jackie MacMullan was blunt. "Just like that... [the Patriots] were just another team again," she wrote in the *Globe* a few days after the season ended. *Miami Herald* writer Tim Casey was on the same page. "Turns out, the Patriots' unlikely [2001 season] journey seems more and more like an aberration," he wrote.

Despite the disappointing final result, Brady still had a solid season statistically, throwing for 28 touchdowns and only 14 interceptions.

"BILL BELICHICK IS POND SCUM AGAIN. ARROGANT, MEGALOMANIACAL, DUPLICITOUS POND SCUM." (2003)

The 2003 season began inauspiciously for the Pats. In the opener, New England was throttled by Bledsoe and the Bills 31–0 at Ralph Wilson Stadium in Buffalo. Brady threw four interceptions and finished with a paltry 20.4 quarterback rating. It was the worst opening day loss in franchise history.

The humiliation at the hands of a Bledsoe-led Bills team was far from the most troubling part of the day. The Patriots were dealing with a bigger distraction that was amplified during and after the game. When Tom Brady stared across the field that Sunday, he saw safety Lawyer Milloy in a Bills uniform. Before 2003, Milloy had played seven seasons with the Patriots, had started 106 consecutive games, and was a key player during their Super Bowl run in the 2001 season.

Six days before that infamous 2003 opener in Buffalo, Milloy was still a member of the Patriots. He was at training camp and played for the Pats in their preseason games. However, he and Belichick were at odds. The Patriots wanted to restructure his contract in a way that would have resulted in a pay cut. Milloy wouldn't budge. According to reports, the Patriots wanted Milloy to take a pay cut from $4.4 million per year to $3 million. Milloy wanted $3.6 million. A mere $600,000 stood between the two parties.

Milloy soon found out that he didn't have as much leverage as he would have liked. New England was already on the books for a $5.25 million salary cap hit with Milloy, and he was coming off the least productive season of his career. The Patriots had also recently signed veteran safety Rodney Harrison from San Diego, and he had been impressive during training camp. He hit hard and brought an edginess that Belichick liked.

As the 2003 regular season approached, Belichick and Milloy were at a standstill. It wouldn't last much longer. On the Tuesday before the Patriots' opener, Belichick pulled the plug and released Milloy. The decision shocked and angered just about everyone, including the Patriots' locker room, the fans, and the media. The *Boston Herald*'s Kevin Mannix made no bones about how he thought Belichick handled the situation. "Bill Belichick is pond scum again," he wrote. "Arrogant, megalomaniacal, duplicitous pond scum."

The Milloy fallout was a distraction during the rest of the week. The veteran safety was a team leader and one of New England's most esteemed players. Right after the team caught wind of the release, Brady confronted Kraft, who had no idea of Belichick's plans, and asked the owner how he could let Belichick do it.

Milloy signed with the Bills a few days later, and, not long thereafter, he was on the field for the season opener in Buffalo, alongside Drew Bledsoe, on the opposite sideline as the Patriots. During pregame introductions, the Bills announced Milloy last to a raucous Ralph Wilson Stadium ovation. It was a sign of things to come. "[During the warmups and introductions], I'm just saying to myself 'oh my god, we are in trouble,'" Damien Woody remembered. "We had no chance that day."

"BILL BELICHICK BASHERS, TODAY IS YOUR DAY. PREPARE TO FEAST" (2003)

With the Patriots vulnerable, and in a distracted, awkward situation, the Bills destroyed them 31–0. Milloy played well. In the second quarter, he tipped one of Brady's passes in the end zone, which was then intercepted by Nate Clements. It was one of four interceptions Brady threw. Milloy also sacked Brady on a safety blitz near the end of the first half. "It was weird. Very weird," Milloy said after the game. "My mother always told me that God doesn't act ugly. I came out on top."

It was an amazing result for a franchise like Buffalo that had been down on their luck for the previous few years. "The script couldn't have been better if the Bills PR department had typed it up and faxed it over to the NFL office," wrote Eric McHugh in the (Quincy, Massachusetts) *Patriot Ledger*. Toward the end of the game, Bledsoe and Milloy were in a great mood and seen hugging, chatting, and looking up at the scoreboard. "We were talking about what you probably think we were talking about," Bledsoe told reporters. "We were both pretty happy with the win."

The loss was also the perfect storm for the media. "Second-guessers unite," wrote Michael Felger in the *Boston Herald*. "Bill Belichick bashers, today is your day. Prepare to feast. The Patriots' humiliating 31–0 loss to the Buffalo Bills is your piece of raw meat." And feast they did. "After the way [Milloy] played for the Buffalo Bills Sunday," wrote Borges in the *Boston Globe*, "maybe the

Patriots couldn't afford not to find a way to afford him. It's too late for that now." On HBO's *Inside the NFL*, analyst Cris Collinsworth compared the New England head coach to "a great doctor with a bad bedside manner." Collinsworth also expressed his bewilderment about the situation: "For [Belichick] to completely misread the pulse of that team and not understand what [Milloy] meant to the locker room, I can't believe he was that far removed from it."

Bill Simmons, an unabashed Boston sports fan, who, at the time, was a popular columnist and media personality with ESPN, wrote that Belichick pushing out Milloy was a disaster, and "indefensible." "They didn't save *that* much in cap space," he added. "It didn't make sense...Sometimes your team makes a move, you hear the news, and it makes you say 'Whaaaaaaaaaaat?????' That was the Milloy release." He continued: "Belichick...screwed up. Big time. Maybe it doesn't change the fact that he won a Super Bowl, but it makes you wonder about him. Just a little."

During the week after the Buffalo debacle, a sense of uneasiness seemed to permeate the Patriots' locker room. Linebacker Tedy Bruschi, one of the Patriots' longest tenured veterans, could not hold in his continuing disappointment about Milloy's release. "How do [I put my heart on the line] in a place where guys who've established what this team is about just come and go?" he asked *Sports Illustrated*'s Peter King. Bruschi was not the only one still troubled about the issue. An unnamed player posed these questions to a *Boston Herald* writer: "What kind of message do you think that sent everyone in here? What does that tell us about what [Belichick] values in a player? What do you think that tells us about what they want in the future?" The team's future, according to *Providence Journal* writer Tom Curran, was heading toward dangerous waters. "For the New England Patriots," he warned, "the next four months might...be as pleasant as an embolism."

Curran also considered the possibility that the relationship between Belichick and his players "may be irreparable." "You ask yourself," Curran wrote, "'Is this when it starts to go bad?'" Longtime ESPN commentator Tom Jackson had a similar line of thinking. The following Sunday after the Bills' blowout, the Hall of Fame offensive tackle said on ESPN's *Sunday NFL Countdown* pregame show that the "emotional devastation" the Patriots players suffered from the Milloy release could cost them their season. Jackson continued, "I want to say this very clearly... They hate their coach."

If Jackson was right, it didn't affect the New England players on that day. The Patriots destroyed the Eagles 31–10.

The Patriots players tried to brush off Jackson's comments. "It's just one outside opinion," said Richard Seymour. Rodney Harrison was a tad less circumspect. "I respect Tom Jackson, but that is one of the stupidest things I ever heard," he said. "He has no idea what we think about Belichick." Wide receiver David Patten was incredulous. "Who is Tom Jackson?" Patten asked a few days later. "Does he sit in at our meetings? Is he in our locker room?"

That loss in Buffalo was the last sign of any Patriots decline for a very long time. New England proceeded to win 14 out of their last 15 regular-season games in 2003, including 12 in a row to close out the regular season. A little over a month later, they captured their second championship title by beating the Carolina Panthers 32–29 in Super Bowl XXXVIII.

New England followed up its 2003 title with another one, the franchise's third, in 2004 as they beat the Eagles 24–21 in Super Bowl XXXIX. The next day, the headline on the front page of the *Boston Globe* simply read "DYNASTY."

Harrison, who took over at strong safety after Lawyer Milloy's release, turned out to be one of the most important players on the

2003 and 2004 championship teams. In both seasons, he led the team in tackles in the regular season and the playoffs. The locker room respected him so much that four months into the 2003 season he was chosen by his teammates as one of the team's captains. In the 2003 Playoffs, he forced three turnovers, including two big ones in the AFC Championship game against the Colts. In the 2004 Playoffs he forced two more, including an interception he returned for 87 yards for a touchdown during the AFC Championship game at Pittsburgh. Harrison went on to play four more seasons with New England, retiring in 2008. He is now considered to be one of the Patriots' most crucial free-agent signings of the Belichick era.

Meanwhile, Drew Bledsoe and the Bills never had any causes to celebrate, as his time with the franchise ended in a thud. Buffalo wasn't able to continue their momentum after the triumph over the Patriots in the 2003 opener, and finished the season 6–10. In 2004, the Bills went 9–7, but missed the postseason after losing a must-win contest in Pittsburgh on the final week of the regular season. Bledsoe played poorly in the game, which was mostly against the Steelers backups as they had already clinched home-field advantage throughout the playoffs. After the 2004 season, Bledsoe was released by the Bills after he refused head coach Mike Mularkey's request that Bledsoe relinquish his starting quarterback role in 2005 to become the backup for up-and-comer J. P. Losman.

"Mularkey and his assistants," wrote Leo Roth in the (Rochester, New York) *Democrat and Chronicle*, "came to the same conclusion most fans and media did with the naked eye: Bledsoe's time has passed."

In his three seasons in Buffalo, Bledsoe started all 48 games, finishing with a 23–25 record, and no playoff appearances. His passer rating declined in each of his second and third seasons. Bledsoe finished his career in Dallas, playing for his first head coach, Bill Parcells. In 2005, he signed a three-year, $23 million deal to be the Cowboys' primary starter. He started all 16 games for Dallas in the 2005 season, leading them to a 9–7 record but came just short of the playoffs. In 2006, he was so erratic and inconsistent that he was benched for young quarterback with tremendous potential: Tony Romo. Romo shined, and took ownership of the job for 10 years. Bledsoe hung up his cleats and retired in April 2007.

"F*CK YOU"

After the triumph over Philadelphia in Super Bowl XXXIX, Belichick was firmly entrenched in the all-time coaching elite. Meanwhile, Tom Jackson's 2003 comment has become infamous. "There is a temptation, especially from guys who played, to try to pretend like they are in [a team's locker room]," Matt Chatham, a linebacker for the Patriots from 2000 to 2005, said in 2020. "But to try to make some sweeping comment about [a group of] 53 men that you're not a part of, is so f*cking stupid to do."

Belichick ended up with the final word. In the 2020 book *The Dynasty*, author Jeff Benedict wrote that right after the Patriots won Super Bowl XXXVIII, their second win in franchise history, beating the Carolina Panthers 32–39 at Houston's Reliant Field, Belichick walked over to the ESPN on-field set for a postgame interview. When he arrived, Tom Jackson extended his hand to him. Belichick looked at Jackson and simply said, "F*ck you."

ACKNOWLEDGMENTS

This project was years in the making. Within six months of creating Freezing Cold Takes, I knew I wanted to write something in a longer form. There are interesting stories behind many of the unprophetic statements I have found throughout the years, and I wanted to share them. With Twitter limiting me to 240 characters per tweet, I couldn't provide much context for any of the posts on the Freezing Cold Takes page.

This book contains hours and hours of research, some of which dates back years from when I started searching for old, inaccurate commentary. Within weeks of starting this project, I knew that I had underestimated the amount of work and energy necessary to write a research-based book. Fortunately, I had tremendous support throughout the process. There is a group of people whose contributions deserve to be recognized.

To start, a hearty thank-you to Justin Spizman, lawyer and writer extraordinaire, who got the ball rolling, assisted me with my proposal, and connected me with John Willig, my agent, to whom I also owe a tremendous debt of gratitude. It didn't take long for John to find the perfect publishing match for me. Also, John advised me during each step of this process, kept me grounded, and made sure I kept my eyes on the prize.

My deep appreciation goes to the folks at Running Press Books, who have been wonderful in guiding me through this journey. In particular, I am tremendously grateful to my spectacular editor at Running Press, Jess Riordan, who turned my proposal into a reality and has had an unwavering belief in my idea, my vision, and me throughout this entire process.

To every journalist, former player, or anybody else who spoke with me for an interview or simply provided advice to a novice writer, thank you for giving me your valuable time.

The support I received during this endeavor extended beyond those directly involved with the publication. I must acknowledge and thank: my friends on the Alerts and Monsoon WhatsApp chat groups for all of your inspiration and for continuing to champion Freezing Cold Takes from the day it launched; my children Brady and Violet, who have provided me with endless amounts of motivation, as they continuously asked me when I would be done (they also proudly told everyone they saw that I was writing a book, which is cool); my brother Stephen and mother-in-law Joni, who have backed me from day one; my mother Ronna, who has been exceptionally supportive and positive about this whole project every time I speak with her, and who will probably buy 50 books before this is all said and done; and my dad Mike, who has been one of my volunteer editors for 30 years and has been my constant advisor from the proposal to the final copy.

My final debt of gratitude goes to my wife Nichole, another superb editor, who has watched me grind away at this for the past two years with unflinching patience and all the love in the world. This book would not exist without you by my side.

Chapter 1: "The Patriots Will Regret Hiring Bill Belichick" (2000 New England Patriots)

page 2: *The six-year contract that*: Bob Glauber, "Why Not Sooner?" (New York) *Newsday*, January 5, 2000.

page 2: *Just prior to stepping*: "12 Hours in Belichick's World," (Bridgewater, New Jersey) *Courier-News*, January 5, 2000.

page 2: *He cited the uncertainty*: Ibid.

page 2: *While Hess and Belichick*: Jake Nisse, "Bill Belichick somehow makes infamous Jets resignation sting worse," *New York Post*, November 10, 2020.

page 2: *The Patriots were looking*: Carlo DeVito, *Parcells, A Biography* (Chicago: Triumph, 2011), 305–306, Scribd.

page 2: *Just before Parcells*: Ibid., 306.

page 3: *However, in contrast to Parcells*: Jeff Benedict, *The Dynasty* (New York: Avid Reader Press, 2020), 113, Scribd.

page 3: *In January 1997*: DeVito, *Parcells*, 265.

page 3: *Since Parcells still*: Ibid., 264.

page 3: *NFL Commissioner Paul Tagliabue*: Rich Cimini and Wayne Coffey, "Tuna forced to stand pat," *New York Daily News*, January 30, 1997.

page 3: *After weeks of unsuccessful*: Rich Cimini, "Parcells comes home & this time it's for reel," *New York Daily News*, February 11, 1997.

page 3: *Three years later, when Belichick*: Rich Cimini, "Belichick bails after one day," *New York Daily News*, January 5, 2000.

page 4: *One of Belichick's prime concerns*: Ian O'Connor, *Belichick: The Making of the Greatest Football Coach of All Time* (Boston: Houghton Mifflin Harcourt, 2018), 276–277, Scribd.

page 4: *Despite Parcells's assurance that Belichick*: Ibid.

page 4: *"He bristles under that kind…"*: Author interview with Bob Glauber, May 12, 2020.

page 4: *"Especially…[with] an opportunity…"*: Ibid.

page 4: *Post columnist George Willis*: George Willis, "Belichick error thankfully over," *New York Post*, January 5, 2000.

page 4: *Willis wrote, "If the Patriots…"*: Ibid.

page 4: *Sports Illustrated's Peter King thought*: Peter King, "The eyes had it in Tennessee," CNNSI.com, January 10, 2000, https://web.archive.org/

web/20020209025645/http://sportsillustrated.cnn.com/inside_game /peter_king/news/2000/01/10/mmqb/ (accessed December 3, 2021); Peter King, "Still adrift, but opinionated: Bob Kraft should shun Belichick," CNNSI.com, January 27, 2000, https://web.archive.org/web/200202080 20725/http://sportsillustrated.cnn.com/inside_game/peter_king/news /2000/01/26/ten_things/ (accessed December 3, 2021).

page 5: *"That yellow line isn't..."*: Jeff Jacobs, "There is no defense for gutless reversal," *Hartford Courant*, January 5, 2000.

page 5: *"It's the color of Belichick's..."*: Ibid.

page 5: *A few weeks later, after Johnson & Johnson heir*: Jeff Jacobs, "Replay it all you want, call still wrong," *Hartford Courant*, January 12, 2000.

page 5: *"Better they find out now..."*: Adrian Wojnarowski, "Resignations leave team in confusion," (North Jersey) *Record*, January 5, 2000.

page 5: *"Belichick belongs..."*: Ibid.

page 5: *He called Belichick*: Ian O'Connor, "A bizarre move by a disheveled man," (Westchester, New York) *Journal News*, January 5, 2000.

page 5: *"He was more negative..."*: Paul Doyle, "A coach's road from failure to genius," *Hartford Courant*, February 6, 2005.

page 5: *"Guys would hate coming to work..."*: Ibid.

page 5: *In the* Dayton (Ohio) Daily News: Greg Simms, "Belichick still scared," *Dayton (Ohio) Daily News*, January 9, 2000.

page 6: *In a column skewering*: Terry Pluto, "No Mr. Bill? Fans of Jets," *Akron (Ohio) Beacon Journal*, January 6, 2000.

page 6: *"Consider Belichick little more..."*: Filip Bondy, "Kraft-y move by Belichick," *New York Daily News*, January 5, 2000.

page 6: *"He is, after all..."*: Ibid.

page 6: *Glauber, in* Newsday: Glauber, "Why Not Sooner?"

page 6: *"He had the perfect..."*: Ibid.

page 6: *In the* Record: John Rowe, "Ungrateful Belichick, lost at sea," (North Jersey) *The Record*, January 9, 2000.

page 6: *"Even if Parcells doesn't..."*: Ibid.

page 6: *Kraft told* Sports Illustrated: Peter King, "Robert Kraft Made a 'Mistake' and Turned it into a Dynasty," *Sports Illustrated*, January 30, 2017, https://www.si.com/nfl/2017/01/30/robert-kraft-patriots-nfl-super -bowl-51-falcons-peter-king (accessed February 24, 2022).

page 6: *Kraft also admitted*: Ibid.

page 6: *Nobody thought it was*: Ibid.

page 6: *He even had media*: Ibid.

page 7: *With the NFL prohibiting*: Gary Myers, "Belichick to file NFL grievance," *New York Daily News*, January 5, 2000.

page 7: *"Why any team would..."*: Dan Pompei, "There is no sane reason for all the fuss over Belichick," *Sporting News*, January 17, 2000.

page 7: *Pompei also hypothesized*: Ibid.

page 7: *"Just because Belichick is…"*: Ibid.

page 7: *"If I'm…Bob Kraft"*: Peter King, "Still adrift, but opinionated: Bob Kraft should shun Belichick," CNNSI.com, January 27, 2000, https://web.archive .org/web/20020208020725/http://sportsillustrated.cnn.com/inside_game /peter_king/news/2000/01/26/ten_things/ (accessed December 3, 2021).

page 7: *King didn't understand*: Ibid.

page 7: *"[Former Carolina Panthers head coach]…"*: Ibid.

page 7: *"Kraft could be headed…"*: Garry Brown, "Belichick would be the wrong call," (Springfield, Massachusetts) *Union-News*, January 7, 2000.

page 7: *"That would be…"*: Ibid.

page 7: *The Patriots gave up*: Rich Cimini, "Tuna, Kraft agree to bury hatchet," *New York Daily News*, January 28, 2000.

page 8: *"I'm kind of a little surprised"*: Bob Duffy, "Mixed reviews from around the league," *Boston Globe*, January 28, 2000.

page 8: *"Giving up a No. 1…"*: Ibid.

page 8: *In the (Rochester, New York)* Democrat and Chronicle: Bob Matthews, "Patriots gave up too much to obtain Belichick," (Rochester, New York) *Democrat and Chronicle*, January 29, 2000.

page 8: *Boston-based radio host Ted*: Jon Couture, "Here's what experts thought of the Patriots hiring Bill Belichick in 2000," Boston.com, January 27, 2019.

page 8: *The* Boston Herald's *Karen Guregian*: Author interview with Karen Guregian, May 9, 2020.

page 8: *Among them: Vince Lombardi*: Karen Guregian, "Pats get their man, Bill just not the ticket," *Boston Herald*, January 28, 2000.

page 8: *Belichick, she concluded*: Ibid.

page 8: *"Sorry folks. Bill Belichick…"*: Ibid.

page 8: *Ian O'Connor, in a*: Ian O'Connor, "Patriots will regret hiring Belichick," (Westchester, New York) *Journal News*, January 28, 2000.

page 8: *"Soon enough," O'Connor added…*: Ibid.

page 9: *"It's turned out to be…"*: Author interview with Karen Guregian, May 9, 2020.

page 9: *"I didn't think he had…"*: Hayden Bird, "A New York sports writer looks back on writing 'Patriots will regret hiring Belichick," Boston.com, January 12, 2017, https://www.boston.com/sports/new-england-patriots /2017/01/12/a-new-york-sports-writer-looks-back-on-writing-patriots -will-regret-hiring-belichick/ (accessed January 6, 2022).

page 9: *With respect to his*: Ibid.

page 9: *In a twist of fate*: O'Connor, *Belichick: The making of the greatest football coach of all time*.

page 9: *"I'm fascinated by how…"*: Ibid.

page 9: *She now believes*: Author interview with Karen Guregian, May 9, 2020.

page 9: *He wrote a column*: Filip Bondy, "Media declare bill of wrongs," *New York Daily News*, February 3, 2005.

page 10: *Bondy posited that*: Ibid.

page 10: *He continued: "Who wanted this…"*: Ibid.

page 10: *"Parcells, who remains…"*: Bill Livingston, "Belichick mumbles an ode to loyalty," *Cleveland Plain Dealer*, January 9, 2000.

page 10: *"Big Tuna would have…"*: Ibid.

page 10: *"It was one of…"*: Author interview with Bob Glauber, May 12, 2020.

page 10: *"I would be the first…"*: Filip Bondy, email message to author, May 7, 2020.

page 10: *"During my long…"*: Ibid.

page 11: *"If there was any proof…"*: Bondy, "Media declare bill of wrongs," February 3, 2005.

Chapter 2: "Trade Dan Marino. Keep Scott Mitchell" (1993 Miami Dolphins)

page 13: *"Trade Dan Marino. Keep Scott Mitchell."*: Greg Cote, "The unthinkable: A trade of Marino," *Miami Herald*, November 1, 1993.

page 15: *Ahead of Miami's upcoming*: Stephen Edelson, "Mitchell looking a lot like Marino," *Asbury Park (New Jersey) Press*, November 5, 1993.

page 15: *"Sometimes you look…"*: Paul Needell, "Great Scott! Miami doesn't miss a beat," *New York Daily News*, November 4, 1993.

page 15: *The day after the Chiefs*: Cote, "The unthinkable: A trade of Marino."

page 15: *In the piece, Cote lamented…*: Ibid.

page 15: *Additionally, he noted…*: Ibid.

page 15: *With Mitchell playing so well…*: Ibid.

page 16: *"I instantly knew what I had written…"*: Author interview with Greg Cote, September 15, 2020.

page 16: *That same day, in the afternoon*: George Diaz, "No one is sacred in sports—football players, sports writers," *Orlando Sentinel*, November 5, 1993.

page 16: *The interview with Cote*: Ibid.

page 16: *As a joke, Cote's face*: Author interview with Greg Cote, September 15, 2020.

page 16: *When he was introduced*: Ibid.

page 16: *"I think they should trade…"*: "Quarterback Audible," (Fort Lauderdale) *Sun-Sentinel*, November 10, 1993.

page 16: *"We have a future…"*: Ibid.

page 16: *A few days later*: Armando Salguero, "Why Marino isn't going anywhere," *Miami Herald*, November 7, 1993.

page 17: *One NFL GM*: Ibid.

page 17: *"It does make some sense"*: "Trading Marino makes sense now," Associated Press, November 2, 1993.

page 17: *"Privately, he probably thought..."*: Author interview with Greg Cote, September 15, 2020.

page 17: *"I've only been out two games..."*: Patrick McManamon, "Stop making sense: Marino trade talks not realistic," *Palm Beach Post*, November 2, 1993.

page 17: *"From a logical standpoint..."*: Ibid.

page 17: *"But from a realistic..."*: Ibid.

page 17: *"There was all kinds..."*: Author interview with Scott Mitchell, May 12, 2020.

page 17: *"The Dolphins had been..."*: Ibid.

page 17: *"No, no, no... not in..."*: Author interview with O. J. McDuffie, October 13, 2020.

page 17: *Later in the week*: Diaz, "No one is sacred in sports."

page 18: *In a follow-up column*: Greg Cote, "About that trade..." *Miami Herald*, November 5, 1993.

page 18: *"I am not an animal!"*: Ibid.

page 18: *"He was not championing..."*: Ibid.

page 18: *"All I'm saying, bottom line..."*: Ibid.

page 18: *"Thank God for one thing"*: Charles Bricker, "Good, we can get off from trade-Marino rot," (Fort Lauderdale) *Sun-Sentinel*, November 9, 1993.

page 18: *"Scott Mitchell's soiree..."*: Ibid.

page 18: *"Whoever wrote that better..."*: Herald Staff, "Esiason: Trade Marino? You are joking, right?," *Miami Herald*, November 8, 1993.

page 18: *"One of the main reasons..."*: Ibid.

page 18: *"I could barely pick"*: Author interview with Scott Mitchell, May 12, 2020.

page 19: *Mitchell did become*: Curt Sylvester, "Lions like what they see, sign Mitchell," *Detroit Free Press*, March 7, 1994.

page 19: *It included a $5 million*: Ibid.

page 19: *At the press conference*: Charlie Vincent, "Great Scott?" *Detroit Free Press*, March 8, 1994.

page 19: *"I had really good years..."*: Author interview with Scott Mitchell, May 12, 2020.

page 19: *"We made the playoffs..."*: Ibid.

page 20: *"If you really understand..."*: Ibid.

page 20: *"The Lions' signing of"*: "Worst Free Agent Signings." *NFL Top 10*. Episode 72, NFL Network, 2011.

page 20: *"Scott Mitchell just..."*: Ibid.

page 20: *"He wasn't as bad..."*: Ibid.

page 20: *"People forget just…"*: Ibid.

page 20: *"In our play-by-play…"*: Ibid.

page 20: *"The way it turned out…"*: Greg Cote, "Revisiting my infamous 'trade Marino' column, 22 years later," Greg Cote's Random Evidence Blog, MiamiHerald.com, March 5, 2016. https://blogs.herald.com/random _evidence/2016/03/xxx-xx.html (accessed November 24, 2021).

page 20: *"Look, they weren't winning"*: Author interview with Greg Cote, September 15, 2020.

page 21: *"It's frustrating because…"*: Author interview with Scott Mitchell, May 12, 2020.

page 21: *"It's just that being…"*: Ibid.

page 21: *"Had I not got injured…"*: Ibid.

page 21: *"Especially of we go…"*: Ibid.

page 21: *"I'm gonna play…"*: Ibid.

page 21: *"Being in the same…"*: Ibid.

Chapter 3: "Chip Kelly Is the Answer to Our City's Prayer" (2013–2015 Philadelphia Eagles)

page 23: *Kelly's offense at Oregon was*: Jason Wolf, "Eagles prepare to debut innovative signs of the times," *USA Today*, September 9, 2013; Duke Ho, "Trojans set focus on speed," DailyTrojan.com, October 19, 2010, https:// dailytrojan.com/2010/10/19/trojans-set-focus-on-speed/ (accessed November 29, 2021).

page 23: *Most no-huddle offenses take*: Ho, "Trojans set focus on speed."

page 23: *Oregon, at its fastest, averaged*: David Wharton, "Webbed fleet," *Los Angeles Times*, August 6, 2011.

page 24: *Centered on tempo, Kelly's offense*: Paul Domowitch, "Eagles coach a Chip off the old inventions," *Philadelphia Daily News*, September 6, 2013.

page 24: *One concept he frequently*: Jeff McLane, "Keeping it simple pays off for Vick," *Philadelphia Inquirer*, August 18, 2013.

page 24: *With an RPO, the quarterback*: Robert Mays, "The RPO Takeover Isn't Complete Just Yet," The Ringer, August 14, 2018, https://www.theringer .com/nfl/2018/8/14/17687896/run-pass-option-evolution-chiefs-eagles -college-offense (accessed September 20, 2021).

page 24: *There have been teams in*: Chris Brown, "The Future of the NFL: More Up-tempo No-huddle," SmartFootball.com, http://smartfootball.com /offense/the-future-of-the-nfl-more-up-tempo-no-huddle#sthash.bp4 NoDM8.kQxQZ4OW.dpbs (accessed September 20, 2021).

page 24: *But by 2013, only Peyton*: Ibid.

page 24: *Most teams in the NFL did not*: Ibid.

page 24: *So much so that it was*: Tim McManus, "Eagles Wake-Up Call: Chip Won't Commit," Phillymag.com, January 7, 2013. https://www.phillymag .com/birds247/2013/01/07/eagles-wake-up-call-chip-wont-commit/ (accessed September 20, 2021).

page 24: *and viewed by some as*: John Kincade (@JohnKincade), "No to Chip Kelly for the Eagles. No gimmick offense college coaches that want to 'try it' in NFL. Google Steve Spurrier," Twitter, December 31, 2012, 8:20, a.m., https://twitter.com/JohnKincade/status/285737183439097856?s=20 (accessed July 18, 2021).

page 25: *"They told us they…"*: *Monday Night Football*, September 9, 2013, aired on ESPN.

page 26: *"Keep in mind these…"*: Kirk Herbstreit (@KirkHerbstreit), "Look at that hole!!! Keep in mind these vaunted NFL Defensive Coordinators have had 8 months to slow down this "gimmick college offense," Twitter, September 9, 2013, 8:42 p.m., https://twitter.com/KirkHerbstreit/status /377230660853071872?s=20 (accessed September 20, 2021).

page 26: *"NFL GMs are sitting…"*: Matt Miller (@nfldraftscout), "NFL GMs are sitting at home drooling over this Chip Kelly offense, and they're gonna want Marcus Mariota to run it for their team," Twitter, September 9, 2013, 8:38 p.m., https://twitter.com/nfldraftscout/status/377229636188 372993?s=20 (accessed September 20, 2021).

page 26: *"Wow, you think Chip…"*: Donovan McNabb (@donovanjmcnabb), "Wow, you think Chip Kelly's offense will work in the NFL? You have your answer now," Twitter, September 9, 2013, 8:43 p.m., https://twitter.com /donovanjmcnabb/status/377230841157414913?s=20 (accessed September 20, 2021).

page 26: *"I kept hearing…"*: Trent Dilfer (@DilfersDimes), "I kept hearing (and strongly disagreeing) all off-season that NFL D coaches would figure out this Saturday offense. Uhmm…I don't think so," Twitter, September 9, 2013, 8:48 p.m., https://twitter.com/DilfersDimes/status/3772320 14287437824?s=20 (accessed September 20, 2021).

page 27: *"Man, every def coordinator…"*: Danny Kanell (@dannykanell), "Man, every def coordinator who has Philly on their schedule is gonna have nightmares tonight. #boogieman," Twitter, September 9, 2013, 9:20 p.m., https://twitter.com/dannykanell/status/377240157893566464?s=20 (accessed September 20, 2021).

page 27: *"This is not an 'after one game'…"*: Lance Zierlein (@LanceZierlein), "This is not an 'after one game' thought. Many of us who followed Oregon knew Chip Kelly's tempo was going to mean to the NFL," Twitter, September 10, 2013, 9:22 a.m., https://twitter.com/LanceZierlein/status /377421857806221313?s=20 (accessed September 20, 2021).

page 27: *"When I talk to guys…"*: Albert Breer (@AlbertBreer), "When I talk to guys who have coached with or against Chip Kelly, the most common reason they think he'll succeed is 'he's too smart to fail,'" Twitter, September 10, 2013, 8:56 a.m., https://twitter.com/AlbertBreer/status/37741 5256953618432?s=20 (accessed September 20, 2021).

page 27: *"Happy National Chip Kelly"*: Bill Reiter (@sportsreiter). "Happy National Chip Kelly NFL Offensive Revolution Day," Twitter, September 9, 2013, 9:16 p.m., https://twitter.com/sportsreiter/status/377239179341 484032?s=20 (accessed September 20, 2021).

page 27: *"Just wait until Chip Kelly"*: Dennis Dodd (@dennisdoddcbs), "Just wait until Chip Kelly gets his quarterback," Twitter, September 9, 2013, 8:51 p.m., https://twitter.com/dennisdoddcbs/status/377232887256723456?s =20 (accessed September 20, 2021).

page 27: *"That sound u hear…"*: Booger McFarland (@ESPNBooger), "That sound u hear is The phone ringing of any spread up tempo offensive coach in college football," Twitter, September 9, 2013, 8:43 p.m., https://twitter .com/ESPNBooger/status/377230741471789056?s=20 (accessed September 20, 2021).

page 28: *"A THING OF DEBUTY"*: "A THING OF DEBUTY," *Philadelphia Daily News*, September 10, 2013.

page 28: *In* Business Insider, *sports*: Tony Manfred, "The NFL Is Freaking Out Over Chip Kelly, the Eagles Coach who Could Change Pro Football Forever," *Business Insider*, September 10, 2013, https://www.businessinsider. com.au/chip-kelly-offense-could-change-nfl-forever-2013-9 (accessed September 20, 2021).

page 28: *Later that week*: John George, "Philadelphia Eagles ticket demand soars after fast start," *Philadelphia Business Journal*, September 13, 2013, https://www.bizjournals.com/philadelphia/news/2013/09/13/demand -for-eagles-tickets-soars.html (accessed September 20, 2021).

page 28: *"The Eagles offense isn't…"*: ESPN Radio (@ESPNRadio), "Hear @ ESPN_Colin #intheHERD: The Eagles offense isn't a fad. They're technology advancing…and we're NEVER going back to dial-up!" Twitter, September 10, 2013, 10:04 a.m., https://twitter.com/espnradio/status/377432 374897696768?s=21 (accessed September 21, 2021).

page 28: *"They're technology advancing…"*: Ibid.

page 28: *"I love it"*: Jarrett Bell, "Kelly sets his own pace," *USA Today*, September 10, 2013.

page 28: *"That was thoroughly impressive…"*: Ibid.

page 28: Toronto Star *columnist*: Cathal Kelly, "Chip Kelly changing the NFL forever," *Toronto Star*, September 16, 2013.

page 28: *"[The Eagles' win] changed…"*: Chris Wesseling, "Is Chip Kelly's Eagles offense revolutionizing the NFL?" NFL.com, September 19, 2013, https://www.nfl.com/news/is-chip-kelly-s-eagles-offense-revolutionizing-the-nfl-0ap2000000247341 (accessed September 21, 2021).

page 28: *"It was spectacular…"*: Ben Volin, "So far, Patriots have not been a driving force," *Boston Globe*, September 15, 2013.

page 28: *"In this offense…"*: Ibid.

page 29: *"These three guys…"*: Ibid.

page 29: *Included in Cataldi's* Metro Philadelphia: Angelo Cataldi, "Chip Kelly Saving Philly Sports," *Metro Philadelphia*, September 11, 2013.

page 30: *"The rest of the NFC…"*: Matt Mullin (@matt_mullin), "Rest of the NFC East should be concerned by this: Chip Kelly isn't going anywhere, and he's only going to get better," Twitter, January 3, 2014, 12:02 p.m., https://twitter.com/matt_mullin/status/419151673492119552?s=20 (accessed January 9, 2022).

page 30: *"A few days after the…"*: Sports Radio 94WIP (@SportsRadioWIP), "[The Eagles] will win a Super Bowl with Chip Kelly. It's going to happen [eventually],"—@RealGlenMacnow, http://bit.ly/94listen, Twitter, January 2, 2014, 10:15 a.m., https://twitter.com/SportsRadioWIP/status/4187624 95344803840?s=20 (accessed September 21, 2021).

page 31: *Cataldi maintained the rosy*: Angelo Cataldi, "Eagles have stability, winning ways with Kelly," *Metro Philadelphia*, January 6, 2014.

page 31: *In* Metro Philadelphia: Mike Greger, "Lurie's gamble on Kelly pays off for Eagles," *Metro Philadephia*, January 5, 2014.

page 31: *In addition (as described…)*: Matt Lombardo, "Former Eagles front office executive: Chip Kelly alienated scouts 'almost immediately,'" NJ.com, January 16, 2019, https://www.nj.com/eagles/2016/03/former_eagles_front _office_executive_chip_kelly_al.html (accessed September 21, 2021).

page 31: *According to a former*: Ibid.

page 32: *Infuriated, Kelly convinced*: Ibid.

page 32: *He even traded Foles*: Fox Sports: NFL (@NFLonFOX), "He's the starting QB for the next 1,000 years here"—Chip Kelly names Nick Foles the Eagles' quarterback through at least 3013," Twitter, December 2, 2013, 5:05 p.m., https://twitter.com/NFLonFOX/status/407631686453559 296?s=20 (accessed September 21, 2021).

page 33: *From then on, the Eagles*: Jeff McLane, "Tempo Secondary to Production," *Philadelphia Inquirer*, January 3, 2014.

page 33: *His drastic roster decisions*: "Report: Kelly's lack of 'people skills ruined holiday party, strained relationship with Lurie," PhillyVoice.com, January 3, 2016, https://www.phillyvoice.com/eagles-chip-kelly-people -skills-lurie-christmas-party/ (accessed September 21, 2021).

page 33: *Numerous people*: Reuben Frank and Dave Zangaro, hosts, "#220 Eagles legend Merrill Reese joins the pod," *Eagle Eye: A Philadelphia Eagles Podcast*, episode 220, NBC Sports Philly, May 21, 2020, https://podcasts

.apple.com/us/podcast/eagle-eye-a-philadelphia-eagles-podcast/id137
6641140.

page 33: *Merrill Reese, the play-by-play*: Ibid.

page 33: *"He was the worst communicator"*: Ibid.

page 33: *Cornerback Brandon Boykin*: Jared Dubin, "Brandon Boykin: Chip
Kelly not racist, but has trouble relating to players," CBSSports.com, August 2, 2015, https://www.cbssports.com/nfl/news/brandon-boykin-chip
-kelly-not-racist-but-has-trouble-relating-to-players/ (accessed September 21, 2021).

page 34: *A few months before*: Elliot Shorr-Parks, "Ex-Eagles coach says
players in locker room sense 'a hint of racism,'" NJ.com, March 10, 2015,
https://www.nj.com/eagles/2015/03/ex-eagles_coach_says_players_in
_locker_room_sense.html (accessed September 21, 2021).

page 34: *While Chip's offensive "revolution"*: Tim McManus, "Eagles pull from
Chip Kelly playbook to awaken 2013 Nick Foles," ESPN.com, January 26,
2018, https://www.espn.com/blog/philadelphia-eagles/post/_/id/24097
/eagles-pull-from-chip-kelly-playbook-to-awaken-2013-nick-foles
(accessed July 19, 2021).

page 34: *Although not the first coach*: Nick Fierro, "Run or pass? Eagles, Foles
have options," *Baltimore Sun*, February 2, 2018.

page 34: *Since 2013, the RPO has*: Mays, "The RPO Takeover Isn't Complete
Just Yet."

page 34: *Kelly's successor in Philadelphia*: McManus, "Eagles pull from Chip
Kelly playbook."

page 34: *In 2017, when Eagles starting quarterback Carson*: Ibid.

page 35: *In 2014, an NFL Films*: Andrew Porter, "Video: Kelly, Foles, Sanchez
Mic'd Up Vs. Giants," CBS Philly, October 16, 2014, https://philadelphia
.cbslocal.com/2014/10/16/video-kelly-foles-sanchez-micd-up-vs-giants/
(accessed November 8, 2021).

Chapter 4: "How Could the Ravens Pass Up Lawrence Phillips, Take OT Jonathan Ogden, and Draft 'Smallish' Ray Lewis?" (1996 Baltimore Ravens)

page 37: *"A"—that's the grade*: Rick Gosselin, "Team-By-Team Analysis," *Dallas Morning News*, April 20, 1998.

page 37: *In 2001, the* Arizona Republic: Kent Somers, "Rams make all the right
moves," *Arizona Republic*, April 23, 2001.

page 37: *In 2005*, Florida Today: Carl Kotala, "NFC draft grades," *Florida Today*, April 27, 2005.

page 38: *Many thought he had*: Arnie Stapleton, "Packers digging for draft
gold," Associated Press, April 20, 1996.

page 38: *Going into his junior*: Jim Corbett, "Jets banking on Johnson as key to their turnaround," Gannett News Service, April 20, 1996.

page 38: *However, after an early September*: Margaret Reist and Ken Hambleton, "Phillips enters plea; Benning exonerated," (Lincoln, Nebraska) *Journal Star*, September 20, 1995.

page 38: *Phillips proceeded to drag her*: Ibid.

page 39: *Eventually, he pled no contest*: Ibid.

page 39: *After six games without Phillips*: Steve Sipple, "NU players welcome back Phillips," (Lincoln, Nebraska) *Journal Star*, October 25, 1995.

page 39: *"Shining moment is tainted"*: Jason Whitlock, "Shining moment is tainted," *Kansas City Star*, January 3, 1996.

page 39: Baltimore Sun *staff writer*: Don Markus, "Sour notes outnumber triumphs," *Baltimore Sun*, January 5, 1996.

page 39: *Going into the 1996*: Gary Lambrecht, "Ravens may seek trade to get Phillips," *Baltimore Sun*, April 12, 1996.

page 40: *Before the draft, the Ravens*: Mike Preston, "Ravens opt to line up with Ogden," *Baltimore Sun*, April 21, 1996.

page 40: *Most mock drafts had him*: Ibid.

page 40: *The Ravens were preparing to choose*: Ibid.

page 40: *They passed on Phillips*: Ibid.

page 40: *Apparently, part of the reason*: Len Pasquarelli, "NFL Draft, day one at a glance," *Atlanta Journal-Constitution*, April 21, 1996.

page 40: *While he was a well-respected prospect*: Ray Lewis, with Daniel Paisner, *I Feel Like Going On: Life, Game, and Glory* (New York: Atria, 2016), 144–149, Scribd.

page 40: *"He didn't have the ideal…"*: Jamison Hensley, "Sizing up a legend: Inside Ray Lewis' draft-day slide to the Ravens," ESPN.com. February 2, 2018, https://www.espn.com/blog/baltimore-ravens/post/_/id/42671 /inside-ray-lewis-fall-to-the-ravens-and-beginning-of-a-hall-of-fame -career (accessed September 17, 2021).

page 41: *"There's a feeling that…"*: Ibid.

page 41: *He admitted that*: Ken Rosenthal, "…but if not for Bidwill, Modell would've strayed," *Baltimore Sun*, April 21, 1996.

page 41: *Even after Arizona*: Preston, "Ravens opt to line up with Ogden."

page 41: *According to Hank Goldberg*: NFL Draft, April 20, 1996, aired on ESPN.

page 41: *"If it helps our team"*: Rosenthal, "…but if not for Bidwill."

page 41: *He made sure to point out*: Preston, "Ravens opt to line up with Ogden."

page 42: *According to Modell*: Bernie Miklasz, "Tale of Two Teams: Blues, Rams Making Headlines," *St. Louis Post-Dispatch*, April 27, 1996.

page 42: *"That doesn't excuse…"*: Ibid.

page 42: *"This was the love…"*: Ibid.

page 42: Tampa Bay Times *NFL reporter*: Rick Stroud, "Rams, Bucs, Oilers make power picks," *Tampa Bay Times*, April 21, 1996.

page 42: Miami Herald *columnist*: Greg Cote, "NFL Draft/Grading the Teams," *Miami Herald*, April 22, 1996.

page 43: *The* Chicago Sun-Times *asked*: Dan Pompei, "Weak Teams Find Strength in Draft," *Chicago Sun-Times*, April 23, 1996.

page 43: *Len Pasquarelli, an* Atlanta Journal-Constitution: Len Pasquarelli, "Rams, Bucs fare best; Jets worst despite top pick," *Atlanta Journal-Constitution*, April 22, 1996.

page 43: Los Angeles Times *columnist*: Bill Plaschke, "Edwards' News is a day late," *Los Angeles Times*, April 22, 1996.

page 43: *"We thought Art Modell…"*: Ibid.

page 43: *"Phillips should have been…"*: Ibid.

page 43: *Randy Lange, a reporter for*: Randy Lange, "Randy Lange's AFC draft analysis," (North Jersey) *Record*, April 28, 1996.

page 43: *"Lewis," Lange wrote, "like [linebacker]…"*: Ibid.

page 43: *Stroud wrote in his next*: Stroud, "Rams, Bucs, Oilers."

page 43: *Plaschke was also lukewarm*: Plaschke, "Edwards' News is a day late."

page 43: *"I really believe that this…"*: NFL Draft, April 20, 1996, aired on ESPN.

page 43: *"I still believe that…"*: Ibid.

page 44: *"It's too deep a year…"*: Ibid.

page 44: *He told Kiper*: Ibid.

page 44: *"We obviously don't…"*: Lorraine Kee, "Running into Trouble?" *St. Louis Post-Dispatch*, April 21, 1996.

page 44: *Banks was thought to have*: Jim Thomas, "Rams Are Putting Quarterback Investment in A Banks," *St. Louis Post-Dispatch*, April 21, 1996.

page 45: *Nevertheless, Brooks saw him as*: Ibid.

page 45: *Pasquarelli gave the Rams*: Pasquarelli, "Rams, Bucs fare best."

page 45: *Stroud listed St. Louis*: Stroud, "Rams, Bucs, Oilers."

page 45: *Stroud also added that*: Ibid.

page 45: *Like many others, he lauded*: Plaschke, "Edwards' News is a day late."

page 45: *Plaschke also gushed that*: Ibid.

page 45: *"Instant offense with RB…"*: Mike O'Hara, "Team by team grades on the draft," *USA Today*, April 21, 1996.

page 45: *"Grade A-minus"*: Ibid.

page 45: *Vinny DiTrani, in the* Record: Vinny DiTrani, "Vinny DiTrani's NFC draft analysis," (North Jersey) *Record*, April 28, 1996.

page 45: *The* Buffalo News's *Milt Northrop*: Milt Northrop, "Four NFC Clubs Get Top Grades, Bills 'C' May Stand For Curious," *Buffalo News*, April 22, 1996.

page 45: *"St. Louis had the nerve…"*: Ibid.

page 45: *The* Dallas Morning News *called*: Miklasz, "Tale of Two Teams."

page 45: *"Could a team have done…"*: Pompei, "Weak Teams Find Strength in Draft."

page 45: *"They got the best…"*: Ibid.

page 47: *Soon after, he was signed*: Jeff Shain, "Dolphins release Phillips," Associated Press, July 26, 1998.

page 47: *to which he eventually pled*: Matthew Stanmyre, "Former NFL running back Lawrence Phillips suspected of killing cellmate," NJ.com, April 14, 2015, https://www.nj.com/giants/2015/04/former_nfl_college_football _star_lawrence_phillips.html (accessed September 18, 2021).

page 47: *But after struggling on the field*: Dennis Georgatos, "Phillips surprised by suspension," Associated Press, November 18, 1999.

page 47: *he was released by the Niners*: John Crumpacker, "49ers cut and run from Phillips," *San Francisco Examiner*, November 24, 1999.

page 48: *"We do not—especially…"*: David Ginsburg, "NFL DRAFT: Ravens to employ tested formula with first-round pick," Associated Press, April 26, 2007.

page 48: *"We factor who's the best player"*: Ibid.

page 48: *"Ozzie is the foundation…"*: Aaron Wilson, "Ozzie Newsome learned from Bill Belichick, Ernie Accorsi," *Baltimore Sun*, January 27, 2013.

page 48: *"Although there is a…"*: "Exploring Ozzie Newsome's Declining Draft Results," FoxSports.com, June 30, 2017, https://www.foxsports.com /stories/nfl/exploring-ozzie-newsomes-declining-draft-results (accessed March 23, 2022).

Chapter 5: "I'm Telling You, [the Chargers] Have Something Special Here [with Ryan Leaf]" (Preseason Performance Traps)

page 51: *Ryan Mallett, a tall*: Mac Engel, "Razorbacks QB ends up right where he started," *Fort Worth Star-Telegram*, September 25, 2010.

page 51: *However, during the 2011*: "Heady times for Ryan Mallett," Associated Press, May 8, 2011.

page 51: *Facing mostly the Jaguars'*: Howard Ulman, "Gabbert Inconsistent in NFL debut for Jaguars," Associated Press, August 12, 2011.

page 51: *NFL Network analyst Bucky Brooks*: Bucky Brooks, "Mallett, Kolb among QBs who shined in preseason debut," NFL.com, August 12, 2011. https://www.nfl.com/news/mallett-kolb-among-qbs-who-shined-in -preseason-debut-09000d5d821688d6 (accessed November 22, 2021).

page 51: *ESPN NFL reporter Chris Mortensen relayed*: Chris Mortensen (@mortreport), "RT @BrandonHartung: how many teams wish they had drafted Mallett already? >> He's in a good spot but already had 1 GM 2nd-guessing himself," Twitter, August 12, 2011, 10:01 p.m., https://twitter

.com/mortreport/status/1021979877798827008?s=20 (accessed November 22, 2021).

page 51: *Fox Sports' NFL writer Peter Schrager*: Peter Schrager (@PSchrags), "Five months after the fact, still shocked and disturbed over Andy Dalton being taken before Ryan Mallett. Everyone was ok with that. Unreal," Twitter, August 12, 2011, 7:58 p.m., https://twitter.com/PSchrags/status /102167053896646656?s=20 (accessed September 11, 2021).

page 51: *To Schrager, the Arkansas*: Peter Schrager (@PSchrags), "Ryan Mallett will have another fantastic outing tonight. The fact he slipped to the third round is MIND BOGGLING. I'll say it every week," Twitter, August 18, 2011, 6:45 p.m., https://twitter.com/PSchrags/status/104323120 978083840?s=20 (accessed September 11, 2021).

page 52: *But unlike the previous example*: Matt Miller (@nfldraftscout), "Would #Bills fans love EJ Manuel this much if the #Jets had drafted him? Doubt it. Realize you drafted a project," Twitter, April 26, 2013, 12:13 p.m., https://twitter.com/nfldraftscout/status/327817629588930560?s=20 (accessed September 11, 2021).

page 52: *"Finally, the Bills…"*: Adam Schein (@AdamSchein), "Finally, the Bills have their QB in @EJManuel3," Twitter, August 12, 2011, http:// thecomeback.com/freezingcoldtakes/nfl/in-2013-after-two-2nd-half -preseason-appearances-many-were-bullish-on-the-ej-manuel-era -in-buffalo.html (Tweet has since been deleted).

page 52: *"EJ Manuel has command…"*: Natalie Pierre (@NataliePierre_), "Warren Sapp on NFL Network: EJ Manuel has command and control of this offense like no rookie I've seen," Twitter, August 16, 2013, 9:46 p.m., https://twitter.com/NataliePierre_/status/368549417235664897?s=20 (accessed September 11, 2021).

page 52: *An article on the website*: Steven Cook, "EJ Manuel's Promising Preseason Debut Signs of Things to Come for Buffalo Bills," BleacherReport .com, August 15, 2013, https://bleacherreport.com/articles/1735810 (accessed September 11, 2021).

page 52: *He started 10 games*: John Wawrow, "Bills still a work in progress," Associated Press, December 31, 2013.

page 52: *Once healthy again*: Sal Maiorana, "Time is right for QB move," (Rochester, New York) *Democrat and Chronicle*, September 30, 2014.

page 53: *Taking advantage of favorable*: Frank Cooney, "Sloppy 49ers are scoreless in Seattle," *San Francisco Examiner*, August 22, 1993.

page 53: *All in all, he went*: Ibid.

page 53: *In his game column*: Steve Kelley, "Starting now, Mirer should be Seahawks' top quarterback," *Seattle Times*, August 22, 1993.

page 55: *"If you think we're making…"*: Nick Canepa, "Sure, it's early, but Ryan Leaf is for real," *San Diego Union-Tribune*, August 16, 1998.

page 55: *"He's going to be…"*: Ibid.

page 55: *Canepa continued*: Ibid.

page 57: *In the Browns' 2010*: Tom Withers, "Browns QBs comfort fans for future," Associated Press, August 17, 2010.

page 57: *About the drive*: Ibid.

page 57: *Two games later*: Steve Doerschuk, "Browns lose, but Delhomme 'outstanding,'" *Canton (Ohio) Repository*, August 29, 2010.

page 57: *during which* Sports Illustrated's: King, Peter (@peter_king). "RT @BrownieTheElf: idk if this goes along ur lines that its only preseason but how bout jake delhomme hes been impressive…Jake's reborn." Twitter, August 29, 2010, 6:51 p.m., https://twitter.com/peter_king/status/22473957268?s=2 (accessed September 11, 2021).

page 57: *In his* Cleveland Examiner *column*: Greg Swartz, "Jake Delhomme just what the doctor ordered for ailing Cleveland Browns," *Cleveland Examiner*, August 28, 2010.

page 57: *Delhomme suffered a high ankle sprain*: Tom Withers, "Browns' Delhomme does football drills," Associated Press, September 30, 2010.

page 58: *A prolific four-year starter*: Jeff Reynolds, "Notebook: Will undersized McCoy prove Browns made right choice?" NFLDraftScout.com, April 24, 2010, https://web.archive.org/web/20130618062741/http://www.cbssports.com/nfl/draft/story/13285393/notebook-will-undersized-mccoy-prove-browns-made-right-choice (accessed September 11, 2010).

page 58: *A few days later, ESPN's*: Evan Silva (@evansilva), "Merril Hoge on Colt McCoy: "Love what I see…Does a great job w/ his eyes. Cleveland may have solidified the position for the next 10 yrs," Twitter, August 17, 2011, 2:29 p.m., https://twitter.com/evansilva/status/103896199651799040?s=20 (accessed September 11, 2021).

page 58: *During the game*: John Clayton (@JohnClaytonNFL), "Colt McCoy continues to show he's might be the most improved QB in football. Working out with B. Favre did pay off," Twitter, August 19, 2011, 7:54 p.m., https://twitter.com/JohnClaytonNFL/status/104702747751878656?s=20 (accessed September 11, 2021).

page 58: *A few days after, Cleveland-based*: Branson Wright, "Colt McCoy was the right choice by the Cleveland Browns," *Blogs. Cleveland Plain Dealer.* August 24, 2011.

page 58: *Later in the preseason*: King, Peter (@peter_king). "RT @CommodorePowers: How do you feel about Colt McCoy this year?…He'll be one of the 5 breakout start in league." Twitter, August 27, 2010, 1:43 a.m., https://twitter.com/peter_king/status/1073273577731352576?s=20 (accessed September 11, 2021).

page 58: *King also requested*: Peter King (@peter_king), "RT @IlGreven: I'm not sold that Holmgren is sold on McCoy…He will be after this year, mark

my words," Twitter, June 8, 2011, 1:21 a.m., https://twitter.com/peter
_king/status/78330696854274048 (accessed September 11, 2021).

page 59: *ESPN's Ed Werder tweeted about*: Ed Werner (@WernerEdESPN),
"Norv Turner impact..RT.'@ESPNNFL: In his 6 drives through 2 preseason
games, QB Brandon Weeden has led the @Browns to 3 TDs, 2 field goals,"
Twitter, August 16, 2013, 12:32 p.m., https://twitter.com/WerderEdESPN
/status/368409955407106050?s=20 (accessed September 11, 2021).

page 59: *Syracuse.com writer*: Ryan Talbot (@RyanTalbotBills), "The Power
of Norv. RT '@PriscoCBS: Weeden looks sharp tonight.'" Twitter, August
15, 2013, 8:26 p.m., https://twitter.com/RyanTalbotBills/status/36816689
4236205057?s=20 (accessed September 11, 2021).

page 59: *Writer Andrea Hangst was so impressed*: Andrea Hangst, "It's Time
to Buy into Brandon Weeden After Another Dominant Preseason Showing," BleacherReport.com, August 16, 2013, https://bleacherreport.com
/articles/1740312-its-time-to-buy-into-brandon-weeden-after-another
-dominant-preseason-showing (accessed September 11, 2021).

page 59: *"Believe it, Browns fans"*: Ibid.

page 60: *"[Kizer] is the future..."*: *Good Morning Football*. Aired August 15,
2017, on NFL Network.

page 60: *"[He] is the next generation..."*: Ibid.

page 60: *Burleson also predicted that Kizer*: *Good Morning Football*. Aired August 28, 2017, on NFL Network.

page 60: *"When I watch him..."*: CBS Sports Network (@CBSSportsNet),
"'When I watch him, he's a special quarterback.' @LFletcher59 on DeShone
Kizer #T2S," Twitter, August 30, 2017, 6:41 p.m., https://twitter.com
/CBSSportsNet/status/903024861349638144?s=20 (accessed November
22, 2021).

page 60: *The day after that game*: Ruiz, Steven. "The Browns' 18-year search
for a quarterback is finally over," For The Win (website). USATODAY.com.
August 28, 2017, https://ftw.usatoday.com/2017/08/nfl-browns-deshone
-kizer-starting-quarterback-hue-jackson (accessed November 22, 2021).

page 60: *In it, he wrote*: Ibid.

page 60: *While he admitted that Kizer*: Ibid.

page 61: *"This time it feels different"*: Ibid.

page 61: *"This time it is different"*: Ibid.

page 61: *While he sometimes showed flashes*: Bryan Manning, "NFL Draft
2014: Logan Thomas' Draft Stock Mirrors His on-Field Play," Bleacher
Report.com, January 25, 2014. https://bleacherreport.com/articles/1934697
-nfl-draft-2014-logan-thomas-draft-stock-mirrors-his-on-field-play
(accessed February 27, 2022).

page 61: *With his freakish physical attributes*: BJ Kissel, "Would Position Change Give Logan Thomas a Better Shot at Sustainable NFL

Career," BleacherReport.com, April 15, 2004, https://bleacherreport.com
/articles/2030830-would-position-change-give-logan-thomas-better
-shot-at-sustainable-nfl-career (accessed December 31, 2021).

page 62: *ESPN's Ron Jaworski called*: Marc Sessler, "Jaws: Cardinals' Logan
Thomas 'best' rookie QB so far," NFL.com, August 13, 2014, https://www
.nfl.com/news/jaws-cardinals-logan-thomas-best-rookie-qb-so-far
-0ap3000000377439 (accessed November 22, 2021).

page 62: *Rivals.com college football analyst*: Mike Farrell (@rivalsmike),
"Jaws says Logan Thomas best rookie QB so far with #Cardinals. I'm one
of few who still thinks he can be very very good. #Hokies," Twitter, August 13, 2014, 9:14 p.m., https://twitter.com/rivalsmike/status/49972575
4117406722?s=20 (accessed November 22, 2021).

page 62: *On NFL.com, media personality*: Adam Schein, "Johnny Manziel, Kel-
vin Benjamin produce preseason excitement," NFL.com, August 11, 2014.
https://www.nfl.com/news/johnny-manziel-kelvin-benjamin-produce
-preseason-excitement-0ap3000000376710 (accessed November 22, 2021).

page 62: *"They're eating a lot…"*: Josh Weinfuss (@joshweinfuss), "Arians on
critics of Logan Thomas who said he'd never make it and should play TE:
'They're eating a lot of crow this week. So that's fun,'" Twitter, August 13,
2014, 3:34 p.m., https://twitter.com/joshweinfuss/status/499640129594
859520?s=20 (accessed November 22, 2021).

page 62: *"So that's fun"*: Ibid.

page 62: *While Thomas may have shined*: Ed Valentine, "Scouting Logan
Thomas: What to know about Giants' new QB," BigBlueReview.com, June 19,
2016, https://www.bigblueview.com/2016/6/19/11970516/scouting-logan
-thomas-what-to-know-about-new-york-giants-new-qb-dophins-cardinals
(accessed December 31, 2021).

page 63: *But he had spent the off-season*: Brett Martel, "Jaguars Showing
Promise," Associated Press, August 20, 2012.

page 63: *During the second game*: Pete Prisco (@PriscoCBS), "Where are all
the Gabbert rippers?" Twitter, August 17, 2012, 8:51 p.m., https://twitter
.com/PriscoCBS/status/236626402634514432?s=20 (accessed November
22, 2021).

page 63: *"To which former Jaguars…"*: Tony Boselli (@TonyBoselli), "It doesn't
fit their script! RT @PriscoCBS: Where are all the Gabbert rippers?" Twitter, August 17, 2012, 8:53 p.m., https://twitter.com/TonyBoselli/status
/236626905409937410?s=20 (accessed November 22, 2021).

page 63: *"Your magic spell is working"*: Peter King, "Luck and Gabbert off to
hot starts, not Kolb; more camp lessons," SI.com, August 20, 2012. https://
www.si.com/more-sports/2012/08/20/mmqb (accessed December 7, 2021).

page 64: *"The Eagles are gonna be…"*: Matthew Berry (@MatthewBerryTMR).
"The Eagles are gonna be awesome this year. I want as many PHI players

as I can get this year." Twitter, August 29, 2015, 8:24 p.m., https://twitter .com/MatthewBerryTMR/status/637782802927353856?s=20 (accessed January 18, 2022).

page 64: *"I want as many [Philadelphia]…"*: Ibid.

page 64: *"Get excited about this Eagles team"*: Andrew Porter, "Didinger: Eagles 'Shock And Awe Offense Best in Team's Preseason History," *philadelphia.cbs local.com*, August 31, 2015. https://philadelphia.cbslocal.com/2015/08/31 /ray-didinger-eagles-offense/ (accessed November 22, 2021).

page 64: *"You're allowed."*: Ibid.

page 64: *"I'm telling you…"*: Ibid.

page 64: *Former Eagles linebacker and Philadelphia*: Eagles (@Eagles), "My mouth is watering, waiting for this offense to take the field Monday Night in Atlanta," @Ike58Reese WATCH: http://bit.ly/TgSqAGem, Twitter, August 29, 2015, 11:17 p.m., https://twitter.com/Eagles/status/637826481104781312 ?s=20 (accessed November 22, 2021).

page 65: *"The chemistry on this squad…"*: Nick Fierro, "Eagles are looking super so far," (Lehigh Valley, Pennsylvania) *Morning Call*, August 31, 2015.

page 65: *"The Eagles should be good…"*: Ibid.

Chapter 6: "No Point in Keeping Tom Coughlin Around" (2004–2007 New York Giants)

page 67: *During the third quarter*: Gary Myers, "Hacking Cough: Reign of error must come to end," *New York Daily News*, December 25, 2006.

page 67: *When the game finally*: Ibid.

page 67: *In the final few*: "Fassel's Fall," *Asbury Park (New Jersey) Press*, December 18, 2003.

page 67: *frequently committed brainless penalties*: Tara Sullivan, "Finding new and creative ways to lose," (North Jersey) *Record*, December 10, 2003.

page 68: *One of the team's principal*: Tom Canavan, "Coughlin signs on as Giants coach," Associated Press, January 7, 2004.

page 68: *As a strict, detail-oriented*: Gary Myers, "Tuna Helper Fits Bill for the Giants," *New York Daily News*, January 7, 2004.

page 68: *As soon as he arrived*: Ralph Vacchiano, "Giants Try Again with Blue Meanie: Coughlin will lay down the law," *New York Daily News*, January 7, 2004.

page 68: *He came armed*: "Coughlin rules," *New York Daily News*, January 7, 2004.

page 68: *If a player ran afoul*: Plaxico Burress and Jason Cole, *Giant: The Road to the Super Bowl* (New York: HarperCollins, 2009), 139, Scribd.

page 68: *However, by the end*: Hays Carlyon, "Coughlin created his own demise," (St. Augustine, Florida) *Record*, December 31, 2002.

page 68: *"At least 10…"*: Michael Strahan, with Veronica Chambers, *Wake Up Happy* (New York: Atria, 2015), 101, Scribd.

page 68: *"Nine out of the 10…"*: Ibid.

page 68: *In September, three*: "3 Giants contest fines over team meetings," Associated Press, September 13, 2004.

page 69: *Strahan was fined*: Ibid.

page 69: *"I absolutely hated…"*: Strahan and Chambers. *Wake Up Happy*, 104.

page 69: *"Guys absolutely hate…"*: "Tipsheet," *St. Louis Post-Dispatch*, December 27, 2004.

page 69: *"He's not the type…"*: Ibid.

page 69: *In early September*: Bob Raissman, "Coughlin Critics Out of Bounds," *New York Daily News*, September 24, 2004.

page 69: *That same Sunday, on CBS's*: Ibid.

page 69: *Around the same time*: Steve Rushin, "Under Tom's Thumb," *Sports Illustrated*, September 27, 2004.

page 69: *Once, during training camp*: Burress and Cole, *Giant*, 139.

page 69: *Coughlin still fined him*: Ibid., 140.

page 69: *"But I told you…"*: Ibid.

page 69: *"Yeah, but you were…"*: Ibid.

page 69: *After the 2006 season*: Steve Serby, "Coughlin Should Be Through With Little Blue," *New York Post*, January 8, 2007.

page 69: *"He just yells to yell"*: Ibid.

page 70: *Perhaps the most disappointing trend*: Keith Idec, "No point in keeping Coughlin around," (North Jersey) *Herald-News*, January 8, 2007.

page 70: *On a few occasions*: Ralph Vacchiano, "Tiki & Big Blue Feel Outfoxed," *New York Daily News*, January 9, 2006.

page 70: *Barber said that he*: Ibid.

page 70: *In July 2006, Shockey professed*: Ralph Vacchiano, "NY Law & Disorder," *New York Daily News*, September 26, 2006.

page 70: *Later that year in September*: Lisa Olson, "A Giant Disgrace," *New York Daily News*, September 25, 2006.

page 70: *A few months earlier*: "Barber will retire at season's end," Associated Press, October 20, 2006.

page 70: *In addition, concerns were growing*: George Willis, "Miserable Manning-Giants' Franchise Quarterback Keep Regressing," *New York Post*, December 25, 2006.

page 71: *Manning, who was in his*: "Young rallies Titans from 21-point deficit to stun Giants," Associated Press, November 26, 2006.

page 71: *From the* Journal News: Ernie Palladino, "The once and future king," (Westchester, New York) *Journal News*, January 7, 2007.

page 71: *"Of course, Tom Coughlin…"*: Stephen Edelson, "Coughlin must go," *Asbury Park (New Jersey) Press*, December 26, 2006.

page 71: *"Regardless of . . . whether the Giants . . .":* Stephen Edelson, "Time for Giants to start over," (Central New Jersey) *Home News Tribune,* December 31, 2006.

page 71: *New York Post Giants beat writer:* Paul Schwartz, "Upheaval of Entire Muddled Operation The Only Salvation," *New York Post,* December 26, 2006.

page 72: *In the* New York Times: Selena Roberts, "Coughlin and His Team Seem to Be a Mismatch," *New York Times,* December 25, 2006.

page 72: *"Barber is on his way out . . .":* Tara Sullivan, "Blue Christmas: Give Coughlin ax," (North Jersey) *Record,* December 25, 2006.

page 72: *"Because it's become . . .":* Ibid.

page 72: *"[John] Mara and Steve Tisch . . .":* Myers, "Hacking Cough."

page 72: *"[The Giants should] go after Weis . . .":* Steve Serby, "Big Bang Theory Fit for Big Blue," *New York Post,* December 26, 2006.

page 72: *"Weis would be . . .":* Ibid.

page 72: *In December 2003:* Steve Serby, "Pats Offensive Genius Is Weis Choice," *New York Post,* December 18, 2003.

page 73: *The loss further highlighted:* Filip Bondy, "Dumb plays from start to finished: Ouster sums up story of season," *New York Daily News,* January 8, 2007.

page 73: *"[Coughlin] is fired . . .":* Bob Raissman, "Fox on prowl to crush Tom," *New York Daily News,* January 9, 2007.

page 73: *"He lost the football team":* Ibid.

page 73: *ESPN commentator Sean Salisbury:* Ibid.

page 73: *In a column later:* Dan Shaughnessy, "Hall of Fame decisions, and some other picks," *Boston Globe,* December 27, 2006.

page 73: *"No point in keeping Coughlin . . .":* Idec, "No Point in Keeping Coughlin Around."

page 73: *"Coughlin must go . . .":* Gary Myers, "Coughlin must go," *New York Daily News,* January 8, 2007.

page 73: *"Too many players . . .":* Ibid.

page 74: *Also, in the* Record: Ian O'Connor, "Don't delay in handing Coughlin a pink slip," (North Jersey) *Record,* January 8, 2007.

page 74: *and in the* New York Post, *Serby pleaded:* Serby, "Coughlin Should Be Through . . ."

page 74: *"Tom Coughlin is our coach . . .":* "Coughlin gets contract extension to coach Giants," Associated Press, January 10, 2007.

page 74: *In reaction to the news:* Steve Serby, "Keeping Coughlin would be a big blue boo-boo," *New York Post,* January 10, 2007.

page 74: New York Post *columnist Mike Vaccaro:* Mike Vaccaro, "Wrong Answer—Keeping Coughlin may land Big Blue in no-man's land," *New York Post,* January 11, 2007.

page 74: *The way he saw it*: Ibid.

page 75: *He concedes that much of*: Tiki Barber, with Gil Reavill, *Tiki: My Life in the Game and Beyond* (New York: Simon Spotlight Entertainment, 2007), 117, 202, Scribd.

page 75: *In February 2017, just over*: Bob Raissman and Leo Standora, "Tiki's Set To Tackle TV News," *New York Daily News*, February 13, 2007.

page 75: *He intimated that*: Bob Raissman, "Tiki TV turns rerun," *New York Daily News*, February 14, 2007.

page 75: *Barber later admitted that*: Barber and Reavill, *Tiki*, 21.

page 75: *"I knew enough about…"*: Ibid.

page 75: *"I needed to make…"*: Ibid.

page 75: *Among many other thoughts*: Ibid., 201.

page 75: *and that "If Tom Coughlin…"*: Ibid., 20.

page 76: *"[He] never uttered…"*: Ibid., 9–10.

page 76: *It was an asset much*: Dennis Waszak Jr., "New York teams traveling different roads to playoffs," Associated Press, January 6, 2007.

page 76: *"He hasn't shown leadership"*: Arthur Staple, "Manning Follows His Lead," *Hartford Courant*, August 22, 2007.

page 76: *"[Manning's] personality hasn't…"*: Ibid.

page 76: *The comments really pissed*: Ralph Vacchiano, *Eli Manning: The Making of a Quarterback* (New York: Sports Publishing, 2012), 233, Scribd.

page 76: *"I guess I could have…"*: Staple, "Manning Follows His Lead."

page 77: *But the most surprising*: Ralph Vacchiano, "Big Blue Happy Family," *New York Daily News*, September 6, 2007.

page 77: *He was committed to becoming*: Burress and Cole, *Giant*, 155.

page 77: *"[Mara and Tisch] were…"*: Author interview with Gary Myers, April 12, 2021.

page 77: *"They told him…"*: Ibid.

page 77: *The defense was porous*: Stephen Edelson, "Coughlin still can't control these guys," *Asbury Park (New Jersey) Press*, September 17, 2007.

page 77: *"How fired is Tom Coughlin?"*: Jim Armstrong, "Lightning can't strike twice? Ask Broncos," *Denver Post*, September 17, 2007.

page 78: *"The housecleaning's coming"*: Edelson, "Coughlin still can't control these guys."

page 78: *"Bringing Coughlin back…"*: Ibid.

page 78: *The following Sunday, on NFL Today*: Aired September 23, 2007, on CBS.

page 78: *"Tom lightened up"*: Burress and Cole. *Giant*, 172.

page 78: *"He was like the…"*: Ibid.

page 78: *When Mara and Tisch*: Vacchiano, *Eli Manning*, 281–282.

page 79: *The owners wanted Coughlin*: Ibid.

page 79: *A day later, Manning*: Tom Canavan, "Eli emotionless following bad loss," Associated Press, November 27, 2007.

page 79: *The following Sunday, on ESPN's*: Neil Best, "Media rushed to judgment," (New York) *Newsday*, December 4, 2007.

page 79: *A few days later*: Ralph Vacchiano, "Apple Sours on Eli," *New York Daily News*, November 28, 2007.

page 79: *"Maybe he should be…"*: Ibid.

page 79: *"New York is going to chew…"*: Ibid.

page 80: *"[Coughlin] needs to…"*: Gary Myers, "Resting Giants a Perfect Plan," *New York Daily News*, December 25, 2007.

page 80: *Bob Glauber, in a* Newsday: Bob Glauber, "Coughlin logically should let his players take a rest against Patriots," (New York) *Newsday*, December 25, 2007.

page 80: *"Anything beyond appearances…"*: Bob Matthews, "Giants would be smart to rest their regulars," (Rochester, New York) *Democrat and Chronicle*, December 26, 2007.

page 80: *"Of course we want…"*: Arthur Staple, "Sirius trash talk: Giants react to Ronde's slight," (New York) *Newsday*, January 3, 2008.

page 81: *"Tampa rested their players"*: *Fox NFL Sunday*. Aired January 6, 2008, on Fox.

page 81: *His fellow co-hosts*: Ibid.

page 81: *Next, despite Johnson, Long, Bradshaw*: *Fox NFL Sunday*. Aired January 13, 2008, on Fox.

page 81: *Bradshaw, who hadn't been*: *Fox NFL Pregame: Super Bowl XLII Pregame*. Aired February 3, 2008, on Fox.

page 81: *One confident New England fan*: Ian Begley, Mark Lelinwalla, and Michael O'Keefe, "Perfect T-Shirt doesn't fit NFL," *New York Daily News*, February 3, 2008.

page 82: *The site started selling*: Ibid.

page 82: *They sold 700 shirts*: Ibid.

page 82: *During media day*: Tom Canavan, "Still outspoken, he predicts a win over Patriots," Associated Press, January 30, 2008.

page 82: *When word about that*: "Brady: Plax Prediction on Pats' points puzzling," Associated Press, January 30, 2008.

page 82: *Spagnuolo changed the Giants*: Glenn Stout and Richard A. Johnson, *The Pats: An Illustrated History of the New England Patriots* (Boston: Houghton Mifflin Harcourt, 2018), 621; Rich Cimini, "Brady bunched up," *New York Daily News*, February 4, 2008, Scribd.

page 83: *Spagnuolo also devised clever coverage*: Hank Gola, "Giant coaches outclass the masters," *New York Daily News*, February 4, 2008.

page 83: *"With [that] three point loss…"*: Gary Myers, "Super Survivors," *New York Daily News*, February 5, 2008.

page 83: *"As it turned out…"*: Ibid.

page 83: *After the game*: *Today*. Aired February 4, 2008, on NBC.

page 84: *When he caught up*: Ibid.

page 84: *From the studio*: Ibid.

page 84: *She then offered him*: Ibid.

page 84: *He praised Manning's performance*: Ibid.

page 85: *"Right after the [2006 season]..."*: Tara Sullivan, "Coughlin shows his sunny side," (North Jersey) *Record*, February 5, 2008.

page 85: *"You have to learn..."*: Ibid.

page 85: *In the days leading up*: Ralph Vacchiano, "Tiki Barber says Tom Coughlin's 'job is in certain jeopardy and his control is slipping away," *New York Daily News*, September 30, 2010.

page 85: *It was no surprise*: Gary Myers, "Losing to Chicago too much to Bear," *New York Daily News*, October 4, 2010.

page 86: *Soon thereafter, he tried*: Gary Myers, "The truth about 2011," *New York Daily News*, September 11, 2011.

page 86: *Barber has said*: Brad Gagnon, "Tiki Barber Doesn't Think Giants Would Have Won Super Bowl XLII Had He Stayed," BleacherReport.com, October 11, 2012, https://bleacherreport.com/articles/1367891-tiki-barber -doesnt-think-giants-would-have-won-super-bowl-xlii-had-he-stayed (accessed September 9, 2021).

page 86: *Regarding his comments about*: Justin Terranova, "5 questions for Tiki Barber," *New York Post*, August 2, 2013.

page 86: *He also contends*: Gagnon, "Tiki Barber Doesn't Think..."

page 86: *"The dynamics of..."*: Ibid.

page 86: *"And at the time..."*: Ibid.

page 86: *In December 2008, he sat*: Toni Monkovic, "Tiki Barber: I Was Wrong About You, Eli," *The Fifth Down* (blog). *New York Times*. December 15, 2008, https://fifthdown.blogs.nytimes.com/2008/12/15/tiki-barber-i-was -wrong-about-you-eli/ (accessed September 9, 2021).

page 86: *"It was entirely based..."*: Author interview with Tara Sullivan, December 8, 2020.

page 86: *"The whole narrative..."*: Ibid

page 86: *"I love the fact..."*: Ibid.

page 86: *"I still contend that..."*: Author interview with Gary Myers, April 12, 2021.

page 87: *"We even shocked ourselves"*: Gary Shelton, "Memorable rewrite of NFL history," *Tampa Bay Times*, February 4, 2008.

Chapter 7: "Brian Brohm has more upside than Aaron Rodgers" (2008 Green Bay Packers)

page 90: *A month before the 2008 Draft*: Bob McGinn, "Brett Favre Retires: Filling a hole in the pocket, Packers are left to restock at quarterback," *Milwaukee Journal Sentinel*, March 5, 2008.

page 90: *To many, he was not*: Todd Finkelmeyer, "In a rush, Badgers fans? You won't top Iowa's run," (Madison, Wisconsin) *Capital Times*, March 8, 2008.

page 90: *In July, he wanted*: Paul Vandermause, "Favre-Packers affair like poker game," *Hattiesburg (Mississippi) American*, July 14, 2008.

page 90: *He said he wanted to*: "Smilin' Brian: Brohm finally relaxed in the spotlight as a senior at Louisville," Associated Press, August 15, 2007, https://www.espn.com/espn/wire?section=ncf&id=2976095 (accessed January 6, 2022).

page 90: *In June 2007, ESPN's premier*: Mel Kiper Jr., "Brohm No. 1, USC places five on initial Big Board," ESPN.com, June 8, 2007.

page 91: *By the time April rolled*: Rick Bozich, "Big East should get No. 2 seed in the NCAAs," *Louisville Courier-Journal*, March 4, 2008.

page 91: *A Cardinals scout told*: Bob McGinn, "What scouts had to say about the Packers' 2008 draft picks," *Milwaukee Journal Sentinel*, April 27, 2008.

page 91: *Another scout told*: Pete Dougherty, "Can the Packers pass on top prospect?" *Green Bay Press-Gazette*, April 22, 2008.

page 91: *Before the draft, Kiper said*: Orlando Ledbetter, "Falcons see lots of QBs after Ryan," *Atlanta Journal-Constitution*, April 20, 2008.

page 91: *The week before the draft*: Rick Bozich, "Love of Ryan over Brohm is puzzling," *Louisville Courier-Journal*, April 21, 2008.

page 92: *"I watched Brohm…"*: Ibid.

page 92: *"One thing I do not see…"*: Ibid.

page 92: *When the Brohm pick*: Naila-Jean Meyers, "N.F.L. Draft: Second Round," *The Fifth Down* (blog), *New York Times*, April 26, 2008, https://fifthdown.blogs.nytimes.com/2008/04/26/nfl-draft-second-round/?searchResultPosition=2 (accessed September 17, 2021).

page 92: *After announcing the Packers*: ESPN News, aired April 26, 2008; "2008 NFL DRAFT Packers Select BRIAN BROHM," YouTube, uploaded by PackersInsider, July 7, 2008, https://www.youtube.com/watch?v=he-0BIKmoq0s (accessed March 2, 2022).

page 92: *Right away, Hoge, the former*: Ibid.

page 93: *"I like him," he told Davis*: Ibid.

page 93: *"I honestly think Brian…"*: Ibid.

page 93: *He then added*: Ibid.

page 93: *He thought Rodgers*: Ibid.

page 93: *Hoge expounded further, stating*: Ibid.

page 94: *"[Packers GM Ted]…"*: Tom Oates, "Rodgers will 'be fine,'" *Wisconsin State Journal*, April 27, 2008.

page 94: *Nevertheless, the same day*: Rob Demovsky, "Brohm seen as 'solid' backup to Rodgers," *Green Bay Press-Gazette*, April 27, 2008.

page 94: *"I think that wasn't…"*: Author interview with Rick Bozich, May 29, 2020.

page 94: *"[Before the NFL]…"*: Ibid.

page 95: *"In retrospect, the NFL…"*: Ibid.

page 95: *"[Ryan] definitely has…"*: Ibid.

page 95: *"I can't believe he didn't…"*: Ibid.

page 95: *"I look at some…"*: Ibid.

Chapter 8: "The Jets Just Got the Steal of the Draft, Their Future Starting QB, Bryce Petty" (NFL Draft Freezing Cold Takes)

page 97: *"The Giants' first-round choice…"*: Larry Fox, "Boo-birds sacking Giant draft of Simms," *New York Daily News*, May 4, 1979.

page 97: *"I don't understand it…"*: NFL Draft, April 26, 1983, aired on ESPN.

page 98: *"After this draft is history…"*: Ibid.

page 98: *"I feel any team that…"*: "Juniors boost QB talent pool," Associated Press, April 19, 1990.

page 98: *"[With Andre Ware at quarterback]"*: Bob Sansevere, "Lions to dominate with Ware at QB," *St. Paul (Minnesota) Pioneer Press*, April 24, 1990.

page 98: *"If I was New England…"*: NFL Draft, April 25, 1993, aired on ESPN.

page 99: *"Everybody should have drafted…"*: "Rookie class much deeper than Manning, Leaf," *Hartford Courant*, August 30, 1998.

page 99: *[Danny Wuerffel's] a winner*: John McClain, "Former teammates deserve look at QB," *Houston Chronicle*, April 13, 1997.

page 99: *"I say it's a no-brainer…"*: Vic Carucci, "Colts may like Manning's head, but Leaf's arm will capture their hearts," *Buffalo News*, April 5, 1998.

page 99: *"Without a doubt, Peyton Manning…"*: Pete Sirianni, "One bad opinion in 140 years isn't the 'biggest flop'" ncnewsonline.com, August 14, 2021, https://www.ncnewsonline.com/news/lifestyles/column-by-pete-sirianni-one-bad-opinion-in-140-years-isnt-the-biggest-flop/article_490e5134-589e-5c0c-ab7d-b022fabed606.html (accessed January 7, 2022); Jason Lisk (@JasonLisk), "For everyone asking, I found this in an article in the *New Castle (Pennsylvania) News* from April 18, 1998. Four writers gave their draft thoughts and that was from someone named Kevin Flowers. I'm doing a project where I'm searching for old scouting comments pre-draft on QBs," Twitter, March 31, 2018, 10:03 a.m., https://twitter.com/JasonLisk/status/980085599058169859?s=20 (accessed January 7, 2022).

page 99: *"He is the quarterback…"*: Jay Mariotti, "A-O-Cade," *Chicago Sun-Times*, April 18, 1999.

page 100: *"Obviously [Tom Brady] has…"*: Alan Greenberg, "Patriots Draft Board Day 2," *Hartford Courant*, April 17, 2000.

page 100: *"I see Brett Favre in…"*: Bob McGinn, "Tulane quarterback seen as Favre-like," *Milwaukee Journal Sentinel*, April 18, 2004.

page 100: *"Will ['draft project' Ben Roethlisberger]…"*: Rick Green, "Steelers' draft quite a project," *Erie (Pennsylvania) Times-News*, April 27, 2004.

page 100: *"In five years we will…"*: Gregg Easterbrook, "Another season of bad predictions," Page 2. ESPN.com, February 14, 2007, https://www.espn.com /espn/page2/story?page=easterbrook/070213 (accessed January 8, 2022).

page 100: *"Dolphins could have had their…"*: Jerry Greene, "It's safe to come out now," *Orlando Sentinel*, April 29, 2007.

page 100: *"Mike Greenberg can't contain his…."*: SportsCenter (@SportsCenter). "Producer: Greeny (Mike Greenberg) can't contain his excitement about the Jets & Sanchez. He really believes Broadway Joe has met his match." Twitter, April 27, 2009, 8:25 p.m., https://twitter.com/SportsCenter /status/1634226055?s=20 (accessed January 15, 2022).

page 100: *"If you are betting…"*: Barry Jackson, "Experts mixed on Dolphins' first-day picks," *Miami Herald*, April 26, 2009.

page 101: *"I love, love, love this…"*: Ian Rapoport (@RapSheet), "I love, love, love this pick for Carolina. Jimmy Clausen. Man, teams are going to be sorry…," Twitter, April 23, 2010, 7:21 p.m., https://twitter.com/RapSheet /status/12730413024?s=20 (accessed January 10, 2022).

page 101: *"If [Tim] Tebow…"*: Tim Brando (@TimBrando), "If Tebow isn't a Jaguar by tonight it's my opinion is the Franchise is gone within 3 years. Not an immediate starter, but a business savior!" Twitter, April 22, 2010, 10:38 a.m., https://twitter.com/TimBrando/status/12642442034?s=20 (accessed September 20, 2021).

page 101: *"I love [Jake] Locker. I'm…"*: NFL Draft, April 20, 1996, aired on ESPN.

page 101: *"LOVE IT. Christian Ponder…"*: Barrett Sallee (@BarrettSallee), "LOVE IT. Christian Ponder to the Vikings. He will have a long successful career in Minnesota. Sleeper of the draft." Twitter, April 28, 2011, 9:18 p.m., https://twitter.com/BarrettSallee/status/63774105849180161?s=20 (accessed January 18, 2021).

page 101: *"The Cardinals should give up…"*: "Path to the Draft: March 30, 2001," WalterFootball.com, March 30, 2011, https://walterfootball.com /pathtothedraft2011_0330.php (accessed January 15, 2022).

page 101: *"I don't see Russell Wilson being…"*: Dave Mahler (@Softykjr), "Hugh Millen: 'I don't see Russell Wilson being anything more than Seneca Wallace. I'm higher on Josh Portis as a prospect.' #Seahawks," Twitter, April 27, 2012, 10:41 p.m., https://twitter.com/Softykjr/status /196066543816282113?s=20 (accessed September 18, 2021).

page 102: *"Dak Prescott is a backup…"*: Colin Cowherd (@ColinCowherd), "Dak Prescott is a backup in NFL. At tight end," Twitter, November 15, 2014, 5:16 p.m., https://twitter.com/ColinCowherd/status/5337452728586 07617?s=20 (accessed January 8, 2022).

page 102: *"Johnny Football will bring…"*: NFL Draft. Aired May 8, 2014 on ESPN.

page 102: *"The Jets just got the steal…"*: Skip Bayless (@RealSkipBayless), "The Jets just got the steal of the draft, their future starting QB, Bryce Petty," Twitter, May 2, 2015, 12:26 p.m., https://twitter.com/RealSkip-Bayless/status/594538452932243456?s=20 (accessed January 8, 2022).

page 102: *"[DeShone] Kizer…is going to…"*: Dan Wolken (@DanWolken), "Kizer handles pressure so well. Going to make millions and millions of dollars. Multiple time Pro Bowler," Twitter, September 4, 2012, 10:12 p.m., https://twitter.com/DanWolken/status/772618360706043904?s=20 (accessed January 20, 2022).

page 102: *"HACKENBERG TO THE JETS!!!…"*: Freezing Cold Takes (@OldTakesExposed), Twitter, April 25, 2019, 10:24 a.m., https://twitter.com/OldTakesExposed/status/1121419799396016128?s=20 (contains screenshots of the tweets that include the quotes to which this citation refers, as the original tweets have been deleted) (accessed January 16, 2022).

page 103: *"Chiefs are STOOPID"*: Tony Massarotti (@TonyMassarotti), "Let me try this again. Chiefs are STOOPID," Twitter, April 27, 2017, 9:41 p.m., https://twitter.com/TonyMassarotti/status/857771598815932417?s=20 (accessed January 20, 2022).

page 103: *"It is unprecedented to see…"*: "1st Round NFL Draft Grades | Bucky Brooks | 2017 Draft." YouTube, uploaded by NFL, April 28, 2017, https://www.youtube.com/watch?v=JIlcF_gj-rg (accessed January 18, 2022).

page 103: *"[The] Chiefs just made…"*: Andrew Holleran, "Recruiting Expert's Old Tweet About QB Patrick Mahomes Is Going Viral," The Spun, *Sports Illustrated,* September 16, 2018, https://thespun.com/news/recruiting-experts-old-tweet-about-qb-patrick-mahomes-is-going-viral (accessed January 20, 2022).

page 103: *"It won't happen, but if"*: Booger McFarland (@espnbooger), "it wont happen but if Louisville were really thinking about Lamar Jackson's future they would move him to wr,thats where he will play in NFL," Twitter, June 20, 2017, 2:25 p.m., https://twitter.com/ESPNBooger/status/877230937284771842?s=20 (accessed January 21, 2022).

page 103: *"I would consider any team…"*: Rodger Sherman, "The Winners and Losers From Round 1 of the NFL Draft," The Ringer, April 27, 2018, https://www.theringer.com/nfl/2018/4/27/17289496/2018-draft-winners-losers-buffalo-bills-josh-allen-lamar-jackson-baltimore-ravens (accessed January 16, 2022).

page 104: *"Cincinnati should keep veteran…"*: "2020 NFL Draft: What SHOULD the Bengals do with the No. 1 pick?" NFL.com, April 3, 2020, https://www.nfl.com/news/2020-nfl-draft-what-should-the-bengals-do-with-the-no-1-pick-0ap3000001108085 (retrieved February 1, 2022).

page 104: *"The…Bears chose Walter Payton"*: Red Smith, "Flesh market," *New York Times,* January 29, 1975.

page 104: *[Emmitt Smith will] be...*": Chris Harry, "If only the Bucs had taken Emmitt," *Orlando Sentinel*, November 30, 2000.

page 104: *"[Emmitt] Smith should be a solid...*": Kevin Lyttle, "Dallas gets draft grade B, as in blew it," *Austin American-Statesman*, April 24, 1990.

page 105: *"Blair Thomas will be...*": Brian Heyman, "Many needs, too few picks," (North Jersey) *Herald-News*, April 22, 1990.

page 105: *"Meet Curtis Enis. I admit...*": Jay Mariotti, "Enis is young anchor Bears need," *Chicago Sun-Times*, April 19, 1996.

page 105: *"Ten years from now...*": Elliott Smith, "Colts soon will regret choice to pass Williams," *Odessa (Texas) American*, April 20, 1999.

page 105: *"Brandon Weeden and Trent Richardson...*": Stewart Mandel (@slmandel), "Brandon Weeden and Trent Richardson in the same backfield next year? That's pretty freaking cool." Twitter, April 26, 2012, 11:07 a.m., https://twitter.com/slmandel/status/195697405851742208?s=20 (accessed January 17, 2022).

page 105: *"Anyone else thinking Trent Richardson...*": Freezing Cold Takes (@OldTakesExposed), "Appreciate u guys sending me all this T-Rich stuff, but this is where it's at," Twitter, August 10, 2017, 9:18 p.m., https://twitter.com/OldTakesExposed/status/895816612397412353?s=20 (contains screenshots of the tweets that include the quotes to which this citation refers) (accessed January 20, 2022).

page 106: *"Wayne Gallman >>>> Derrick Henry...*": Todd Fuhrman (@Todd Fuhrman), "Wayne Gallman >>>> Derrick Henry when it comes to their careers at the next level." Twitter, January 11, 2016, 11:53 p.m., https://twitter.com/ToddFuhrman/status/686772996711661569?s=20 (accessed January 22, 2022).

page 106: *"I would rather have Kenneth...*": Matt Miller (@nfldraftscout), "I would rather have Kenneth Dixon than Derrick Henry. @Carlos_Danger," Twitter, March 23, 2016, 11:07 a.m., https://twitter.com/nfldraftscout/status/712657108915720192?s=20 (accessed January 8, 2022).

page 106: *"[Dolphins third-round draft pick]...*": Jason Cole, "J.J. will take Shannon over Moss any time," (Fort Lauderdale) *Sun-Sentinel*, April 20, 1998.

page 106: *"[The] Colts reached*": Warner Hessler, "Grading the NFL Draft," (Newport News, Virginia) *Daily Press*, April 24, 2001.

page 106: *"This was the easy part...*": Bob Wojnowski, "Rogers' talent running routes not his roots, warrants selection," *Detroit News*, April 27, 2003.

page 107: *"I'll see you at his...*": Jim Weber, "Mel Kiper's Top 10 NFL Draft Blunders," Awful Announcing, April 10, 2017, https://awfulannouncing.com/espn/mel-kipers-top-10-nfl-draft-blunders.html (accessed January 20, 2022).

page 107: *"Matt Jones, a WR-TE hybrid...*": Walter Cherepinsky, "2005 NFL Draft Grades and Re-Grades, AFC Re-Grades," WalterFootball.com, June

3, 2008. https://walterfootball.com/draft2005Gafc.php (accessed January 25, 2022).

page 107: *"Jay Cutler says THANK YOU..."*: Skip Bayless (@realSkipBayless), "Jay Cutler says THANK YOU. Kevin White will be a BEAST. Extremely confident and backs it up. Big/strong/fast/tough. #CHIpick," Twitter, April 30, 2015, 8:57 p.m., https://twitter.com/RealSkipBayless/status/59394217 9166363648?s=20 (accessed January 22, 2022).

page 107: *"[Rickey] Dudley will be..."*: John Marvel, "John Marvel looks at the first day of the NFL Draft," *Contra Costa (California) Times*, April 21, 1996.

page 107: *"People are high on Arizona TE..."*: Freezing Cold Takes (@OldTakes Exposed). "DELETION: Looks like @GregABedard recently reached his breaking point with this classic (Thx @thoughtsnprayer)," Twitter, March 28, 2016, 9:18 a.m., https://twitter.com/OldTakesExposed/status /714441634780430336 (contains a screenshot of the tweet that has the quote to which this citation refers, as the original tweet has been deleted) (accessed January 8, 2022).

page 108: *"The thought of the New England..."*: Gregg Easterbrook, "Is the NFL draft science or lottery," Page 2, ESPN.com, April 27, 2010, http://www .espn.com/espn/page2/story?page=easterbrook/100427_tuesday_morning _quarterback_draft_review (accessed January 19, 2022).

page 108: *"[Buffalo Bills]: Worst Pick..."*: "Rough draft—but not for Shula," (Fort Lauderdale) *Sun-Sentinel*, May 2, 1985.

page 108: *"[Chris Doleman] is a projection..."*: "Schemes and Dreams | 1985 Caught in the Draft," YouTube, uploaded by NFL Films, April, 22, 2021, https://www.youtube.com/watch?v=LWtUS8arQbA&t=895s (accessed January 19, 2022).

page 109: *"Should the Panthers use..."*: Dan Arkush, "With the draft's No. 2 overall pick, Carolina faces a tough decision," *Pro Football Weekly*, April 10, 2002.

page 109: *"Charles Woodson... won't have the..."*: Jason Lisk (@JasonLisk), "and for those saying someone couldn't be more wrong. Well, I couldn't fit all of it in the screen grab. Here was his Best Bet." Twitter, March 31, 2018, 10:23 a.m., https://twitter.com/JasonLisk/status/980085599058169859 ?s=20 (accessed January 7, 2022).

page 109: *"Let's face it: [Ed] Reed..."*: Mike Preston, "Let's face it: Reed is a pick without pizazz," *Baltimore Sun*, April 21, 2002.

page 109: *"With [Defensive tackle Vernon] Gholston..."*: Matt Sohn, "Rare athlete fits in perfectly with Jets' complex 'D,'" April 26, 2008.

page 109: *"[The Houston Texans] will rue..."*: Chris Baldwin, "Texans will rue the night they took Pizza Boy J. J. Watt over Nick Fairley, Houston lover," Culture Map (Houston), April 29, 2011, https://houston.culturemap.com/news /sports/04-29-11-texans-will-rue-the-night-they-took-pizza-boy-watts -over-nick-fairley-houston-lover/#slide=0 (accessed January 7, 2022).

page 109: *"Luke Kuechly at No. 10…"*: Andrew Perloff (@andrewperloff), "Luke Kuechly at No. 10 to Panthers is not going to work out well. Tacklers are easy to find. I know he can cover TEs, but cmon," Twitter, April 26, 2012, 8:54 p.m., https://twitter.com/andrewperloff/status/195677331174596610?s=20 (accessed January 20, 2022).

Chapter 9: "Tony Mandarich Is in a Class by Himself … It Doesn't Get Any Better Than This" (1989 Green Bay Packers)

page 111: *In 2009, former Rutgers*: Kory Kozak, "Steroids fueled spectacular rise and fall," April 17, 2009, https://www.espn.com/nfl/news/story?id=4073575 (September 21, 2021).

page 112: *"He's faster than any…"*: Rick Telander, "The Big Enchilada," *Sports Illustrated*, April 24, 1989.

page 112: *"There's probably nobody…"*: Ibid.

page 112: *Joe Wooley, the director*: Bob McGinn, "Mandarich: A man among children," *Green Bay Press-Gazette*, April 18, 1989.

page 112: *The Browns did give*: Don Pierson, "Mandarich's size and skills block reality off the film," *Chicago Tribune*, April 21, 1989.

page 113: *"A once-in-a-lifetime…"*: "Packers steady on Mandarich," United Press International, April 16, 1989.

page 113: *"A freak of nature"*: McGinn, "Mandarich: A man among children."

page 113: *"The best offensive…"*: "Mandarich tops talented group of lineman available in draft," Scripps Howard News Service, April 19, 1989.

page 113: *"Mandarich is out…"*: Brian Allee-Walsh, "Lineman Mandarich Has No Peer," (New Orleans) *Times-Picayune*, April 18, 1989.

page 113: *"A surer thing…"*: Don Pierson, "'89 class not good, but better than '90," *Chicago Tribune*, April 21, 1989.

page 113: *"An instant starter…"*: Larry Dorman, "Safety, first: Oliver likely Dolphin pick," *Miami Herald*, April 22, 1989.

page 113: *"I've been in football…"*: "Packers hit jackpot with No. 2 draft pick," Associated Press, April 23, 1989.

page 114: *"Could be the best…"*: Brian White, "Dr. W's draft," (Southwest Florida) *News-Press*, April 23, 1989.

page 114: *"He's the best I've…"*: Steve Schoenfeld, "Despite glitz at top, draft field bottoms out," *Arizona Republic*, April 16, 1989.

page 114: *"He's the finest pure…"*: Jack Sheppard, "Experts agree: Mandarich blocks out the competition," *Tampa Bay Times*, April 19, 1989.

page 114: *"Mandarich is in a class…"*: Vinny DiTrani, "Superman of the NFL Draft," (North Jersey) *Record*, April 17, 1989.

page 114: *The workout astonished…*: Jack Ebling, "The Incredible Bulk," *Lansing State Journal*, February 18, 1989.

page 114: *"Someday, we'll be able to...":* Ibid.

page 114: *Mandarich weighed in:* Ibid.

page 114: *He also bench-pressed:* Ibid.

page 114: *It was described by:* Gary Long, "Mandarich looms over linemen," *Miami Herald,* April 15, 1989.

page 115: *"[Packers General Manager] Tom...":* McGinn, "Mandarich: A man among children."

page 115: *"You can get quarterbacks...":* Ibid.

page 115: *While he didn't:* Telander, "The Big Enchilada."

page 115: *Less than a year earlier:* Tommy Chalkin with Rick Telander, "The Nightmare of Steroids," *Sports Illustrated,* October 24, 1988.

page 115: *Chalkin also alleged:* Ibid.

page 116: *A subsequent internal investigation:* Brant Newman, "South Carolina avoids major punishment for steroids mess," United Press International, July 26, 1990.

page 116: *Three South Carolina coaches:* Ibid.

page 116: *When he arrived at:* Cody J. Tucker, 'Eventually he saw the light," *Lansing State Journal,* April 26, 2018.

page 116: *By the time he left:* "Morning Line," *Detroit Free Press,* January 16, 1989.

page 116: *When prompted, he would cite:* Art Kabelowsky, "Mandarich on his best behavior," *Racine (Wisconsin) Journal Times,* April 24, 1989.

page 116: *He attributed his:* Telander, "The Big Enchilada."

page 116: *"Our trainer talked...":* Bob McGinn, "Team not scared by Mandarich steroid talk," (Appleton, Wisconsin) *Post-Crescent,* April 15, 1989.

page 117: *Five days before:* Bob McGinn, "Mandarich reaches deal," (Appleton, Wisconsin) *Post-Crescent,* September 5, 1989.

page 117: *When Mandarich finally reported:* John Aehl, "Mandarich weight becoming heavy issue for Packers," *Wisconsin State Journal,* December 14, 1989.

page 117: *He rarely played, and there were:* Greg Garber, "Green Bay shows it can stay ahead of the pack," *Hartford Courant,* December 3, 1989.

page 117: *Rumors were rampant:* Ibid.

page 117: *The speculation heated up:* "MSU officials refute report of widespread steroid use by football players," United Press International, March 21, 1990.

page 117: *It also alleged:* Ibid.

page 117: *MSU officials denied:* Ibid.

page 118: *Instead, he moved back to Michigan:* Kozak, "Steroids fueled spectacular rise and fall."

page 118: *Six months later:* "Outside the Lines, Where Are They Now? Tony Mandarich." *SportsCenter,* April 19, 2009, aired on ESPN.

page 118: *According to Mandarich:* Rick Telander, "Tony Mandarich is very, very sorry," *Sports Illustrated,* March 9, 2009.

page 118: *He lost 20 pounds, and*: Jill Lieber, "Tony the Terrible," *Sports Illustrated*, September 28, 1992.

page 119: *After coming clean in 2008*: Sharon Shaw Elrod and Tony Mandarich, *My Dirty Little Secrets—Steroids, Alcohol & God: The Tony Mandarich Story* (Ann Arbor, Michigan: Loving Healing Press, 2009), chap. 6, iBook.

page 119: *He claimed he was not sober*: "Where Are They Now? Tony Mandarich." *SportsCenter*, April 19, 2009, aired on ESPN.

page 119: *"Playing half in the bag…"*: Kevin Mitchell, "Mandarich's life a cautionary tale," (Saskatoon, Saskatchewan) *Star Phoenix*, August 26, 2015.

page 119: *"You think it's helping…"*: Ibid.

page 119: *After the Showtime interview*: Rick Telander, "A couple of sorry tales," *Chicago Sun-Times*, October 24, 2008.

page 119: *A couple of months later*: Telander, "Tony Mandarich is very, very sorry."

page 119: *"I was wrong. I conned you…"*: Ibid.

page 119: *Jack Ebling, who covered*: Cody Tucker, "Tony Mandarich, 23 years sober, still can't escape 'incredible bust' moniker," *Lansing State Journal*, April 25, 2018, https://www.lansingstatejournal.com/story/sports/2018/04/25/michigan-state-tony-mandarich-nfl-draft/548646002/ (accessed September 21, 2021).

page 119: *It was a phrase*: Eric Lacy, "Mandarich on MSU," *Detroit News*, October 2, 2008.

page 119: *According to (Appleton, Wisconsin)* Post-Crescent: Tim Froberg, "The truth about Mandarich's drug use surfaces 20 years later," (Appleton, Wisconsin) *Post-Crescent*, March 13, 2009.

page 120: *"Collegiate steroid abuse…"*: Matt Hinton, "Tony Mandarich fails to stun the world with heads-slappingly obvious admission of steroid abuse at Michigan State," YahooSports.com, September 30, 2008, https://sports.yahoo.com/blogs/ncaaf-matt-hinton/tony-mandarich-fails-stun-world-head-slappingly-obvious.html (accessed September 22, 2021).

page 120: *"Boy, there's a real…"*: "2 minute drill," *Philadelphia Daily News*, October 3, 2008.

page 120: *"What next? An admission…"*: Ibid.

page 120: Kenosha (Wisconsin) News *writer Mike Larsen*: Mike Larsen, "Still hope Brewers, Cubs fans," *Kenosha (Wisconsin) News*, October 2, 2008.

page 120: *Even then, it only tested*: Shaw and Mandarich. *My Dirty Little Secrets*, chap. 3.

page 120: *So as soon as the Michigan State*: Ibid.

page 120: *During his 2009 ESPN*: "Outside the Lines, Where Are They Now? Tony Mandarich." *SportsCenter*, April 19, 2009, aired on ESPN.

page 121: *Mandarich also admitted to*: Ibid.

page 121: *In 2008, Mandarich said*: Shannon Shelton, "Mandarich tells about his juicing," *Detroit Free Press*, October 3, 2008.

page 121: *"I'm big, I'm strong…"*: Jack Sheppard, "Experts agree: Mandarich blocks out the competition."

page 121: *After the draft*: Rob Schultz, "Mandarich seems happy to join Packers organization," (Madison, Wisconsin) *Capital Times*, April 24, 1989.

page 121: *"I called [Lovelace] 'Linda'…"*: Telander, "The Big Enchilada."

page 122: *"I ripped his helmet…"*: Ibid.

page 122: *"I knew he…"*: Telander, "Tony Mandarich is very, very sorry."

page 122: *"There was nothing…"*: Telander, "A couple of sorry tales."

page 122: *In 2020, Telander explained*: Author interview with Rick Telander, October 9, 2020.

page 122: *Until the NCAA*: Thomas P. Simon, "Reforming the NCAA Drug-Testing Program to Withstand State Constitutional Scrutiny: An Anaylsis and Proposal," *University of Michigan Journal of Law Reform* (1990): 289–290, https://repository.law.umich.edu/cgi/viewcontent.cgi?article=1751&context=mjlr (accessed September 21, 2021).

page 122: *NCAA Executive Director*: Ibid.

page 123: *"Unfortunately, I think…"*: Ibid.

page 123: *One suggested that*: Tim Froberg, "The truth about Mandarich's drug use surfaces 20 years later," (Appleton, Wisconsin) *Post-Crescent*, March 13, 2009.

page 123: *According to Braatz in 1989*: McGinn, "Team not scared by Mandarich steroid talk."

page 123: *Braatz essentially admitted as much*: Ibid.

page 123: *Braatz said, "The point is moot…"*: Ibid.

page 124: *Bob McGinn, who covered the Packers*: McGinn, "The McGinn Files. How Mandarich duped the scouting world and the Packers," *The Athletic*, October 2, 2019.

page 124: *According to McGinn, shortly before*: Ibid.

page 124: *When Washington general manager*: Robert Sansevere, "Skimming the top: A look at the cream of the NFL Draft crop," (Minneapolis) *Star Tribune*, April 21, 1989.

page 124: *"The hype was bigger…"*: Jill Lieber, "Tony the Terrible."

page 124: *"There isn't anybody…"*: Ibid.

Chapter 10: "When It Comes to Winning That One Critical Game, Bill Cowher Can't Do It" (1992–2005 Pittsburgh Steelers)

page 127: *With his famous long*: Timothy W. Smith, "A Style That's Written in His Face," *New York Times*, January 28, 1996.

page 127: *While some opponents found*: Michael Madden, "Steelers' iron leader," *Boston Globe*, January 9, 1998.

page 127: *The media touted him*: Ibid.

page 127: *His teams sometimes looked unprepared*: "Steelers Report Card," *Pittsburgh Post-Gazette*, September 18, 2000; "Bengals' Fake Drove Spike Into Steelers' Hearts," Associated Press, October 13, 1998.

page 127: *In mid-December 1999, after Pittsburgh's*: Ron Cook, "Comedy of errors gets poor rating," *Pittsburgh Post-Gazette*, December 13, 1999.

page 128: *"The talent should be there."*: Ibid.

page 128: *"It's safe to say…"*: Ibid.

page 128: *During the 1998 season*: Bill Cowher, with Michael Holley, *Heart and Steel* (New York: Atria Publishing Group, 2021), chap. 11, iBook.

page 128: *"Tom and Bill disagreed…"*: Dan Rooney, as told to Andrew E. Masich and David F. Halas, *My 75 Years with the Pittsburgh Steelers and the NFL.* (Cambridge, MA: Da Capo Press, 2017), 246.

page 128: *"Bill didn't want Donahoe…"*: Ibid.

page 128: *"We were beyond mediation…"*: Cowher and Holley, *Heart and Steel*, chap. 11.

page 128: *"I could not and did not"*: Ibid.

page 128: *According to team vice-president*: "Donahoe quits Steelers," *Pittsburgh Post-Gazette*, January 15, 2000.

page 128: *"It would be an upset…"*: Thomas George, "For Some, End of Season Is End of Line," *New York Times*, January 1, 2000.

page 128: *In the* Los Angeles Times: Houston Mitchell, "Welcome to the Basement, 49ers," *Los Angeles Times*, December 6, 1999.

page 128: *In the* Post-Gazette, *Cook*: Ron Cook, "Cowher, Steelers should part ways," *Pittsburgh Post-Gazette*, January 9, 2000.

page 129: *The growing theory among Steelers fans*: Jason Cole, "Parcells' tricks not fair to a loyal Belichick," *Miami Herald*, January 9, 2000.

page 129: *He wrote: "The Steelers…"*: Mark Madden, "Cowher under fire, but won't be fired," *Pittsburgh Post-Gazette,* December 18, 1999.

page 129: *"On January 12, 2000…"*: Pete Dougherty, "Cowboys may pass on Davis," *Green Bay Press-Gazette*, January 12, 2000.

page 129: *A few days later*: Alan Robinson, "Steelers begin search for successor," Associated Press, January 16, 2000.

page 129: *Rooney only accepted Donahoe's*: Ibid.

page 129: *Not long thereafter, the Steelers*: Gerry Dulac, "Donahoe's forced resignation comes as surprise to players," *Pittsburgh Post-Gazette,* January 15, 2000.

page 129: *Donahoe's departure was described*: Tim Graham, "Donahoe comes with sterling reputation," *Buffalo News*, January 11, 2001.

page 129: *"I just wanted a collaborative…"*: Cowher and Holley, *Heart and Steel*, 310.

page 130: *"I am writing to express…"*: "Did the Steelers keep the wrong guy?" *Pittsburgh Post-Gazette*, January 22, 2000.

page 130: *"Giving more power…"*: Ibid.

page 130: *"This stunning decision…"*: Bob Smizik, "Donahoe departs; Steelers lose," *Pittsburgh Post-Gazette*, January 15, 2000.

page 130: *"The chances of the Steelers…"*: Ibid.

page 130: *"They had two men"*: Ibid.

page 130: *"It was their job"*: Ibid.

page 130 *"The Steelers signed…"*: T. J. Simers, "Again, Beathard Saves His Best For Last," *Los Angeles Times*, April 17, 2000.

page 130: *"Choosing between personnel…"*: Ibid.

page 130: *After the second game, a 23*: Bob Smizik, "How low can the Steelers go?" *Pittsburgh Post-Gazette*, September 18, 2000.

page 131: *In the* Californian, *writer*: Jay Paris, "NFL Rankings," (Temecula, California) *Californian*, September 29, 2000.

page 131: *"During the CBS broadcast…"*: Chuck Finder, "CBS almost pulls plug on Steelers," *Pittsburgh Post-Gazette*, September 25, 2000.

page 131: *"Former Washington Pro Bowl offensive"*: Ibid.

page 131: *"The following day…"*: Houston Mitchell, "Two-Minute Drill," *Los Angeles Times*, September 25, 2000.

page 131: *"Cowher is toast…"*: Jay Paris, "A few more NFL coaches likely on the way out," (Temecula, California) *Californian*, September 29, 2000.

page 131: *"The only question is if…"*: Ibid.

page 131: *"The guess here is…"*: Ron Cook, "It's Cowher vs. Donahoe again," *Pittsburgh Post-Gazette*, January 12, 2001.

page 132: *"After Pittsburgh lost…"*: "Caught on the web," *Pittsburgh Post-Gazette*, September 24, 2002.

page 133: *For years, Cowher had been criticized*: Ron Cook, "Is Cowher wearing thin on his coaches," *Pittsburgh Post-Gazette*, January 16, 1997; Ed Bouchette, "Gailey leaves void: Gets Dallas job while Steelers launch search to replace him," *Pittsburgh Post-Gazette*, February 13, 1998.

page 133: *but this time reports of*: Mark Madden, "Cowher gets bad marks for abuse of assistants," *Pittsburgh Post-Gazette*, January 10, 2004.

page 133: *Curti wrote that other coaches*: Chuck Curti, "Cowher can't win the big one," *Beaver County (Pennsylvania) Times*, January 25, 2005.

page 133: *He added: "When it…"*: Ibid.

page 134: *"The Steelers will never…"*: "Sports Mailbag," *Pittsburgh Post-Gazette*, December 9, 2005.

page 134: *Another wrote, "I have a solution…"*: Ibid.

page 134: *"Is the season over?"*: Ed Bouchette, "IS THE SEASON OVER?" *Pittsburgh Post-Gazette*, December 5, 2005.

page 134: *Right before the Steelers' Super Bowl*: John Altavilla, "Jaws returns," *Hartford Courant*, February 4, 2006.

page 134: *He said he trusted*: Ibid.

page 134: *"We're about stability..."*: Alan Robinson, "Rooney's patience pays off as Cowher returns to title game," January 27, 2002.

page 134: *"We know what..."*: Ibid.

Chapter 11: "The 49ers Should Do Everyone a Favor. Trade Steve Young. The Myth. And the Man" (1987–1994 San Francisco 49ers)

page 138: *As one local columnist*: Art Spander, "Bay Area just can't get enough of Joe," *San Francisco Examiner*, December 18, 1992.

page 139: *Later coined the "West Coast Offense"*: Richard Goldstein, "Bill Walsh, Innovator of West Coast Offense, Dies at 75," *New York Times*, July 31, 2007.

page 139: *It also prioritized ball control*: Michael Lombardi, "The Genius of Bill Walsh," The Ringer, September 6, 2018, https://www.theringer.com/nfl/2018/9/6/17822756/gridiron-genius-mike-lombardi-bill-walsh (accessed February 20, 2022).

page 139: *The quarterback needed to think*: Ibid.

page 139: *He had a natural ability*: Keith Dunnavant, *Montana: The Biography of Football's Joe Cool* (New York: Thomas Dunne Books, 2016), chap. 6, iBook.

page 139: *While not noticeably fast*: Ibid., 244.

page 140: *During training camp*: Frank Cooney, "Montana due back for opener," *San Francisco Examiner*, August 24, 1985.

page 140: *In June 1986, he underwent*: "Montana recovering from secret surgery," Associated Press, June 13, 1986.

page 141: *In the first game*: "Montana on the mend after back surgery," Associated Press, September 18, 1986.

page 141: *Local papers immediately*: Charles Bricker, "Walsh faces major rebuilding job, there's little help in sight," (San Jose, California) *Mercury News*, January 6, 1987.

page 141: *Some of the Niners*: Ibid.

page 141: *Walsh was beginning to believe*: Dunnavant, *Montana*, chap. 8, iBook.

page 141: *He needed not just*: Ibid.

page 141: *He quickly focused on*: Ibid.

page 142: *After a stellar career at*: "$40 million bid to Young reported," Associated Press, March 4, 1984.

page 142: *Announced as a four-year deal*: Ken Peters, "Express sign Young for $40 million," Associated Press, March 6, 1984.

page 142: *But by the time*: Jim Selman, "Buccaneers sign Young to contract," *Tampa Tribune*, September 11, 1985.

page 142: *He later recalled*: Spence Checketts, host, "Steve Young," *Reality Check with Spence Checketts*, February 13, 2019.

page 142: *After Tampa Bay used its first pick*: Ira Miller, "Walsh 'stole' Young," SFGate.com, January 18, 2012, https://www.sfgate.com/sports/article/Walsh-stole-Young-2618265.php (accessed August 8, 2021).

page 142: *Walsh couldn't understand why*: Ibid.

page 142: *He was convinced that Tampa*: Ibid.

page 143: *"Steve, you don't come…"*: Steve Young, with Jeff Benedict, *QB: My Life Behind the Spiral* (Boston: Houghton Mifflin Harcourt, 2016), 188, Scribd.

page 143: *"Joe might wander…"*: Ibid.

page 143: *On his first day*: Ibid, 192.

page 143: *He looked healthy*: Ibid.

page 143: *He referred to Young*: Don Pierson, "Montana vs. Young: Day of Reckoning here," *Chicago Tribune*, September 11, 1994.

page 143: *According to Young's agent, Leigh*: Leigh Steinberg and Michael Arkush, *The Agent: My 40-Year Career Making Deals and Changing the Game* (New York: St. Martin's Griffin, 2015), 206, Scribd.

page 144: *"Steve Young is…"*: Glenn Dickey, "Viking Win Didn't Surprise Everyone," *San Francisco Chronicle*, January 6, 1988.

page 144: *"He does the same…"*: Ibid.

page 144: *"In the present tense"*: Dave Albee, *USA Today*, December 28, 1987.

page 144: *The consensus was that*: Lowell Cohn, "The Obstacle Is Removed," *San Francisco Chronicle*, January 4, 1988.

page 144: *But when the Minnesota Vikings*: Bob Padecky, "No one else will stop them, either," (Santa Rosa, California) *Press Democrat*, December 28, 1987.

page 144: *Soon after, Walsh*: Jim Jenkins, "Montana not worried about Young," *Sacramento Bee*, January 12, 1988.

page 145: *In November 1987,* San Francisco Chronicle *columnist Glenn Dickey*: Glenn Dickey, "Joes Good, But Not the Best," *San Francisco Chronicle*, November 17, 1987.

page 145: *"Montana's local reputation rests…"*: Ibid.

page 145: *Dickey also essentially labeled Montana*: Ibid.

page 145: *"Montana has been, indisputably…"*: Ibid.

page 145: *He then added that*: Ibid.

page 145: *Dickey also believed that*: Ibid.

page 146: *He told NBC's Merlin Olsen*: Ralph Leef, "Walsh admits to QB Controversy, (Santa Rosa, California) *Press Democrat*, August 3, 1988.

page 147: *To him, it was bittersweet*: Young and Benedict, *QB: My Life Behind the Spiral*, 253.

page 147: *He did not want to wait*: Ibid., 253–254.

page 148: *If that wasn't ominous enough*: Tom Jackson, "Young should ask 49ers to trade him," *Sacramento Bee*, August 22, 1990.

page 148: *In late August 1990*: Ibid.

page 148: *"He's running out of time"*: Ibid.

page 148: *"And he darn well ought…"*: Ibid.

page 148: *Also, Jackson surmised that*: Ibid.

page 148: *Against the advice of many*: Young and Benedict, *QB: My Life Behind the Spiral*, 266.

page 148: *He thought that the 49ers' offense*: Ibid.

page 149: *According to a witness*: Bob Padecky, "49ers are losing games and class," (Santa Rosa, California) *Press Democrat*, October 16, 1991.

page 149: *It became so bad*: Charles Haley, with Joe Layden, *All the Rage: Life of an NFL Renegade* (Kansas City: Andrews McMeel Publishing, 1997), 63, Scribd.

page 149: *Niners' reps had to ask*: Padecky, "49ers are losing games and class."

page 149: *"He was such a whiner"*: Haley and Layden, *All the Rage*, 79.

page 149: *"He was always moping"*: Ibid., 78.

page 149: *After the game, former 49ers receiver*: Padecky, "49ers are losing games and class."

page 149: *"I'm just glad Joe Montana…"*: Mark Purdy, "A bad trend haunts Young," (San Jose, California) *Mercury News*, October 14, 1991.

page 150: *That evening, while narrating*: NFL Primetime. Aired December 1, 1991, on ESPN.

page 150: *Bono's performance also spawned a media narrative*: Bob Padecky "Bono brings back flashes of Joe," (Santa Rosa, California) *Press Democrat*, December 2, 1991; Bruce Jenkins, "Revived 49ers Should Keep Bono at QB," *San Francisco Chronicle*, December 2, 1991.

page 151: *"[Bono] is quickly…"*: Joe Santoro, "Niners find substitute Joe in Bono," *Reno Gazette-Journal*, December 2, 1991.

page 151: *"He's right handed… he throws…"*: Ibid.

page 151: *Hall of Fame quarterback…*: Frank Cooney, "Bono no bonehead for 49ers, leaves Young waiting again, *San Francisco Examiner*, December 4, 1991.

page 151: *"Bono is Montana's surrogate"*: Larry Minner, "Sorry, Mr. Young," *Modesto (California) Bee*, December 3, 1991.

page 151: *"He runs the system…"*: Ibid.

page 151: *"Believe me," Vitt said*: Claire Farsnworth, "'Oh No, Bono,' Third-String QB Becoming a 49er Savior," *Seattle Post-Intelligencer*, December 5, 1991.

page 151: *"[Steve Young's stock] has…*: Lowell Cohn, "Invest in Bono—His Stock Is Way Up," *San Francisco Chronicle*, December 5, 1991.

page 151: *"The brutal truth is…"*: Ibid.

page 151: *He continued, "It is a fact…"*: Ibid.

page 152: *A few days later, (Santa Rosa, California)*: Michael Silver, "Starting Bono over Young is bonkers," (Santa Rosa, California) *Press Democrat*, December 4, 1991.

page 152: *"I definitely wasn't anti-Bono…"*: Author interview with Michael Silver, December 17, 2020.

page 152: *"Get ready for the Montana/Bono..."*: "49ers vs. Seahawks," *NFL on CBS Sports*, December 8, 1991, aired on CBS.

page 153: *Various scribes likened*: Bob Padecky, "49ers have a new master architect," (Santa Rosa, California) *Press Democrat*, December 9, 1991; John Crumpacker, "Receiver hauls in the game-winner against Seattle as S.F. stays in hunt," *San Francisco Examiner*, December 9, 1991.

page 153: *"Steve Bono can play..."*: Jim Van Vliet, "Kings give pay-per-view a trial run," *Sacramento Bee*, December 10, 1991.

page 153: *"Bono has the obvious..."*: Ibid.

page 153: *As the* San Francisco Examiner*'s*: Ray Ratto, "Losing touch with reality," *San Francisco Examiner*, May 11, 1992.

page 153: *Near the end of the 1991 season*: John Crumpacker, "Perpetual backup QB expects to remain with 49ers," *San Francisco Examiner*, December 22, 1991.

page 154: *One plugged-in writer*: Ira Miller, "49ers must trade Young for safety, running back," *San Francisco Chronicle*, December 12, 1991.

page 154: *"There was a lot of pressure"*: Frank Cooney, "49ers' best trade of the year was the one they didn't make," *San Francisco Examiner*, November 22, 1992.

page 154: *"There were many factors..."*: Ibid.

page 154: *The morning of the 1992 NFL Draft*: Ibid.

page 154: *They wanted two first-round*: Ibid.

page 154: *"I'm not going to accept..."*: "Young won't accept being Joe's backup," Associated Press, May 9, 1992.

page 154: *"That would be like running..."*: Ibid.

page 154: *"Time to say so long..."*: Bruce Jenkins, "Time for 49ers to Say So Long to Steve Young," *San Francisco Chronicle*, May 11, 1992.

page 154: *"It doesn't look that complicated..."*: Ibid.

page 154: *(San Jose, California)* Mercury News *columnist*: Mark Purdy, "49ers have no choice: Young must be traded," (San Jose, California) *Mercury News*, May 10, 1992.

page 154: *"Steve Young is not..."*: Bob Padecky, "49ers need to trade Young," (Santa Rosa, California) *Press Democrat*, May 10, 1992.

page 154: *"The 49ers should do..."*: Ibid.

page 155: *"Steve Young has a better..."*: Bob Padecky, "For good of 49ers, a case pro Bono," (Santa Rosa, California) *The Press Democrat*, August 26, 1992.

page 155: *In a column, he declared*: Ibid.

page 155: *Although he admitted*: Ibid.

page 155: *He theorized that the 49ers'*: Ibid.

page 155: *On CBS, Randy Cross explained*: Rudy Martzke, "Less proves to be better for CBS and Chirkinian," *USA Today*, August 17, 1992.

page 155: *In an interview with Cross*: Rudy Martzke, "Valvano finds comfort from friends, colleagues," *USA Today*, August 14, 1992.

page 156: *"To put it mildly"*: John Crumpacker, "Montana throws—a fit," *San Francisco Examiner*, August 28, 1992.

page 156: *When Montana heard that Young would*: Lowell Cohn, "Montana's Behavior is Just Plain Undignified," *San Francisco Chronicle*, September 1, 1992.

page 156: *On the sidelines*: Art Spander, "Montana doesn't want to pass the torch," *San Francisco Examiner*, August 30, 1992.

page 156: *"Steve Bono should…"*: Chris Mortensen, "49ers Can't Escape QB Problems," *Sporting News*, September 13, 1992.

page 156: *One of the common criticisms*: Larry Minner, "The right Steve," *Modesto (California) Bee*, December 15, 1991.

page 157: *Many felt he should stay*: Santoro, "Niners find substitute Joe in Bono."

page 157: *Shanahan worked with him*: Young and Benedict, *QB: My Life Behind the Spiral*, 299.

page 158: *"I hope Steve Young…"*: Paola Boivin, "Joe vs. Steve, Who should Start? 49ers Fans Take Sides," *Los Angeles Daily News*, January 8, 1993.

page 158: *Just prior to the game*: Young and Benedict, *QB: My Life Behind the Spiral*, 212–213.

page 158: *"And all is right with…"*: "Lions vs. 49ers," *Monday Night Football*, December 28, 1992, aired on ABC.

page 159: *"It might be raining…"*: Ibid.

page 159: *"Now. All is well"*: Ibid.

page 159: *"Yes, if it is possible…"*: Bob Padecky, "Yet another return to greatness," (Santa Rosa, California) *Press Democrat*, December 29, 1992.

page 159: *"You hate to say it but now…"*: Ibid.

page 159: *"Montana moves his team…"*: Ibid.

page 159: *According to 49ers, play-by-play*: Boivin, "Joe vs. Steve, Who should Start?"

page 159: *A few days before*: Chris Dufresne, "His Support is Hardly the Size of Montana," December 27, 1992.

page 159: *"Last week, these guys…"*: Boivin, "Joe vs. Steve, Who should Start?"

page 159: *"I asked someone what…"*: Ibid.

page 160: *Michael Wilbon, in his*: Michael Wilbon, "Big Young year can't stop chant: 'We want Joe!'" *Washington Post*, January 7, 1993.

page 160: *Despite acknowledging that*: Ibid.

page 160: *"What would be the harm…"*: Ibid.

page 160: *"Something that would leave him…"*: Ibid.

page 160: *From Lowell Cohn's next day* Chronicle: Lowell Cohn, "Don't Say This Was Young's Fault," *The San Francisco Chronicle*, January 18, 1993.

page 160: *Within a few hours*: John Crumpacker, "Now Young will have to elude blitzing fans," *San Francisco Examiner*, January 18, 1993.

page 161: *After the game, Seifert*: Gary Swan, "Rice Hopes Montana Returns," *San Francisco Chronicle*, January 19, 1993.

page 161: *Young's agent, Leigh Steinberg*: "MVP could bolt 49ers," United Press International, January 19, 1993.

page 161: *Young countered those statements*: "49ers' Young still not able to put comparisons to rest," Associated Press, January 20, 1993.

page 161: *His contract was about to expire*: Ibid.

page 161: *The day after the loss*: R. E. Graswich, "For 49ers, it's now next season, 1993 will be the Joe Show," *Sacramento Bee*, January 18, 1993.

page 161: *Frank Cooney, in the* San Francisco Examiner: "Trading Young would be the smarter move for 49ers," *San Francisco Examiner*, April 10, 1993.

page 161: *Montana wanted a fair shot*: Gary Myers, "Joe picks K.C., but S.F. balks," *New York Daily News*, April 18, 1993.

page 161: *They told Montana to look*: Gary Swan, "Bono Signs, Montana Starts His Search," *San Francisco Chronicle*, April 8, 1993.

page 161: *Then, a plot twist*: Frank Cooney and Larry D. Hatfield, "Montana: Departure best for all involved," *San Francisco Examiner*, April 19, 1993.

page 161: *Seifert announced that Montana*: "Montana says he'll go to K.C.," Associated Press, April 19, 1993.

page 162: *Ray Ratto, in the* Examiner: Ray Ratto, "It was all one big silly charade," *San Francisco Examiner*, April 19, 1993.

page 162: *"I think it was meant..."*: Ibid.

page 162: *"Joe Montana gets..."*: Ibid.

page 162: *The* Sacramento Bee*'s Mark*: Mark Kreidler, "Something about this deal smells," *Sacramento Bee*, April 19, 1993.

page 162: *"Listen does Mr. Toad..."*: Ibid.

page 162: *In the* New York Daily News: Gary Myers, "L'affaire Montana an embarrassment," *New York Daily News*, April 20, 1993.

page 162: *"Moe, Larry and Curly..."*: R. E. Graswich, "Moe, Larry and Curly would be proud of this bunch," *Sacramento Bee*, April 20, 1993.

page 162: *"The 49ers insist they..."*: Ibid.

page 162: *He said it was*: Gary Myers, "Joe's choice? Chiefs," *New York Daily News*, April 20, 1993.

page 163: *Shortly thereafter, the 49ers*: "The deal: what the Chiefs, 49ers get," *Kansas City Star*, April 22, 1993.

page 163: *"[Seifert] just lost..."*: Bruce Jenkins, "Tearful day for 49ers fans—or a Chance to Rebuild," *San Francisco Chronicle*, April 21, 1993.

page 163: *"Now he's stuck with..."*: Ibid.

page 163: *He continued: "The fans might be the biggest losers of all..."*: Ibid.

page 163: *The* New York Times *summed up*: Tom Friend, "SF mourns the departure of Montana," *New York Times*, April 22, 1993.

page 164: *To* Chronicle *writer*: Scott Ostler, "'Magical' Joe Gets Better and Better," *San Francisco Chronicle*, September 12, 1994.

page 165: *Young had been violently brought*: John Crumpacker, "Few bright spots for team as Eagles deliver beating," *San Francisco Examiner*, October 3, 1994.

page 165: *Young threw a fit on*: Bob Padecky, "Young correctly expresses anger," (Santa Rosa, California) *Press Democrat*, October 3, 1994.

page 165: *"Management for the best…"*: Kevin Lyons, "Big money free agents little help for 49ers," *Washington Times*, October 3, 1994.

page 166: *"If you were watching carefully…"*: "They wrote it," (Spokane, Washington) *Spokesman Review*, January 30, 1995.

page 166: *Glenn Dickey saw enough*: Glenn Dickey, "Young as good as Montana ever was," *San Francisco Chronicle*, January 30, 1995.

page 166: *"Yesterday was the final proof"*: Ibid.

page 167: *"What about all the people…"*: John Eisenberg, "Finally, out of shadows, into his own," *Baltimore Sun,* January 30, 1995.

page 167: *"To hell with them"*: Ibid.

Chapter 12: "Why would we give up a first-round pick for [Brett Favre]?" (1992–1998 Green Bay Packers)

page 169: *Wolf was known as*: Don Pierson, "Bears will find Packers' Wolf at their door," *Chicago Tribune*, December 8, 1991.

page 169: *A real "football man"*: Ibid.

page 169: *Wolf knew that, to turn*: Michael Bauman, *Ron Wolf and the Green Bay Packers* (Champaign, IL: Sports Publishing, 2019), 14–16, Scribd.

page 169: *Moreover, he wanted it*: Ibid., 16.

page 170: *A Bill Walsh disciple*: John Clayton, "Gruden and Reid have come a long way," ESPN.com, 2002, https://www.espn.com/nfl/playoffs02/columnist/2003/0116/1493923.html (accessed September 25, 2021).

page 170: *The "hot" candidate of the*: Steve Hubbard, "Stanford's Green new name on Steelers' list," *Pittsburgh Press*, January 4, 1992.

page 170: *Joseph Dill, the sports editor*: Joseph Dill, "Defense warrants attention," *Oshkosh (Wisconsin) Northwestern*, January 14, 1992.

page 170: *He also grumbled*: Ibid.

page 171: *One doubter, Tom Silverstein*: Tom Silverstein, "Holmgren era about to begin. But is he an Infante clone?" *Milwaukee Sentinel*, January 11, 1992.

page 171: *"In a lot of ways…"*: Ibid.

page 171: *"They're going from…"*: Ibid

page 171: *"It was George Santayana…"*: Tom Oates, "Packers return to failed path," *Wisconsin State Journal*, January 13, 1992.

page 171: *"It appears the Packers…"*: Ibid.

page 171: *Chris Mortensen, in the* Sporting News: Chris Mortensen, "Holmgren will strive to pack a wallop," *Sporting News,* February 17, 1992.

page 171: *"In that division, you've…"*: Silverstein, "Holmgren era about to begin."

page 172: *"You're not playing half…"*: Ibid.

page 172: *In the press box at Atlanta–Fulton County Stadium*: Bauman, *Ron Wolf and the Green Bay Packers,* 20–21.

page 172: *During the 1990 season*: Ibid., 18.

page 172: *He came back extremely impressed*: Ibid.

page 172: *"Favre was always late…"*: Rob Demovsky, "The Great Gamble," ESPN.com, August 4, 2016, https://www.espn.com/espn/feature/story/_/id /17211520/how-brett-favre-landed-green-bay-packers-made-happen (accessed September 25, 2021).

page 172: *"[He] couldn't even run…"*: Ibid.

page 173: *A few days after the Atlanta game*: Ron Wolf, interview with Jason Wilde and Mark Tauscher, *Wilde and Tausch,* WTMJ Packers Flagship Podcast, September 17, 2019.

page 173: *"[The Executive Committee] had no idea…"*: Rob Reischel, *Leaders of the Pack: Starr, Favre, Rodgers, and Why Green Bay's Quarterback Trio is the Best in NFL History.* (Chicago: Triumph Books, 2015), p. 85, Scribd.

page 173: *"But they were all…"*: Ibid.

page 173: *"I sure would have liked to"*: Ron Wolf, interview with Wilde and Tauscher.

page 173: *Because I'm sure that those guys*: Ibid.

page 173: *Team president Harlan recalled that*: Bob Harlan, with Dale Hoffman, *Green and Golden Moments: Bob Harlan and the Green Bay Packers* (Stevens Point, WI: KCI Sports Publishing, 2007), 102.

page 173: *Wolf would sometimes have*: Don Pierson, "Pack's Favre not just your average kid QB," *Chicago Tribune,* February 16, 1992.

page 173: *"Some of the worst mail…"*: Mark Beech, *The People's Team: An Illustrated History of the Green Bay Packers* (Boston: Houghton Mifflin Harcourt, 2019), 563, Scribd.

page 173: *"Who is this Wolf guy…"*: Bauman, *Ron Wolf and the Green Bay Packers,* 143.

page 173: *"People thought Wolf was nuts"*: Curt Brown "Out of Nowhere, Packers' rising star Favre has funny name but serious talent," (Minneapolis) *Star Tribune,* December 20, 1992.

page 174: *"I'll never forget…"*: Ibid.

page 174: *According to Mark Scheifelbein*: Bauman, *Ron Wolf and the Green Bay Packers,* 377.

page 174: *"We…made a stupid trade…"*: Chris Havel, "Some Packers fans are never pleased," *Green Bay Press-Gazette,* February 22, 1992.

page 174: *When Jon Gruden, Holmgren's*: Jon Gruden, with Vic Carucci, *Do You Love Football?!* (New York: HarperCollins, 2004), 123–124, Scribd.

page 174: *"Who the hell is [he]?"*: Brown, "Out of Nowhere…"

page 174: *"What in the world…"*: "They also said it, Members of the media," *Green-Bay Press-Gazette*, April 26, 1993.

page 174: *"Prove it to us"*: "Our Opinion," (Fond du Lac, Wisconsin) *Commonwealth Reporter*, February 17, 1992.

page 174: *"Pardon our raised eyebrows…"*: Ibid.

page 174: *"So now we will find…"*: Len Wagner, "Could UWGB-Badgers game get Bennett twist?" *Green Bay Press-Gazette*, February 13, 1992.

page 174: *Describing what he thought the Packers*: John Lindsay, "Bumper crop of talent is lined up for the draft," Scripps Howard News Service, April 24, 1992.

page 175: *Some writers, like the* Wausau (Wisconsin) Daily Herald's: Jay Lillge, "Taking the professional approach," *Wausau (Wisconsin) Daily Herald*, April 5, 1992.

page 176: *In his* Cincinnati Enquirer *game report*: Tim Sullivan, "Loss proves Bengals have long way to go," *Cincinnati Enquirer*, September 21, 1992.

page 176: *According to Favre's wife Deanna*: Deanna Favre, with Angela Hunt, *Don't bet against me!* (Carol Stream, IL: Tyndale House, 2007), 44, Scribd.

page 177: *"A confused rattled…"*: Tom Kessenich, "What has happened to the Packers?" *Oshkosh (Wisconsin) Northwestern*, October 8, 1993.

page 177: *"The book on Favre appears…"*: Ibid.

page 177: *One fan, writing*: "Sports Forum," *Green Bay Press-Gazette*, October 9, 1993.

page 177: *"At least [Detmer is]…"*: "Sports Line," (Appleton, Wisconsin) *Post-Crescent*, November 9, 1993.

page 177: *Another fan derided*: "Callers rip Favre, want Detmer," *Wasau Daily Herald*, November 9, 1993.

page 177: *"Stick Ty Detmer in and…"*: Ibid.

page 177: *Another wrote a letter to*: "Letters to the Sports Editor," *Wisconsin State Journal*, December 24, 1993.

page 178: *"[Favre] is struggling…"*: Chuck Carlson, "Questions abound over Green Bay's quarterback of the future," (Appleton, Wisconsin) *Post-Crescent*, November 9, 1993.

page 178: *"For the first time…"*: Ibid.

page 178: *According to Woelfel, the second-year*: Gary Woelfel, "Holmgren's playcalling defies logic," (Racine, Wisconsin) *Journal Times*, December 21, 1993.

page 178: *"Why are some members…"*: Ibid.

page 178: *"Is it because some…"*: Ibid.

page 178: *That summer, the Packers*: "A very rich QB," Associated Press, July 15, 1994.

page 181: *A couple of weeks later*: Mike Freeman, "Three Players File Suit, Seek Free Agency in '93," *Washington Post*, September 22, 1993, https://www .washingtonpost.com/archive/sports/1992/09/22/three-players-file -suit-seek-free-agency-in-93/bff3d01b-7474-40bc-b83a-05114df0b9e0/ (accessed March 23, 2022).

page 181: *Prior to the settlement*: Manny Topol, "NFL Trial Kicks Off," (New York) *Newsday*, June 15, 1992.

page 181: *At first, the concern was*: Ibid.

page 182: *However, as part of the settlement*: "NFL deal draws mixed reviews," Associated Press, January 8, 1993.

page 182: *One general manager*: Greg Garber, "What is the price of free agency?" *Hartford Courant*, December 13, 1992.

page 182: *"Players will go to the large markets..."*: "Speaking of free agency...," *Hartford Courant*, December 13, 1992.

page 182: *"Look at the dynasties..."*: Ibid.

page 182: *In 1987, Buffalo*: "What they say about free agency," *Fort Worth Star-Telegram*, January 20, 1987.

page 182: *That same year, Cleveland*: Ibid.

page 183: *"The players...will gravitate..."*: Tim Kawakami, "New World of Free Agency Looms on the Horizon for the NFL," *Los Angeles Times*, August 29, 1991.

page 183: *Ironically, when Packers head coach*: Ron Wolf and Paul Attner, *The Packer Way* (New York: St. Martin's Press), 101.

page 183: *They argued that it made no logical sense*: Phil Anastasia, "Free agency remains crux of NFL's problems," (Camden, New Jersey) *Courier-Post*, March 8, 1992.

page 183: *"Not everyone is going to break to the Rams..."*: Ibid.

page 183: *"You think all the running backs..."*: Ibid.

page 183: *Another issue frequently mentioned*: Robert Klemko, "How Reggie White Made Green Bay Cool," *Sports Illustrated*, December 6, 2016.

page 183: *"It was...the whitest community in the NFL"*: Ibid.

page 183: *He asked, "Why would a player..."*: Gale Sayers, "Gale Sayers on Sports: Free Agency and the NFLPA," (Mountain Home, Arkansas) *Baxter Bulletin*, February 1, 1989.

page 183: *From 1989 to 1992, the Packers signed*: Bob McGinn, "Weather no turnoff to free agents," *Green Bay Press-Gazette*, February 16, 1989.

page 184: *Just before the free agency period*: Bauman, *Ron Wolf and the Green Bay Packers*, 57.

page 184: *"I didn't think we had a prayer..."*: Ibid., 57.

page 184: *Defensive coordinator Ray Rhodes*: John Morton, "Green Bay trip was more than just a courtesy visit," *Green Bay Press-Gazette*, April 20, 1998.

page 184: *He wanted to play for*: Peter King, "Trip to Bountiful," *Sports Illustrated*, March 15, 1993.

page 184: *The Reggie White free agency*: Kris Schwartz, "Reverend Head-Slap Reggie," ESPN.com, https://www.espn.com/classic/biography/s/White _Reggie.html (accessed September 26, 2021).

page 185: *Cleveland Browns owner Art Modell*: King, "Trip to Bountiful."

page 185: *In Atlanta, the Falcons*: "The Atlanta Falcons took free agent Reggie White to meet Gov. Z," Associated Press, March 9, 1993.

page 185: *Falcons cornerback Deion Sanders*: Ibid.

page 185: *When White visited the Jets*: Hal Bock, "Jets take White's suggestion, get Esiason in trade," Associated Press, March 17, 1993.

page 185: *A day later*: Ibid.

page 185: *When he first visited the Packers*: "Reggie's words," *Green Bay Press-Gazette*, April 20, 1998.

page 185: *But his agent Jimmy Sexton*: Reggie White, with Jim Denney, *Reggie White: In the Trenches* (Nashville: Thomas Nelson Publishers, 1997), 139.

page 185: *The Packers were only finally*: Beech, *The People's Team*, 305.

page 185: *When he arrived in Green Bay*: Ibid.

page 185: *His recruitment meal was*: Ibid.

page 185: *White pointed out that Green Bay*: "Green Bay, coach impress White more than expected," Associated Press, March 12, 1993.

page 185: *But Holmgren and Wolf told*: White and Denney, *Reggie White: In the Trenches*, 141.

page 185: *They assured him that the organization*: Ibid,

page 186: *"It shouldn't happen"*: Chuck Carlson, "White's price not right for the Packers," (Appleton, Wisconsin) *Post-Crescent*, March 14, 1993.

page 186: *"The Packers need Reggie White like a horse…"*: Ibid.

page 186: *Carlson continued*: Ibid.

page 186: *"For the good of the Packers…"*: Ibid.

page 186: *"It would not make much sense"*: Ed Meyer, "It's high time for the Browns to put it on the line," *Akron (Ohio) Beacon Journal*, February 28, 1993.

page 186: *"When exactly did Reggie…"*: Mike Lupica, "Reggie's a Prize, Not a Franchise" *New York Daily News*, March 21, 1993.

page 186: *"This silliness… is over the top…"*: Ibid.

page 186: *"I do not believe Reggie White…"*: Ibid.

page 186: *When all the writers*: Author interview with Chuck Carlson, September 23, 2020.

page 187: *"To spend that kind of money…"*: Ibid.

page 187: *"Taking shots at the city…"*: Ibid.

page 187: *White said one day*: Barbara Barker, "Is White destined for 49ers?," (North Jersey) *Record*, March 26, 1993.

page 187: *"I've got to go where God wants me to go"*: Ibid.

page 187: *"Reggie," Holmgren said*: Bauman, *Ron Wolf and the Green Bay Packers*, 62.

page 187: *"This is God. You ought..."*: Ibid.

page 187: *He came away impressed*: Rick Gano, "Packers' green White's gold," (Madison, Wisconsin) *Capital Times*, April 7, 1993.

page 187: *He was attracted to*: Phil Anastasia, "White returns to Philadelphia for final award," (Camden, New Jersey) *Courier-Post*, March 25, 1993.

page 187: *Rhodes and Holmgren even flew*: White and Denney, *Reggie White: In the Trenches*, 140.

page 187: *But, ultimately, when it came*: Mike Florio, "Wolf says money led Reggie White to Green Bay," ProFootballTalk.com, February 8, 2015, https://profootballtalk.nbcsports.com/2015/02/08/ron-wolf-says-money -led-reggie-white-to-green-bay/ (accessed September 27, 2021).

page 187: *At that point, White recalled*: White and Denney, *Reggie White: In the Trenches*, 141.

page 188: *However, the five-year deal*: Ibid.

page 188: *That, to Reggie, was*: Ibid.

page 188: *White was getting $9 million total*: Wolf, *The Packer Way*, 110.

page 188: *"It was an amazing..."*: Author interview with Chuck Carlson, September 23, 2020.

page 188: *"Everybody who covered..."*: Ibid.

page 188: *And what about God*: White and Denney, *Reggie White: In the Trenches*, 142.

page 188: *Four years later*: Ibid., 143.

page 189: *"From a business point of view..."*: Bill Lyon, "A hero leaves us disillusioned," *Philadelphia Inquirer*, April 11, 1993.

page 189: *"They felt he did not..."*: Ibid.

page 190: *White is still considered*: "Top 20 free-agent signings in NFL history," NFL.com, March 25, 2018.

page 190: *In 1992, while the free agency issue*: Phil Anastasia, "Free agency remains crux of NFL's problems," (Camden, New Jersey) *Courier-Post*, March 8, 1992.

Chapter 13: "The Vikings Fleeced the Cowboys to Get Herschel Walker" (1989–1993 Dallas Cowboys)

page 192: *"We didn't have enough players"*: Jimmy Johnson, interview by Dan Patrick, *The Dan Patrick Show*, January 14, 2020.

page 192: *On Thursday evening, February 23*: Peter Golenbock, *Landry's Boys: An Oral History of a Team and an Era* (Chicago: Triumph Books, 2005), 736, Scribd.

page 192: *They learned about it*: Ibid.

page 192: *The big news didn't deter*: Denne H. Freeman, "Holding Head High, Landry Says So Long," Associated Press, February 27, 1989.

page 192: *While Landry was in his office*: Golenbock, *Landry's Boys*, 736.

page 193: *According to Don, Johnson told*: Ibid.

page 193: *Johnson then offered David*: Ibid.

page 193: *On Saturday morning*: "Landry firing shakes 'family,'" Associated Press, March 5, 1989.

page 193: *"If you would have taken..."*: Author interview with Gary Myers, April 12, 2021.

page 194: *In what Jones described*: Berry Tramel, "Jerry Jones fired Tom Landry 30 years ago Monday; the right decision in the wrong way," (Oklahoma City) *Oklahoman*, February 26, 2019.

page 194: *"They didn't show..."*: "To some fans, coaching change a tragedy; to others, a necessity," Associated Press, February 27, 1989.

page 194: *"Here he is, a legend..."*: Ibid.

page 194: *Dave "Kidd" Kraddick*: "Tom Landry has lost his job but not the respect of fans," United Press International, March 3, 1989.

page 194: *Some of the lyrics*: Ibid.

page 194: *"We've all felt the magic..."*: KXAS-NBC 5, 10 p.m. News, Television newscast, February 28, 1989.

page 194: *"To see the man..."*: Ibid.

page 195: *"Firings are hard..."*: Verne Lundquist, *Play by Play: Calling the Wildest Games in Sports* (New York: HarperCollins, 2009), 117, Scribd.

page 195: *In late April*: Golenbock. *Landry's Boys*, 741.

page 195: *Fifty thousand people showed up*: Ibid.

page 196: *"[He] could be..."*: Robert Sansevere, "Skimming the top: a look at the cream of the NFL Draft crop," (Minneapolis) *Star Tribune*, April 21, 1989.

page 196: *"Even Broncos personnel..."*: Ibid.

page 196: *"If [the Cowboys]..."*: "Experts: Dallas blunders," *Gannett News Service*, April 21, 1989.

page 196: *"They're taking Aikman..."*: Ibid.

page 196: *"But Aikman's not..."*: Ibid.

page 196: *"The Cowboys blew it"*: Al Carter, "Cowboys have Aikman, but where are the defenders?" *Houston Chronicle*, April 24, 1989.

page 196: *He thought they went for...*: Ibid.

page 196: *"Had the Cowboys been able to live with Steve Pelleur..."*: Ibid.

page 197: *According to Aikman's agent*: Leigh Steinberg and Michael Arkush, *The Agent: My 40-Year Career Making Deals and Changing the Game* (New York: St. Martin's Griffin, 2015), 194, Scribd.

page 197: *Upon learning that the Cowboys*: Ibid.

page 197: *Jones assured him that they*: Ibid., 195.

page 198: *He believed Walker*: Gordon Forbes, "Vikings GM enjoys trade's early success," *Gannett News Services*, October 16, 1989.

page 198: *Former Washington general manager*: "Quoteboard," *Fort Worth Star-Telegram*, October 13, 1989.

page 198: *For the same reason*: Peter King, "Sudden Impact," *Sports Illustrated*, October 23, 1989.

page 198: *The next day, Johnson*: "Quoteboard," *Fort Worth Star-Telegram*.

page 199: *"Yes, we have a prime suspect…"*: Randy Galloway, "NO WAY: Grins won't last for long," *Dallas Morning News*, October 13, 1989.

page 199: *"The Vikings got Herschel Walker…"*: Ibid

page 199: *"[They] gave up nothing…"*: Ibid.

page 199: *"It's a textbook example of…"*: Ibid.

page 199: *Longtime Dallas scribe Frank Luksa*: Steve Wulf, "The run that birthed Dallas' dynasty," ESPN.com, October 8, 2014, https://www.espn.com/nfl/story/_/id/11659891/herschel-walker-trade-25th-anniversary-run-birthed-dallas-cowboys-dynasty (accessed September 28, 2021).

page 199: *"It's a lot like giving…"*: Skip Miller, "Hurricane Jerry ravaging the Cowboys," Newport News (Virginia) *Daily Press*, October 17, 1989.

page 199: *"The Dallas rebuilding job…"*: Ibid.

page 200: *"The town is just about ready…"*: Jerry Magee, "Dallas 'Jaybirds' off to a rocky start," (Oklahoma City) *Oklahoman*, October 29, 1989.

page 200: *"It's sad to see…"*: Ibid.

page 200: *"Darryl Clack is our guy…"*: Ed Werder, "Rest of life without Herschel begins today for Cowboys," *Fort Worth Star-Telegram*, October 15, 1989.

page 200: *"We'll have the same offense…"*: Ibid.

page 200: *"To build a team…"*: Author interview with Randy Galloway, September 1, 2020.

page 200: *"I just didn't respect…"*: Ibid.

page 200: *"I didn't have a sample size"*: Ibid.

page 201: *On the CBS Broadcast*: Packers at Vikings, October 15, 1989, aired on CBS.

page 201: *"He's here"*: Ibid.

page 202: *At one point during the game broadcast*: Ibid.

page 202: *"That is Chuck Foreman"*: Ibid.

page 202: *"Until this afternoon, perhaps…"*: Ibid.

page 202: *According to Peter King*: King. "Sudden Impact."

page 202: *"Maybe the Minnesota Vikings…"*: Michael Wilbon, "Walker's 148 yards make Vikings look super," *Washington Post*, October 16, 1989.

page 202: *"What a bargain. The Cowboys…"*: Ibid.

page 202: *"The Vikings just found…"*: Rudy Martzke, "World Series ratings might be the worst ever," *USA Today*, October 17, 1989.

page 202: *Later in the evening*: KARE-11 Minneapolis, 10 p.m. News, Television newscast, October 15, 1989, https://tcmedianow.com/kare-tv-october-15-1989-10pm/ (accessed November 20, 2021).

page 202: *During his report from the Metrodome*: Ibid.

page 202: *Daly also spoke with famed*: Ibid.

page 203: *During another segment later in*: Ibid.

page 203: *A deli at the Riverplace Market*: Cheryl Johnson and Eric Eskola, "Bigwigs throw their buddies to the 'Wolves'" (Minneapolis) *Star Tribune*, October 19, 1989.

page 203: *At a St. Paul Elementary*: Cheryl Johnson and Eric Eskola, "Jim Loken's name keeps resurfacing at White House," October 31, 1989.

page 203: *The Vikings, who had used*: Jon Roe, "I-formation suited perfectly to Walker," (Minneapolis) *Star Tribune*, October 19, 1989.

page 203: *"We were a two-back..."*: Jamie Aron, "20 years later, Herschel Walker trade still reverberates," Associated Press, October 9, 2009.

page 203: *"Things just didn't work out..."*: Ibid.

page 203: *"Sometimes you think that you..."*: "Chris Doleman on Herschel Walker's arrival with Vikings in 1989," YouTube, uploaded by Mad Sports Radio—Mike Damergis, December 19, 2017, https://www.youtube.com/watch?v=4TqiZl5b4Oc (accessed February 3, 2021).

page 203: *"I think that's what happened"*: Ibid.

page 204: *When Minnesota acquired Walker*: Robert Sansevere, "Vikings not planning major defensive changes Sunday," (Minneapolis) *Star-Tribune*, October 14, 1989.

page 204: *But when that day came*: Jim Souhan, "Vikings give Herschel his walking papers," (Minneapolis) *Star-Tribune*, May 30, 1992.

page 204: *"On that glorious October afternoon..."*: Packers at Vikings, October 15, 1989, aired on CBS.

page 204: *"The team I left at UCLA..."*: *A Football Life*, season 6, episode 11, "Troy Aikman," December 2, 2016, aired on NFL Network.

page 205: *"I distribute liquor in Grand Prairie..."*: "You make the call," *Fort Worth Star-Telegram*, December 25, 1989.

page 205: *"These high-paid guys..."*: Ibid.

page 205: *Another fan wrote...*: Ibid.

page 205: *He had been trying to trade*: Gary Myers, *Coaching Confidential: Inside the Fraternity of NFL Coaches* (New York: Crown, 2013), 133, Scribd.

page 205: *Despite the appearances*: Randy Galloway, "Aikman gets the start? No joke, Jimmy," *Dallas Morning News*, November 11, 1989.

page 205: *Johnson later admitted*: *A Football Life*, "Troy Aikman."

page 206: *The whole charade wore on*: "Modesty is Big Part of the Aikman Package," Associated Press, September 22, 1991.

page 206: *"It's almost like a vendetta"*: Eric Celeste, "Troy Aikman won't dance," *D Magazine*, September 1992, https://www.dmagazine.com/publications /d-magazine/1992/september/troy-aikman-wont-dance/ (accessed September 28, 2021).

page 206: *There's very few days*: Ibid.

page 206: *He categorically detests*: Kevin Draper, "Troy Aikman Hates Skip Bayless, and Fox Sports Loves It," Deadspin.com, September 6, 2016. https://deadspin.com/troy-aikman-hates-skip-bayless-and-fox-sports -loves-it-1786256067 (accessed July 9, 2021).

page 206: *In early 1996*: Skip Bayless, "What's Killing America's Team?" *D Magazine*, September 1996.

page 206: *Aikman had been embroiled*: Mike Kiley, "Aikman, Switzer 'Feud Just Won't Die," *Chicago Tribune*, January 27, 1996.

page 207: *There had been leaks*: Jim Reeves, "Aikman vs. Switzer overshadows game," *Fort Worth Star-Telegram*, January 25, 1996.

page 207: *Further, staff members told*: Bayless, "What's Killing America's Team?"

page 207: *Aikman steadfastly denied all*: Ibid.

page 207: *When Bayless published* Hell-Bent: Bryan Curtis, "What Skip Bayless Really Wrote about Troy Aikman," The Ringer, September 6, 2016, https://www.theringer.com/2016/9/6/16041924/what-skip-bayless-really -wrote-about-troy-aikman-8aade8f5a612 (accessed July 9, 2021).

page 207: *But many, especially Aikman, thought*: Ibid.

page 207: *"It's not fair to print..."*: Dan Shaughnessy, "The fact is, rumors about Aikman are cheap shots," *Boston Globe*, August 16, 1996.

page 207: *"It's unattributed gossip..."*: Ibid.

page 207: *To Skip, Walsh was the "un-Troy"*: Skip Bayless, "Aikman was lucky, and good," ESPN.com, August 2006, http://www.espn.com/espn/page2 /story?page=bayless/060807 (accessed September 28, 2021).

page 208: *[Aikman] didn't have Walsh's*: Ibid.

page 208: *Bayless also wrote that*: Celeste, "Troy Aikman won't dance."

page 208: *and has repeatedly written*: Skip Bayless (@RealSkipBayless), "Steelers won 2 Super Bowls w/ QB they didn't care for. Cowboys won 3 while majority of players could not stand Aikman. Just doesn't matter," Twitter, February 1, 2011, 2:53 p.m., https://twitter.com/RealSkipBayless /status/32526965982363648?s=20 (accessed September 28, 2021).

page 208: *Also, according to Bayless*: "SportsNation Chat," Skip Bayless, May 2007, ESPN.com, http://m.espn.com/general/chat/chat?eventId=15762&src =desktop (accessed September 28, 2021).

page 208: *In a September 1992 profile*: Celeste, "Troy Aikman won't dance."

page 208: *Fans sometimes brought*: Staff Reports, "Update," *Dallas Morning News*, October 16, 1989.

page 208: *Or the one with*: Staff Reports, "Update," *Dallas Morning News*, November 6, 1989.

page 209: *Throughout the 1989 season, Landry*: Denne H. Freeman, "Jerry Jones keeps seeing Tom Landry in his sleep," Associated Press, January 28, 1990.

page 209: *In one interview with ESPN*: "Sports Briefly," *Fort Worth Star-Telegram*, September 27, 1989.

page 209: *At a speech in Virginia*: Jennings Culley, "Tom Landry is enjoying his season on the sidelines," *Richmond Times-Dispatch*, October 6, 1989.

page 209: *After the Walker trade, Landry*: Denne H. Freeman, "Landry wouldn't make trade with Minnesota," Associated Press, October 13, 1989.

page 209: *and questioned the value of the draft picks*: Sam Blair, "Landry questions value of draft picks," *Dallas Morning News*, October 13, 1989.

page 209: *Landry told the media*: Mark Johnson, "This time, Landry will be just another fan in the stands," *Dallas Morning News*, December 15, 1989.

page 209: *"It shows they haven't forgotten me"*: Freeman, "Jones keeps seeing Landry."

page 209: *Some fans showed up*: Staff Reports, "Update," *Dallas Morning News*, October 16, 1989.

page 209: *In January 1990, Galloway*: Randy Galloway, "Landry's fame is causing Jones endless blame," *Dallas Morning News*, January 14, 1990.

page 210: *"Johnson could have kept…"*: Kevin Lyttle, "Cowboys future is promising," *Austin American-Statesman*, February 23, 1990.

page 210: *"Big deal. Instead he made a move…"*: Ibid.

page 211: *Aikman did not take it well*: Vito Stellino, "QB Aikman struggles in chaotic atmosphere swirling about Cowboys," *Baltimore Sun*, September 23, 1990.

page 211: *In late September 1990, in what may have been*: Brian Allee-Walsh, "Saints get QB Walsh for 3 picks," (New Orleans) *Times-Picayune*, September 26, 1990.

page 211: *Their regular starter Bobby Hebert*: Ralph Malbrough, "Bobby Hebert holdout in 1990 altered Saints, NFL history," wwltv.com, September 14, 2017, https://www.wwltv.com/article/sports/nfl/saints/bobby-hebert-holdout-in-1990-altered-saints-nfl-history/289-474806788 (accessed September 29, 2021).

page 211: *But Saints general manager*: Ibid.

page 211: *In his game report,* Daily Advertiser: Kevin Foote, "Walsh just what the doctor ordered for the Saints," (Lafayette, Louisiana) *Daily Advertiser*, October 15, 1990.

page 211: *Another area writer, the* Hattiesburg (Mississippi) American's: Stan Caldwell, "Thank Hebert's agent for Walsh's deliverance," *Hattiesburg (Mississippi) American*, October 15, 1990.

page 212: *"This was one of Troy Aikman's…"*: Tim Cowlishaw, "Cowboys report card," *Dallas Morning News*, October 15, 1990.

page 212: *"Even Troy will tell you…"*: Ibid.

page 212: *The next day, writers*: Allan Malamud, "Notes on a Scorecard," *Los Angeles Times*, October 16, 1990; Gary Myers, "Giants–49ers lone Super matchup," *New York Daily News*, October 16, 1990.

page 212: *That summer, Finks caved*: "QB Hebert ends holdout, becomes a Saint again," *Baltimore Sun*, June 5, 1991.

page 213: *First, finding the offense too inconsistent*: Mike Fisher, "Shula demoted; Landry aides Lowry, Nolan axed," *Fort Worth Star-Telegram*, January 10, 1991.

page 213: *He initially wanted Miami Dolphins offensive coordinator*: Craig Barnes, "Stevens staying in Miami," (Fort Lauderdale) *Sun-Sentinel*, January 18, 1991.

page 213: *He settled on Norv Turner*: Mike Fisher, "Cowboys hire Rams' Turner to run offense," *Fort Worth Star-Telegram*, February 2, 1991.

page 213: *They traded up from the 11th pick*: Mike Fisher, "Cowboys swap for draft's top pick," *Fort Worth Star-Telegram*, April 20, 1991.

page 214: *"Did someone mention playoffs?"*: Rick Gosselin, "Sacked," *Dallas Morning News*, September 16, 1991.

page 214: *"Not this Sunday, and certainly…"*: Ibid.

page 214: *"The look on the face of…Norv…"*: Jim Reeves, "Pride, tradition, take extra helping of lumps," *Fort Worth Star-Telegram*, September 16, 1991.

page 214: *The previous two seasons*: Barry Jackson, "Cowboys' rebuilding plan goes offensive," *Miami Herald*, August 18, 1991.

page 214: *Under Turner, Aikman started releasing*: Barry Jackson, "Cowboys' rebuilding plan goes offensive," *Miami Herald*, August 18, 1991.

page 214: *Also, Aikman developed a friendship*: Thomas George, "N.F.L PREVIEW; For Aikman, a Mid-Career Crisis," *New York Times*, September 6, 1998.

page 215: *His knee wasn't 100 percent*: Lee Williams, "Aikman not happy on Cowboys sidelines," *El Paso Times*, January 1, 1992.

page 215: *After Aikman made clear to reporters*: Celeste, "Troy Aikman won't dance."

page 215: *A few days later*: Dave Goldberg, "Forget Earlier Rout, But Still Take Skins," Associated Press, January 3, 1992.

page 216: *"To say it doesn't bother me…"*: Williams, "Aikman not happy."

page 216: *"I feel like I should…"*: Ibid.

page 216: *Ed Werder, the* Orlando Sentinel's: Ed Werder, "Cowboys' Aikman upset as backup," *Orlando Sentinel*, January 2, 1992.

page 216: *After the game, Randy Galloway*: *A Football Life*, "Troy Aikman."

page 216: *However, the next day, Aikman*: Ibid.

page 217: *Haley and 49ers head coach*: Kevin Sherrington, "Haley coming back to haunt San Francisco," *Dallas Morning News*, January 13, 1993.

page 218: *As* Hartford Courant *columnist*: Alan Greenberg, "Johnson and Jones did it their way," *Hartford Courant*, February 2, 1993.

page 218: *After the Super Bowl Triumph, Cowboys radio voice*: "Dallas' Jones makes his mark," Associated Press, February 1, 1993.

page 218: *[Jones has] taken more*: Ibid.

page 219: *"The Dallas Cowboys are not…"*: Tony Kornheiser, "Time to bury Switzer," *Washington Post*, December 2, 1995.

page 219: *The column offered this fateful analogy*: Editorial, "So long, Herschel," *Longview (Texas) News Journal*, October 14, 1989.

Chapter 14: "Turns Out, the Patriots' Unlikely 2001 Season Journey Seems More and More Like an Aberration" (2000–2005 New England Patriots)

page 223: *Belichick had a stellar*: Jon Gelberg, "Belichick a defensive mastermind," *Asbury Park (New Jersey) Press*, October 14, 1990.

page 223: *but his ability and temperament*: Alan Greenberg, "Regardless of Title, Belichick Has Final Say," *Hartford Courant*, January 29, 2000.

page 223: *A large sign*: Michael Madden, "Belichick has scary return to old haunts," *Boston Globe*, November 13, 2000.

page 223: *The next day, veteran*: Dan Shaughnessy, "With this effort, are we seeing a re-Pete?" *Boston Globe*, November 13, 2000.

page 223: *He added, "Bill Belichick…"*: Ibid.

page 224: *"I was just having…"*: Author interview with Dan Shaughnessy, October 31, 2020.

page 224: *But when Kraft*: Carlo DeVito, *Parcells, A Biography* (Chicago: Triumph, 2011), 249–250, Scribd.

page 224: *"It was a little…"*: Author interview with Dan Shaughnessy, October 31, 2020.

page 224: *"Like, alright smarty…"*: Ibid.

page 224: *From the* Boston Herald*'s Year in Review*: "For Patriots, Belichick hiring turns out to be the change for the worse," *Boston Herald*, December 31, 2000.

page 225: *At the time, it was hailed*: "Drew Bledsoe Elected Into Patriots Hall of Fame," CBS Boston, May 16, 2011, https://boston.cbslocal.com/2011/05/16/drew-bledsoe-elected-into-patriots-hall-of-fame/ (accessed August 5, 2021).

page 225: *owned almost all*: David Halberstam, *The Education of a Coach* (New York: Hyperion, 2005), 250.

page 225: *"I saw this as an opportunity…"*: Alan Greenberg, "Bledsoe's Record Deal: 10 Years, $103 Million," *Hartford Courant*, March 8, 2001.

page 225: *In March 2001, a month*: Joel Buchsbaum, "Patriots the team most set up for failure," *Pro Football Weekly*, March 5, 2001.

page 225: *The publication also added: "When [the Boston media]…"*: Ibid.

page 226: *On MSNBC.com, he torched Belichick*: "Seymour helped push Gerard Warren to New England," *Pro Football Talk*, May 4, 2010, https://profootballtalk.nbcsports.com/2010/05/04/seymour-helped-push-gerard-warren-to-new-england/ (accessed September 30, 2021).

page 226: *He wrote that Seymour*: Ibid.

page 226: *Additionally, Borges thought*: Ibid.

page 226: *"[Receiver] was a low priority"*: Alan Greenberg, "Belichick's Building Blocks," *Hartford Courant*, April 23, 2001.

page 226: *"We just didn't feel…"*: Ibid.

page 226: *The (Fort Lauderdale)* Sun-Sentinel's: Chris Perkins, "Grading the 2001 NFL Draft," (Fort Lauderdale) *Sun-Sentinel*, April 23, 2001.

page 226: *Alan Greenberg of the* Hartford Courant: Alan Greenberg, "Rating the AFC," *Hartford Courant*, April 23, 2001.

page 227: *Jason Cole, in the* Miami Herald: Jason Cole, "Jason Cole Grades the Draft," *Miami Herald*, April 23, 2001.

page 227: *By taking Seymour, he concluded*: Kevin Mannix, "Club digs out again, Uses backfill to plug holes," *Boston Herald*, April 22, 2001.

page 227: *According to him, he's now*: Ron Borges (@RonBorges), "I'll be doing my best. Ty and Big Sey remain good friends. Richard and I laugh a lot about how some folks love to bring up that David Terrell thing. He always says, 'Seems to bother your critics more than it ever bothered me.'" Twitter, March 31, 2020, 9:16 p.m., https://twitter.com/RonBorges/status/1245158153198723072?s=20 (accessed September 30, 2021).

page 227: Sports Illustrated *projected*: "Scouting reports, how they'll finish," *Sports Illustrated*, September 3, 2001.

page 227: *"I would be very surprised if they don't find…"*: "Patriots Got No Respect," *Philadelphia Inquirer*, February 5, 2002.

page 228: *"It's going to be another…"*: Ibid.

page 228: *"The Patriots have been in reverse…"*: Bob Matthews, "Football Preview 2001," (Rochester, New York) *Democrat and Chronicle*, September 2, 2001.

page 228: *"So, what's with that?"*: Kevin Mannix, "The NFL Draft: Brady pick hard to figure. QB picture out of whack," *Boston Herald*, April 17, 2000.

page 228: *"The Patriots have their franchise…"*: Ibid.

page 228: *Alan Greenberg, in the* Hartford Courant: Alan Greenberg, "Patriots Draft Board Day 2," *Hartford Courant*, April 17, 2000.

page 229: *The coaches noticed*: Halberstam, *The Education of a Coach*, 221.

page 229: *By the start of the regular season*: Ibid.

page 229: *But according to Borges, who has*: Bill Simmons, "I really hate the Colts," Grantland.com, November 6, 2000, http://grantland.com/features /i-really-hate-the-colts/ (accessed November 19, 2021); Aaron Schatz, "The End is Here for Once-Great Bledsoe," Footballoutsiders.com, November 15, 2014, https://www.footballoutsiders.com/extra-points/2004 /end-here-once-great-bledsoe (accessed November 19, 2021).

page 230: *"The New England Alliance…"*: Ron Borges, "Now it's team's turn to take the lumps," *Boston Globe*, September 25, 2001.

page 230: *"It will get to see…"*: Ibid.

page 230: *Without Drew Bledsoe…the Patriots*: Terry Bannon, "NFL Picks," *Chicago Tribune*, September 28, 2001.

page 230: *[The Patriots are] even*: Jason Schaumberg, "NFL Power Rankings," (Woodstock, Illinois) *Northwest Herald*, September 28, 2001.

page 230: *New England's fortunes*: Phillip B. Wilson, "Patriots QB Brady steps up for 1st NFL start," *Indianapolis Star*, September 30, 2001.

page 230: *Honestly, I don't know*: "Dr. Z's Power Rankings Week 3," CNNSI .com, September 25, 2001, http://web.archive.org/web/20111228105918 /http://sportsillustrated.cnn.com/football/news/2001/09/25/power _rankings/ (accessed October 1, 2021).

page 230: *Afterwards, rumblings started to be heard*: Howard Ullman, "Brady relishes win in first start," Associated Press, October 2, 2001.

page 230: *In his next-day* Globe: Ron Borges, "Brady exposed to a tough D," *Boston Globe*, October 8, 2001.

page 231: *He continued*: Ibid.

page 231: *In the* Boston Herald: George Kimball, "Debate ends quickly," *Boston Herald*, October 8, 2011.

page 231: *On the CBS game broadcast*: Chargers at Patriots, October 14, 2001, aired on CBS.

page 231: *Belichick did not seem*: Jeff Benedict, *The Dynasty* (New York: Avid Reader Press, 2020), 300, Scribd.

page 232: *He has always maintained*: "Bledsoe heads to Buffalo for 2003 pick," ESPN.com, April 21, 2003, https://www.espn.com/nfl/news/2002 /0421/1371887.html (accessed January 21, 2022).

page 232: *While some gave the impression*: Nick Cafardo, "Quarterback keeper: Kraft fanning flames," *Boston Globe*, January 31, 2002.

page 232: *Belichick clarified that Brady*: Nick Cafardo, "Brady chosen one," *Boston Globe*, January 31, 2002.

page 232: *"The only reason…"*: Author interview with Damien Woody, November 13, 2020.

page 232: *"This was Brady's team…"*: Ibid.

page 233: *After Brady threw three interceptions*: Michael Gee, "Fans home in on Brady," *Boston Herald*, October 14, 2002.

page 234: *"Tom Brady looks nothing…"*: Charles Bricker, "Denver Broncos (5–2) at New England Patriots (3–3)," (Fort Lauderdale) *Sun-Sentinel*, October 25, 2002.

page 234: *"How could Belichick, the widely proclaimed…"*: Jim Donaldson, "Basically speaking, Patriots falling down on the job," *Providence Journal*, October 14, 2002.

page 234: *In the* Boston Herald: Kevin Mannix, "Patriots Report Card, Brain drain plagues Pats," *Boston Herald*, October 15, 2002.

page 234: *On NFL.com, former*: Pat Kirwin, "Favre tops midseason awards," NFL.com, October 30, 2002, https://web.archive.org/web/20021030085525/http://www.nfl.com/ (accessed January 13, 2022).

page 234: *He also awarded*: Ibid.

page 235: *In late September, on Boston-area*: Bruce Allen, "A couple of thoughts while waiting," *Boston Sports Media Watch* (blog), September 29, 2002, https://bostonsportsmedia.com/2002/09/29/a-couple-thoughts-while-waiting/ (accessed January 15, 2022).

page 235: *A week later, veteran*: Bruce Allen, "With the Giants/Braves playoff game," *Boston Sports Media Watch* (blog), October 6, 2002, https://bostonsportsmedia.com/2002/10/06/with-the-giantsbraves-playoff-game/ (accessed January 15, 2022).

page 235: *"I don't understand why…"*: Carl Kotala, "Bledsoe lifeline for Bills," (Cocoa) *Florida Today*, October 19, 2002.

page 235: *"It was kind of…"*: Ibid.

page 235: *(Rochester, New York)* Democrat and Chronicle *Bills writer*: Sal Maiorana and Leo Roth, "Drew Bledsoe or Tom Brady? Did the Patriots make the right choice?" (Rochester, New York) *Democrat and Chronicle*, October 29, 2002.

page 235: *"I just think that he…"*: Ibid.

page 235: *"Bledsoe is only 30…"*: Ibid.

page 235: *At the end of October*: Bud Poliquin, "Bledsoe Continues Brilliance," (Syracuse, New York) *Post-Standard*, October 28, 2002.

page 235: *"The New England Patriots got…"*: Ibid.

page 235: Buffalo News *columnist*: Bucky Gleason, "Bledsoe evens our score with New England," *Buffalo News*, October 29, 2002.

page 235: *"We knew Bledsoe was…"*: Ibid.

page 235: *"Lucky for us…Belichick…"*: Ibid.

page 237: *"Just like that…[the Patriots]…"*: Jackie MacMullan, "A time for sober reflection," *Boston Globe*, January 1, 2003.

page 237: *"Turns out, the Patriots' unlikely [2001 season] journey…"*: Tim Casey, "Darling status of Patriots has short shelf life," December 25, 2002.

page 238: *However, he and Belichick*: Nick Cafardo, "Rival revival: Milloy signs with Bills," *Boston Globe*, September 4, 2003.

page 238: *The Patriots wanted to*: Ibid.

page 238: *Milloy wouldn't budge*: Ibid.

page 238: *According to reports, the Patriots*: Kevin Mannix, "Self-paralysis: Belichick's gamble on Milloy could cut legs out from under him, Pats," *Boston Herald*, September 7, 2003.

page 238: *Milloy wanted $3.6 million*: Ibid.

page 238: *New England was already on the books*: John Wawrow, "Buffalo brings in Milloy," Associated Press, September 4, 2003.

page 238: *The Patriots had also recently*: Benedict, *The Dynasty*, 349–351.

page 238: *He hit hard, and brought an edginess*: Ibid., 350.

page 238: *"Bill Belichick is pond scum again"*: Mannix, "Self-paralysis."

page 238: *"Arrogant, megalomaniacal…"*: Ibid.

page 238: *Right after the team caught wind of the release*: Benedict, *The Dynasty*, 352.

page 238: *During pregame introductions*: Scott Pitioniak, "Bills' message to Belichick: You blew it," (Rochester, New York) *Democrat and Chronicle*, September 8, 2003.

page 239: *"[During the warmups and…"*: Author interview with Damien Woody, November 13, 2020.

page 239: *"We had no chance…"*: Ibid.

page 239: *"It was weird. Very weird"*: "Sidelights to the game," *Boston Globe*, September 8, 2003.

page 239: *"My mother always told me that God…"*: Ibid.

page 239: *"The script couldn't…"*: Eric McHugh, "Backlash: Patriots' castoffs, Bledsoe and Milloy, sting their old team," (Quincy, Massachusetts) *Patriot Ledger*, September 8, 2003.

page 239: *"We were talking about…"*: "Bledsoe, Milloy savor one," Associated Press, September 8, 2003.

page 239: *"We were both pretty happy"*: Ibid.

page 239: *"Second-guessers unite"*: Michael Felger, "All the wrong moves," *Boston Herald*, September 8, 2003.

page 239: *"Bill Belichick bashers, today is:"* Ibid.

page 239: *"After the way [Milloy] played for the Buffalo Bills…"*: Ron Borges, "An unheeded safety alert," *Boston Globe*, September 8, 2003.

page 240: *On HBO's Inside the NFL*: Jim Baker, "Dierdorf: Forget it," *Boston Herald*, September 12, 2003.

page 240: *Collinsworth also expressed his bewilderment*: Ibid.

page 240: *Bill Simmons, an unabashed Boston*: Bill Simmons, "One happy Sports Guy: NFL picks return," Page 2, ESPN.com, September 2003, https://www.espn.com/espn/page2/story?page=simmons/030926 (accessed November 28, 2021).

page 240: *"They didn't save that…"*: Ibid.

page 240: *"It didn't make sense..."*: Ibid.

page 240: *He continued: "Belichick...screwed up..."*: Ibid.

page 240: *"How do [I put my heart on the line]..."*: Peter King, "Surprise! Surprise!," *Sports Illustrated*, September 15, 2003.

page 240: *An unnamed player posed these*: Karen Guregian, "Bill's bomb has to be diffused," *Boston Herald*, September 9, 2003.

page 240: *"For the New England Patriots..."*: Tom E. Curran, "Perfectly good team has been allowed to crumble from within," *Providence Journal*, September 9, 2003.

page 241: *Curran also considered the possibility*: Ibid.

page 241: *"You ask yourself," Curran wrote..."*: Ibid.

page 241: *The following Sunday*: Benedict, *The Dynasty*, 357.

page 241: *Jackson continued, "I want..."*: Ibid.

page 241: *"It's just one outside opinion..."*: Nick Cafardo, "Patriots won't fan any flames," *Boston Globe*, September 16, 2003.

page 241: *"I respect Tom Jackson..."*: "Around the League," *Chicago Tribune*, September 16, 2003.

page 241: *"He has no idea..."*: Ibid.

page 241: *"Who is Tom Jackson"*: Alan Greenberg, "No word on Colvin," *Hartford Courant*, September 17, 2003.

page 241: *"Does he sit in at our meetings?"*: Ibid.

page 242: *"Mularkey and his assistants..."*: Leo Roth," Mularkey correct to turn the ball over to Losman," (Rochester, New York) *Democrat and Chronicle*, February 17, 2005.

page 243: *"There is a temptation..."*: Author interview with Matt Chatham, October 29, 2020.

page 243: *"But to try to..."*: Ibid.

page 243: *In the 2020 book*: Benedict, *The Dynasty*, 372.

page 243: *Belichick looked at Jackson*: Ibid.

INDEX

ABOUT THE AUTHOR

Fred Segal is an attorney who practiced law full-time for more than eight years before retiring to pursue other opportunities. He currently operates the popular social media brand Freezing Cold Takes. He has appeared on numerous national radio and TV shows, podcasts, and local shows across the country to discuss his feeds. Major publications such as The Athletic, *Sports Illustrated*, and *USA TODAY* have profiled Fred and Freezing Cold Takes. Segal grew up in Miami and has lived in Florida almost his entire life.